ISBN 978-1-5280-4939-9
PIBN 10022724

This book is a reproduction of an important historical work. Forgotten Books uses
state-of-the-art technology to digitally reconstruct the work, preserving the original format
whilst repairing imperfections present in the aged copy. In rare cases, an imperfection in
the original, such as a blemish or missing page, may be replicated in our edition. We do,
however, repair the vast majority of imperfections successfully; any imperfections that
remain are intentionally left to preserve the state of such historical works.

Carnegie Endowment for International Peace
DIVISION OF ECONOMICS AND HISTORY
John Bates Clark, Director

ECONOMIC PROTECTIONISM

BY JOSEF GRUNZEL

EDITED BY

EUGEN VON PHILIPPOVICH

PROFESSOR OF POLITICAL ECONOMY IN THE UNIVERSITY OF VIENNA

OXFORD: AT THE CLARENDON PRESS
London, Edinburgh, New York, Toronto, Melbourne and Bombay
HUMPHREY MILFORD
1916

5

ᴅ'ᵞ.

INTRODUCTORY NOTE BY THE DIRECTOR

THE Division of Economics and History of the Carnegie Endowment for International Peace is organized to ' promote a thorough and scientific investigation of the causes and results of war '. In accordance with this purpose a conference of eminent statesmen, publicists, and economists was held in Berne, Switzerland, in August 1911, at which a plan of investigation was formed and an extensive list of topics was prepared. The programme of that Conference is presented in detail in an Appendix. It will be seen that an elaborate series of investigations has been undertaken, and the resulting reports may in due time be expected in printed form.

Of works so prepared, some will aim to reveal direct and indirect consequences of warfare, and thus to furnish a basis for a judgement as to the reasonableness of the resort to it. If the evils are in reality larger and the benefits smaller than in the common view they appear to be, such studies should furnish convincing evidence of this fact and afford a basis for an enlightened policy whenever there is danger of international conflicts.

Studies of the causes of warfare will reveal, in particular, those economic influences which in time of peace bring about clashing interests and mutual suspicion and hostility. They will, it is believed, show what policies, as adopted by different nations, will reduce the conflicts of interest, inure to the common benefit, and afford a basis for international confidence and good will. They will further serve to reveal the natural economic influences which of themselves bring about more and more harmonious relations and tend to substitute general benefits for the mutual injuries that follow unintelligent self-seeking. Economic internationalism needs to be fortified by the mutual trust that just dealing creates; but just conduct itself may be favoured by economic conditions. These, in turn, may be created partly by a natural evolution and partly by the conscious action of governments; and both evolution and public action are among the important subjects of investigation.

An appeal to reason is in order when excited feelings render armed conflicts imminent; but it is quite as surely called for when no excitement exists and when it may be forestalled and prevented from developing by sound national policies. To furnish a scientific basis for reasonable international policies is the purpose of some of the studies already in progress and of more that will hereafter be undertaken.

The publications of the Division of Economics and History are under the direction of a Committee of Research, the membership of which includes the statesmen, publicists, and economists who participated in the Conference at Berne in 1911, and two who have since been added. The list of members at present is as follows :

EUGÈNE BOREL, Professor of Public and International Law in the University of Geneva.

LUJO BRENTANO, Professor of Economics in the University of Munich; Member of the Royal Bavarian Academy of Sciences.

CHARLES GIDE, Professor of Comparative Social Economics in the University of Paris.

H. B. GREVEN, Professor of Political Economy and Statistics in the University of Leiden.

FRANCIS W. HIRST, Editor of *The Economist*, London.

DAVID KINLEY, Vice-President of the University of Illinois.

HENRI LA FONTAINE, Senator of Belgium.

His Excellency LUIGI LUZZATTI Professor of Constitutional Law in the University of Rome; Secretary of the Treasury, 1891-3; Prime Minister of Italy, 1908-11.

GOTARO OGAWA, Professor of Finance at the University of Kioto, Japan.

Sir GEORGE PAISH, Joint Editor of *The Statist*, London.

MAFFEO PANTALEONI, Professor of Political Economy in the University of Rome.

EUGEN PHILIPPOVICH VON PHILIPPSBERG, Professor of Political Economy in the University of Vienna; Member of the Austrian Herrenhaus, Hofrat.

PAUL S. REINSCH, United States Minister to China.

His Excellency BARON Y. SAKATANI, recently Minister of Finance; Present Mayor of Tokio.

THEODOR SCHIEMANN, Professor of the History of Eastern Europe in the University of Berlin.

HARALD WESTERGAARD, Professor of Political Science and Statistics in the University of Copenhagen.

FRIEDRICH, FREIHERR VON WIESER, Professor of Political Economy at the University of Vienna.

The function of members of this Committee is to select collaborators competent to conduct investigations and present reports in the form of books or monographs; to consult with these writers as to plans of study; to read the completed manuscripts, and to inform the officers of the Endowment whether they merit publication in its series. This editorial function does not commit the members of the Committee to any opinions expressed by the writers. Like other editors, they are asked to vouch for the usefulness of the works, their scientific and literary merit, and the advisability of issuing them. In like manner, the publication of the monographs does not commit the Endowment as a body or any of its officers to the opinions which may be expressed in them. The standing and attainments of the writers selected afford a guarantee of thoroughness of research and accuracy in the statement of facts, and the character of many of the works will be such that facts, statistical, historical, and descriptive, will constitute nearly the whole of their content. In so far as the opinions of the writers are revealed, they are neither approved nor condemned by the fact that the Endowment causes them to be published. For example, the publication of a work describing the attitude of various socialistic bodies on the subject of peace and war implies nothing as to the views of the officers of the Endowment on the subject of socialism; neither will the issuing of a work, describing the attitude of business classes toward peace and war, imply any agreement or disagreement on the part of the officers of the Endowment with the views of men of these classes as to a protective policy, the control of monopoly, or the regulation of banking and currency. It is necessary to know how such men generally think and feel on the great issue of war, and it is one of the purposes of the Endowment to promote studies which will accurately reveal their attitude. Neither it nor its Committee of Research vouches for more than that the works issued by them contain such facts; that their statements concerning them may generally be trusted, and that the works are, in a scientific way, of a quality that entitles them to a reading.

JOHN BATES CLARK,
Director.

CONTENTS

PART ONE

THE GENESIS OF ECONOMIC PROTECTIONISM

PART TWO

THE DIRECTIONS ASSUMED BY ECONOMIC PROTECTIONISM

PART THREE

THE EFFECTS OF ECONOMIC PROTECTIONISM

PART ONE

THE GENESIS OF ECONOMIC PROTECTIONISM

THE GENESIS OF ECONOMIC PROTECTIONISM

1. National Economy and World Economy

The Classification of Economic Activity. The essentials of economic protectionism can be understood only in the light of a clear comprehension of the relations between private economy, national economy, and world economy. By economic activity in general we mean conscious endeavour directed to providing for the satisfaction of human wants. This provision, however, is not incumbent upon the individual human being alone ; in many respects the burden is entirely taken out of his hands or essentially lightened by the various social groups in which his life is lived. Private economy includes the economic activities, on the one hand, of persons who are bound together by the natural ties of the family into a consumption unit or household, and, on the other hand, of those whose similar or mutually complementary activities unite them into an industrial unit with efforts directed, not toward the most advantageous utilization of goods, but toward the most effective means of procuring them. The national economy embraces the economic activity of the politically organized state, within which under present-day conditions the private-economy units occupy a position similar to that of the cells in a plant or animal body. Economic society, moreover, is not a mere spatial proximity of the constituent units, but an organism directed by a common will, and whose development may come into conflict with that of its individual members. Transactions between societies are carried out by the private-economy units, yet by no means independently, but subject always to limitations imposed by the obligations and interests of the

B

larger group. Society, and especially society organized as a state, possesses its own interests, which frequently clash with those of the individual, but which none the less are to be distinguished fundamentally from altruism.[1] The expression 'world economy', in turn, denotes the interlacing of economic interests which results from the extension of the economic activities of individuals and societies beyond national boundaries.

Private Economy. The development of these three fields of economics has been very unequal. Only in recent years has the theory of the private economy been treated to any extent, and at best the discussions contain chiefly material belonging to commercial technology. It is none the less a matter for scientific investigation, since economic phenomena are to be judged by different standards according to whether the private-economy standpoint of the individual or the national-economy standpoint of the political society is adopted; but the private interest is at every point so dependent upon the social that the latter must be regarded as predominant. For the individual entrepreneur, a destructive exploitation of human labour may be a useful means of increasing his competitive efficiency, as also any other sort of unfair competitive methods, but the opposing standpoint of the social whole must prevail. Under these circumstances it is of little practical value to investigate the relations to one another of the private-economy units composing a politically organized society, or even their relations to the political power viewed from below upward instead of from the standpoint of the whole. The private entrepreneur will be likely to treat the national-economy factors as fixed quantities in his own calculations and only call them in question where the issue is raised as to the most suitable organization for utilizing them. The private-economy consumption unit, the family, requires in general no elaborate organization;

[1] Emanuel Sella, *Der Wandel des Besitzes*, German translation by J. Blumstein, Munich and Leipsic, 1912, p. 3.

but it is otherwise with the modern corporate productive unit working to supply an ever-extending trade, which is forced to maintain on the inside a complicated office-system and on the outside an equally complex mechanism for meeting competition, utilizing the common means of trade and commerce, &c. It is therefore comprehensible that only modern large-scale industry has led to the development of a theory of private economy which has taken on the form of a commercial technology.

World Economy. The theory of world economy is also in a stage of development so primitive that languages other than German have not yet a generally recognized word for it, and this in spite of the fact that in cases where water transportation was convenient economic relations between different countries developed earlier than those within a country itself. The subject-matter of this science, in contrast with that of national economy, can only be a descriptive economics, seeking to analyse and explain international economic transactions. Thus it serves merely to supplement the treatment of national economy, forming with the latter the material for a theory of national-economic policy as opposed to world-economic policy. There cannot be a world economy or international economy, because a world-will which would rank above the national wills and in which they would find expression does not exist. International relations are not regulated in accordance with an ideal of the human race, but according to the wills of the nations concerned. Regulation by international agreement is essentially different from regulation by laws of states, in that the treaty embodies no higher organic will, but merely a summation of separate will-units to the extent to which they are in agreement in certain particulars. In a commercial treaty a state seeks to further, not the commerce of the world, but merely its own foreign trade, and will consequently annul the agreement without regard to the effect on the world economy the moment it finds such a course consonant with its own interests. The agreement only is international; the economic policy which finds expression in it is strictly national. We have not an international economic policy; we have only an economic foreign policy which is part of the national economic policy. World-economic processes hold an ancillary, not a dominant, position in regard to the various national-economic bodies of the world, which thus find a new field of activity outside the sphere of their political jurisdiction.

For this reason the quest for a principle of world economics is also vain. The classical political-economy found such a principle in international division of labour, in consequence of which, every forward step in world economy meant an increase in national welfare and national-economic and world-economic ideals coincided. But the necessary presupposition of this argument from the international division of labour is false, the assumption, namely, that the wealth production in any country is permanently restricted to its natural resources. Nevertheless, as world-economic relations increase in complexity, they undergo more and more thoroughgoing regulation by international agreements, treaties, and trade congresses. In this movement we may recognize the beginnings of an international organization, but such a union must remain as distinct from political organization as free association is from compulsory. Just as a free association can never succeed in binding together all the members of an interest group and completely subordinating their special interests to the common aim, so an international organization can only mitigate conflicts of interest, never make them entirely subservient to a higher principle of economic policy. Only the national-economy principle of the greatest possible development of productive forces is finally decisive.

National Economy. The question remains, why the politically organized nation in particular should form so conspicuous a landmark in the economic life that all other forms of organization are overshadowed and dwarfed in comparison.

In glancing over the course of human development we see four types of social structure following one another, the later never entirely displacing the earlier, it is true, and all to a certain extent continuing to subsist side by side, .yet varying sharply in their relative significance. These four are blood communities, language communities, religious communities, and political communities. In European countries in recent times, or since the appearance of mercantilistic ideas in the sixteenth century, the political community has pushed the others more and more into the background, for the simple reason that this form is best adapted to the requirement of a more perfect socialization of the process of satisfying wants. If the principle of nationalism was especially emphasized in the nineteenth century, it was because the bond of a common nationality served, in the two European countries Germany and Italy, as a useful implement in advancing political organization. That the principle is no longer dominant is best explained by the consideration that it has not been strong enough to disrupt existing well-established political states.

The progressive socialization of the want-satisfying activities causes discontent with the original condition in which peoples were distinguished by race, language, or religion, and demands the union of the population of a territory among themselves and with their home-land into a coherent economic body by means of a political constitution. Political institutions form a common basis for economic activity, which increases in importance, and by its characteristics soon comes to distinguish one political community from another. Other communities are not combated or eliminated, but utilized. Common descent is decisive for the character of wants, since the life-habits of persons of the same stock are much alike; it is also decisive for the specializations in production, because human aptitudes are also fairly uniform within the same race-group. A common language facilitates exchange among the inhabitants and thus furthers the imitative impulse so important economically, leading to the formation of common usages and customs which impose manifold conventional requirements on the individual. Religious views influence the pursuit of culture, which involves the production and consumption of economic values. But once the state has been forged, an assimilation process goes on within it, often furthered, too, by external change and chance. In friendly business competition and on the field of battle a common store of experiences is accumulated by the whole politically organized population. Thus we speak of a ' people ', not in the ethnographic sense of a homogeneous nationality or in the legal sense of the citizenship of a state, but with the economic meaning of the population of a certain territory. It therefore includes all persons who actually dwell within the area under the political jurisdiction in question. Germans belong to France when and so long as they remain in France, even though they do not renounce their nationality or give up their German citizenship. In countries with a nationally homogeneous population the term ' nation ' is often used for the political community, but there also the nation is unmistakably and always more than simply the cultural community implied in nationality. The formation of an independent national economy may possibly be impeded but it cannot be checked by the circumstance that different nationalities inhabit contiguous portions of the territory under a common political constitution. Dissimilarities in physical characteristics of the people signify little economically, and differences in spiritual qualities are more and more pushed aside by the influence of the unavoidable common commercial language and the sledge-hammer blows of a common political destiny. The Austrian, Swiss, and Belgian economic societies are very real entities in spite of the national contrasts within those states.

Economic Protectionism. The national economy, then, is to-day the dominant economic unit to which other groups and factors must subordinate themselves. Sometimes narrower territorial units may exist within and wider ones beyond that of the national economy, possessing some of the characteristics of the latter. Thus in federal states the component states have a certain economic independence, and it is possible to speak of a Prussian or Saxon national economy as well as of the German. So again, a customs union combines politically independent states into a higher economic unit, and there is an Austro-Hungarian national economy in addition to the Austrian and Hungarian. In all these cases we are dealing merely with a division of the national-economic functions between different territorial units which behave externally as one. The goods or the travellers entering German territory across the Saxon boundary are affected at once by the German and Saxon national economics ; on entering Austria they are subject at the same time to the merely Austrian railway rates and to the Austro-Hungarian customs regulations, &c.

Economic protectionism represents the logical consequences of the situation created when world-economy relations break into the national-economy sphere. It is not therefore a policy of world economics, but a detail of the external policy of the national economy. It is neither more nor less than the sum total of the measures adopted by the national-economy unit for the purpose of advancing its interests in the field of world economy.

2. The Development of Protectionistic Economic Theory

The Mercantilistic Theory of National Enrichment. Mercantilism, as the first scientific movement in economics, assigned economic functions to the state, and so laid the foundation of the present conception of political economy. The theory regarded world-economy relations purely as a means of enriching the national-economy group. Each state should sell as much as possible to foreign countries and buy as little as possible from them, so that its national wealth might be increased through a large excess of exports over imports. Commercial treaties were regarded as a means of taking advantage of other nations and to be desired only by politically powerful countries and feared by all others. The consequent closing of the gates against foreign goods involved a general shrinkage of world-economic activity, though this was richly compensated by the abolition of internal customs lines which set free domestic trade in every country.

The Classical World-Economics. The physiocratic-classical school, under the influence of the cosmological viewpoint of the dominant nature-philosophy, emphasized the necessity of the widest possible extension of economic relations, to the end that the division of labour, which had been so conspicuously triumphant in national industry, should become international as well, and that each country should devote itself to the production of those goods for which it found itself most favoured by natural conditions. In this way each country would operate with the lowest possible production-costs and exchange its products for others produced in other countries under the same favourable conditions. Thus each would reap a twofold advantage, being in a position at once to sell as dearly and buy as cheaply as possible. The interests of humanity and of the nations were viewed as identical, and hence national boundaries should not be allowed to have any bearing on economic relations. Holding such views, the classical school found no place for an economic policy ascribing any sort of activity in this field to the state as an organic body. It would have nothing to do with citizens of different countries, but only with economic individuals. Its task was to consist exclusively in the discovery of those natural laws which govern the economic process as carried on by the human race as a whole.

Fichte's 'Closed Commercial State'. The philosopher

Fichte came to a very different conclusion.[1] If the task is imposed upon the state of protecting every one in the possession of his property, it must first give to every one his own. To this end Fichte constructed a socialistic ideal state in which every person should have his part in economic activity assigned to him according to a definite plan. Such an organization, of course, could be maintained only by making impossible any disturbance from without of the equilibrium between the various productive classes. Hence the state would be forced to take over all trade with foreign countries and would become as isolated as a commercial body as it had previously been juridically and politically. To this end all gold and silver money would first of all have to be withdrawn from circulation, because it is a universal medium, and for it would be substituted a new national currency made from a new substance whose composition should be kept secret so that it could circulate only within the country. At the same time the state would monopolize all foreign trade, but only for the purpose of reducing imports by the development of substitute industries and would cut down exports by restrictions from year to year until a condition of complete economic independence of foreign countries should be reached. Foreign travel should be permitted only to scholars and artists, when its cost would be borne by the state. ' Idle curiosity and quest of diversion should no longer be allowed to drag their tedium about through every country on the globe.'

The newer Conception of National Economics. By way of the two extremes, the classical idea of a world economy and the fantastic socialist dream of a closed commercial state— ' the two leading types of political nonsense', as Adam G. Müller says [2]—thinkers finally reached the concept of national economy. Irresistible, that is, as were the doctrines of Adam

---

[1] Johann Gottlieb Fichte, *Der geschlossene Handelsstaat*, Tübingen, 1800.
[2] ' Historische Übersicht der Entwicklung,' in Bernhard Harms, *Volkswirtschaft und Weltwirtschaft*, Jena, 1912.

Smith and his immediate successors in cultured circles, yet in the long run the truth forced recognition outside of England that, in the economic relations of the world, states are after all independent units between which opposition as well as community of interests subsists. In consequence, the alleged natural laws of economic exchange undergo modifications in each country, which must be taken into account in all political calculations. Especially the older historical school in Germany began to perceive that countries more retarded in their development could not expect to profit by the free play of economic forces in the same degree as could England, where industrial progress had been carried much farther. The somewhat obscure Reichsgraf von Soden, who first employed the term 'national economy' (*Volkswirtschaft*), uses it, it is true, to designate those very economic doctrines which follow from cosmopolitan principles and hence relate to humanity as a whole ; he distinguishes from it under the name of political economy (*Staats-Wirtschaftskunde*) the science based on political organization and relating to economic welfare within the scope of the state. The correct view was brought forward by Karl Heinrich Rau, who acknowledges that the exchange of goods extends beyond the borders of the individual state, but contends that in so doing it constitutes an economy of a higher order. The subject-matter of the science can in his view be only the economic life within the state, even though occasional international relations be taken into account. This national science of economics, or political economy, he divided again into two branches, pure and applied. Pure economics, as the theoretical part, treats of the natural economic laws ; the applied or practical branch, on the other hand, deals with the means of promoting the economic welfare of a people. The conceptions of Karl Knies and Wilhelm Roscher were similar to that of Rau. They emphasized particularly the special character certain to be imparted to the economic life of any people by the distinctive natural resources of the ˙

country and the national history. It is quite possible to suppose that the science would set applied or practical 'political' economy more in the foreground as soon as it dropped the quest for eternal natural laws of world economy and took up rather the temporally and spatially conditioned bases of national welfare, regarding individual states as economic units as well as political, and comparing them as such. Pursuit of this course led to the first sharp conflict with the classical school. If the economic life of the race is to be differentiated along national lines, there can be no uniform recipe valid under all conditions for increasing the 'wealth of nations'. Hence the German List and the American Carey raised their voices in opposition to the free-trade principles advocated by the classical economists, which they contended were suited only to requirements such as those of England. Other countries should in their view still make use of protective duties as an educational expedient until their industries could hold their own with the English in a freer competition. The classical writers had taken a mere fiction for a reality and were bound to meet with disaster in the practical application of their doctrines.

Present-day Views concerning National Economics and World Economics. We may divide into three groups the views now held regarding the relations between national and world economy. The first group includes theories which assume an increasing isolation of national economy from world economy by trade restrictions, and hence approach the idea of a 'closed commercial state', though perhaps on other than the original grounds. The second group of theories assumes on the contrary a progressive assimilation of the two economies and regards a perfect world economy as the ultimate ideal and the goal to be striven for. The third group assumes no displacing of either system by the other, but a continued existence of both side by side, each supplementing the other in their constant interchange, though of course further distinctions arise in the treatment of these relations.

The continuous spread of economic protectionism led to the adoption, especially in agricultural circles, of the maxim that the goal of future progress must be the supply of the home demand by the country itself. Heavy manufactures also, always closely related to agriculture in respect of commercial policy preferences, incline to the same view. For example, the chamber of commerce of Essen, one of the greatest industrial regions in Germany, declares in its annual report for the year 1912, that it is as important to Germany to place on a plane of safety the provision by her own activities of the most important necessaries of life, especially bread and meat, as it is to produce the implements of external power. In the literature of the subject the same thought was represented in the controversy carried on a few years ago on the subject of the agricultural versus the industrial state.[1] It was contended that when the countries formerly devoted to the production of raw materials develop manufactures and increase in population, they will necessarily purchase smaller quantities of manufactured goods while their exportation of raw materials will be less. Their commerce with the great states of older civilization will therefore gradually fall off. Perhaps the most pointed statement of the case is that of Kropotkin, who says: 'Every nation to be its own farmer and manufacturer; every individual to be a field labourer and some sort of technologist; every individual to be in the possession of scientific knowledge and technical skill—this, according to our view, is the tendency of the civilized nations.' And in another place he explains[2]: 'In proportion as the nations of western Europe meet with increasing difficulty in

---

[1] R. Oldenberg, *Über Deutschland als Industriestaat*, Göttingen, 1897; H. A. Wagner, *Agrar- und Industriestaat*, Jena, 1902; J. Méline, *Retour à la terre*, Paris, 1906; L. Brentano, *Schrecken des übersiegenden Industriestaates*, second edition, Munich, 1907; Gerhard Hildebrand, *Die Erschütterung der Industrieherrschaft und des Industrie-Sozialismus*, Jena, 1910.

[2] P. Kropotkin, *Landwirtschaft, Industrie und Handwerk*. Authorized German translation by Gustav Landauer, second edition, Berlin, 1910, pp. 18, 52.

finding a market for their goods in foreign countries and in obtaining in exchange for them the means of life, they will be compelled to produce those means of life within their own territory; they will be compelled to rely upon domestic purchasers for a market for their goods and upon domestic producers for the necessaries of life—and the sooner they do it, the better.' Sombart [1] also has expressed his belief in ' the decreasing significance of world-economy relations '. On the other hand, it has justly been pointed out that the increasing industrialization of the characteristically raw-material-producing countries has not at all lessened their foreign trade, but has even increased it. Especially striking is the fact, shown by commercial statistics, that in general, imports increase more rapidly than exports. This is to be traced in part to the increasing demand for raw materials and for food-stuffs, but the imports of manufactures also have increased instead of diminishing. In France the Tariff Commission of the Senate, on the occasion of the tariff revision of 1910, established the fact that in the period from 1899 to 1908 imports increased from 4,518,000,000 to 6,091,000,000 francs while exports increased only from 4,229,000,000 to 4,615,000,000. Of manufactured goods alone, the imports increased from 728,000,000 francs to 1,151,000,000 or fifty-eight per cent, the exports only from 2,077,000,000 to 2,619,000,000 or twenty-five per cent. Germany, England, the United States of America, and Belgium lead the world in iron industries, yet their imports of iron and iron goods have increased instead of decreasing. The most intensive commercial activity is carried on not between the industrial nations and colonial or agricultural countries, but among the most highly developed industrial states. Germany exports three-fourths of her goods to western Europe; more than half the exports of France are taken up by England, Germany, and Belgium; England's best customers, with the exception of

[1] Werner Sombart, *Die deutsche Volkswirtschaft im neunzehnten Jahrhundert*, Berlin, 1903, p. 427.

British India, are Germany and the United States, and Belgium carries on more than half her foreign trade with Germany, Great Britain, France, and the Netherlands. In the trade of Belgium with Germany, too, almost the same classes of goods make up the imports and exports, as iron and steel, textile manufactures, chemical products, and the like. The efficiency of an industry does not preclude the importation of similar products, but often enough is the occasion of it. Thus Germany, in spite of her high industrial development, is dependent upon foreign sources for her supply of certain classes of yarns and of machinery, for tin plate, for many kinds of leather, &c. But the fear of dependence will lead to no restrictions, for the dependence is mutual, and peace is much more safely based on an economic community of interests than on political treaties.

In diametric opposition to the foregoing, the views of the second group regard world economy as representing a higher stage of development than national economy. The group is again divided between views which connect this higher development with a change in political organization and those which leave political organization entirely out of account. Those thinkers who assume no essential change in the present political communities or social order are closely connected with the classical school. Friedrich List himself, the founder of economic nationalism, regards the condition of national economy merely as a transitional stage preliminary to a world economy in which all nations will form but a single society. The classical school, he thinks, erred only in assuming as actually present a state of affairs which had first to be brought about. 'The idea of universal union can be realized only when many nationalities have risen to as nearly as possible a uniform stage of industry and civilization and of political development and power.' Yet the union is, like eternal peace, 'commanded by reason as well as religion.' That the adherents of the classical tendency in various literatures profess a similar faith needs not to be discussed at greater length. The attempt of Dietzel [1] might be mentioned, to construct above the concrete political economy a ' theoretical social economy ' treating of the economic individual as such. He argued for the growth alongside of the national economic organisms of a world-economic organism before which the former should recede more and more into the background. In connexion with the political organization, the world-economy idea appears earliest in Schmoller's theory of economic stages. [2] In his view, village economy, city economy, national economy, and world economy follow in succession in the historic development. He does not say explicitly whether a corresponding political organization is to be thought of as forming the basis of this world economy, or whether the original principle of division suddenly drops out. Kobatsch also has worked out a law of stages of his own for the historical evolution, summarizing the most important advances in the field of intellectual and material culture. He calls the period of the later antiquity and the middle ages the stage of ' monetarism ', that of the fifteenth and sixteenth centuries mercantilism, that of the eighteenth and nineteenth centuries, liberalism ; the middle of the nineteenth century is the period of nationalism, and that of the second half of the century continentalism and imperialism, while the twentieth century is designated as the period of internationalism. [3] The last period he characterizes by saying that in it the communities of interest involved in the trade relations of the national-economy groups become perceptibly stronger than the conflicts of interest. Among the socialists, such as Karl Marx, Werner Sombart, &c,. the higher development toward world economy follows as a matter of course from the demand for a complete change in the social order, through a socialization of the means of production which shall not stop at national

---

[1] Heinrich Dietzel, *Theoretische Sozialokonomie*, Leipsic, 1895.

[2] Gustav Schmoller, *Grundriss der allgemeinen Volkswirtschaftslehre*. 2 vols., Leipsic, 1904 and 1908.

[3] Rudolph Kobatsch, *Internationale Wirtschaftspolitik*, Vienna, 1907, p. 315.

boundaries. Finally, those thinkers who, like Bluntschli, the great student of international law, look forward to the coming of a great world-state in which all humanity will be organized, and also the peace advocates who urge a union of the nations to prevent war,—all these are compelled to look upon the progress toward world economy as in part the cause and in part the effect of political union on the international plane.

The third group is composed of those theories which regard national economy and world economy as destined to continue side by side. Here also a distinction is made as to whether world economy and national economy are generically similar concepts. Bernhard Harms represents the opinion that the relation between the two economies is to be regarded as a permanent condition and not as a matter of historic development, and that the standpoint for the treatment of both must be the same. National economy, in his view, includes the relations of the private-economy units among themselves and with the political authority, while world economy covers the mutual relations of all the private-economy units of the world. The following facts he regards as characteristic of national economy.[1] '(1) Its territorial scope is limited to the political domain of a single state. (2) It consists of a multiplicity of private economies, among which complete freedom of trade subsists within the boundaries of the given political jurisdiction. (3) It possesses technological media of exchange and transportation which permit such a utilization of the legal right of freedom of intercourse that even the spatially more widely separated private-economy units are able to supplement each other in their want-satisfying activities while carrying on the productive operations best suited to their respective localities. (4) It promotes more efficient activities on the part of the constituent units by measures of legal, commercial, economic and business policy.' The same

[1] Bernhard Harms, *Volkswirtschaft und Weltwirtschaft*, Jena, 1912, p. 100.

essential conditions obtain, according to Harms, in the case of the world economy. That the multiplicity of individual economy units and the highly evolved commercial relations are present admits of no dispute. The spatially limited field, also, corresponding to the political domain of the state, is furnished by the whole surface of the earth. Further, the exchange of goods is promoted by the activity of the state in the world sphere as well as within its own borders. So far well and good; but Harms passes over the condition he himself has laid down of a unified control of the whole field—in this case the earth's surface—and substitutes for such control the interaction of the various measures of economic policy of the various states. But these may not necessarily so much as strive toward unity, and their foreign trade measures may therefore not only fail to promote but may even obstruct world commerce. Treaties between nations do not constitute a source of juridical authority at all analogous to the legislation of autonomous states, for in such agreements it is not two wills of different order, state-will and world-will, which find expression, but merely the same state-will manifested in two different directions. The intelligent direction by a higher will, from which all other characteristics of the national economy follow of themselves, is wanting in the world economy. If the world-economic policy is defined as ' the international regulation and promotion of the commercial relations between the private economy units of different political states ',[1] then it is simply that part of national-economic policy which is concerned with foreign trade. Even in international treaties dealing with ocean navigation, in spite of the international character of the high seas, the ships must be strictly national, and hence the nationalistic element is so exclusively dominant that any agreement of this nature is concluded only when, and allowed to remain in force only so long as, it corresponds to the interests of the treaty power in question. The present writer, therefore, as already

[1] Op. cit., p. 393.

C

explained, assumes that national economy and world economy will continue to exist side by side. We define national economy, however, as an organism ruled by a unified will and world economy as mere community of trade relations. With this view too the conception of Philippovich seems in substantial agreement ; he says : [1] ' We cannot yet speak at the present time of a world-economy as an independent economic organism, since the various national economies which form the members of this world-economy are bound together only by commerce and not by a unified political constitution.' The words, ' not yet, at the present time ', seem, it is true, to indicate that in the light of the historic progress such a stage is posited as coming or perhaps only as probable ; but the condition laid down of a ' unified political constitution ' for the whole world shows that reference is merely made to a Utopian reflection. Karl Bücher [2] likewise rejects the doctrine of an evolutionary tendency toward a world economy : ' For on the one hand, no stage of economic development has ever permanently guaranteed independent control of the want-satisfying process ; every one has left certain gaps open which were to be filled in various ways. On the other hand, the alleged world-economy has thus far at least never produced any phenomena to be distinguished in essential characteristics from those of national economy, and it is to be seriously doubted whether any such phenomena will be manifested in any future time that we can now foresee.'

[1] Eugen von Philippovich, *Grundriss der politischen Oekonomie*, seventh edition, Tübingen, 1908, p. 19.

[2] Karl Bücher, *Die Entstehung der Volkswirtschaft*, eighth edition, Tübingen, 1911, p. 142.

II

THE SUBJECTS OF WORLD ECONOMY

1. The Great Economic Spheres

The Sphere of the State, the Customs Sphere, and the Economic Sphere. The sphere of the state and the customs sphere do not coincide, because political boundaries are determined by all sorts of historical accidents, and hence the political authority is frequently impelled by economic motives to draw the tariff boundary along other lines. It occasionally leaves part of the territory of the state outside the customs line (customs exclusions) or in pursuance of treaties includes contiguous foreign territory within the line (customs incorporations). These arrangements at present usually represent, however, trifling exceptions only ; in general it is the aim to embrace the entire territory of the state in a uniform customs line and so to secure also a uniform economic domain. A closer consideration of the development since the nineteenth century shows, however, that although that century was so favourable to the establishment of large customs divisions, yet the effort in this direction was not always successful ; for the real unification of an economic sphere much more is required than a common customs boundary. Just as duties do not guarantee the founding of industries, so also a customs line affords no assurance of the development of a unified economic sphere. To the first a certain stage of culture must be added, to the second a certain community of culture. The systems of wants and mechanisms of their satisfaction, also the potentialities of production, must be reasonably similar as well as the government and legislation affecting the various arms brought within the customs line, if the necessary homogeneity of interests is to be brought about.

Since as to this point culture is always the more and nature always the less decisive factor, we must seek the tests of similarity less in the natural features of the country and much more in the cultural make-up of the inhabitants. Viewed in this light, the great customs divisions present themselves as a politico-economic fiction, for as a matter of fact they fall into several economic spheres. These, it is true, manifest in some degree a tendency to increase in size, but the limits of this process fall well short of those gigantic national complexes which have been marked out by customs legislation, which has run far in advance of existing conditions. On the contrary, the effort becomes more and more conspicuous to take account of these factual conditions by at least tacitly drawing inter-mediate customs lines, and by the use of substitutes for tariff protection. Hence, though it is calculated that approximately four-fifths of the habitable land surface of the globe and of the total population now belong to the larger customs divisions, this signifies neither progress in the direction of a world-economic organism nor an approach toward ' a common, universal freedom of trade '[1], but only an arming for the conflict on the world-economy plane. Even the summation of the greater customs spheres, which are opposed to one another in a multitude of ways, is misleading. A world war could be characterized by general alliances among the military powers just as well as could a progress toward world peace be so characterized. All such structures lead to no other end than the strengthening of the subjects of world economy.

The Division of the greater Customs Districts into Economic Spheres. It is hardly possible to give a complete picture of the present development in the direction of stable economic spheres ; each country, true to the old maxim of ' one state one customs unit ', is struggling to obliterate such movements toward independence, although they combat symptoms rather than causes. The evidence at hand is sufficient,

---

[1] Sigmund Schilder, *Entwicklungstendenzen der Weltwirtschaft*, Berlin, 1912, vol. i, p. 233.

however, to demonstrate that the great customs units are very far from being unified economic divisions, hence the tendency toward subdivision of customs units continues.

The British world-empire comprehends the greatest national complex of all. Its composition is shown in the following table :

BRITISH DOMINIONS

	Area in square kilometres.	Population.
Mother Country	314,511	45,216,665
Colonies and Protectorates . .	29,332,981	373,630,089
Total	29,647,492	418,846,754

But in the first place the colonies with responsible governments, namely, Canada, the South African Union, the Australian Commonwealth, and New Zealand, must be separated from the enormous English possessions. These all pursue a completely independent national economic policy and protect themselves even against the competition of the mother country, though recently they have begun to favour England as against foreign countries by preferential duties. Canada is in fact more influenced by the tariff policy of the United States of America, as shown by the history of the commercial agreement of 1911, and only restrained by political considerations from closer relations with that country. Within the colonies themselves, again, we observe efforts toward the formation of independent economic divisions. In Canada an opposition manifests itself between the industrial East and the agricultural West. In Australia the development of transcontinental railways will be insufficient to overcome the natural separation of the North and West from the South by wide stretches of desert. The English Government has been able longest to ward off an autonomous economic policy in the crown colony of India; but in spite of its great ethnographic and religious heterogeneity, the population has succeeded, through the *swadeshi* movement which set in about the year 1905, in making their special

interests felt. In England itself there is a growing con-
viction that only by economic concessions can the English
political influence be maintained.   It was a notable utterance
which Lord Crewe addressed to an assemblage of Liberals in
Cheltenham in the fall of 1912, when he said that a protectionistic government in England would not have the right,
and in the long run not the power, to prevent India from
introducing protective duties to the same degree to which the
self-governing English dominions apply them to goods coming
from England. To whatever extent, moreover, protective
duties might be applied in India, they would be directed
primarily against England, for England is the chief rival of
Indian domestic industry.   Thus an area of 23,900,000 square
kilometres and a population of 314,200,000 are already cut off
in an economic sense from the English colonial domain.   The
remainder is divided among colonies in the tropics, many of
which naturally gravitate toward other markets, as West
India toward the United States of America and Rhodesia
toward the Belgian Congo, among free-port districts such as
Gibraltar, Malta, Hongkong, Weihaiwei, the Straits Settlements, Aden, and Walfish Bay, and ' open door ' dominions
like the Pacific Islands and British East and West Africa.
All these are as accessible to any other country as they are
to England.

But even the small mother country itself is not a unified
economic division, for Ireland also is struggling for a special
situation in economic respects. As early as the eighteenth
century a notable movement was on foot encouraging the
people to use Irish products.[1] At that time the industrial
positions of England and Ireland, previously on the same
plane, were beginning to shift at the expense of the latter
country in consequence of England's wealth in coal and iron.
On the occasion of the Home Rule debates in the 1912–13

---

[1] A. E. Murray, *A History of the Commercial and Financial Relations
between England and Ireland from the Period of the Restoration*, London,
1903, p. 202.

session of Parliament, it was repeatedly brought out that an economic issue was involved in the separatist movement in Ireland ; the new bill leaves two economic divisions under a common tariff system while aiming to make them independent in their factory legislation and general social policy. In the meantime the Irish have resorted to independent action, and by the introduction of national marks for merchandise (to which subject we shall later recur) have organized a system of protection for the national products.

The second largest domain under European rule is Russia. The extent of the Russian dominions is shown in the table below.

RUSSIAN DOMINIONS

	Area in square kilometres.	Population.
Mother Country	22,031,727	160,095,200
Protectorates	265,000	2,000,000
Total	22,296,727	162,095,200

Here we find a division into customs districts in the mother country itself ; Finland is completely independent as to tariff policy, although efforts to assimilate it with the rest of the country have been carried on for decades and are opposed not by political but by merely economic obstacles ; eastern Siberia also was free territory down to the year 1908 and still occupies a peculiar position. But in addition to these divisions the work of Kowalewsky [1] names and describes for us no fewer than twenty-one economic divisions, fundamentally different in every characteristic affecting the economic life, their outer nature, the character of their population, and the political and economic institutions which they have developed in the course of their histories. Another interesting general characteristic of these economic divisions is that they become smaller as we approach the more densely populated region of western Europe, coming down finally to an area of 100,000 square kilometres, and, on

---

[1] W. Kowalewsky, *La Russie à la fin du 19ᵉ siècle*, Paris, 1900, p. 37.

the other hand, they increase greatly in extent toward eastern Europe and Asia.

France has increased her dominions in area and population in much larger proportions than Russia through her colonial activities, as shown in the table below.

FRENCH DOMINIONS

	Area in square kilometres.	Population.
Mother Country	536,464	39,601,509
Colonies and Protectorates . .	10,293,835	46,125,510
Total	10,830,299	85,727,019

But of these the Asiatic colonial possessions at least form economically an entirely separate division, with an area of 664,209 square kilometres and a population of 16,600,000. Algeria, with an area of 890,000 square kilometres and a population of 5,200,000, has perforce retained to a certain extent its separate position as to tariff policy in spite of the fact that it is legally and administratively treated as a French department and not as a colony. The same applies in a much greater degree to the protectorate of Tunis, with an area of 167,400 square kilometres and a population of 1,800,000. The remaining African colonies are widely separated geographically from these by the Sahara, and further, in some of them, as French Congo, the ' open door ' policy is maintained.

Even in the great European countries which have not laid the principal stress on colonial possessions we find the national customs domain cut up into various separate economic divisions. We note in Germany, for example, that from 1816 to 1871 the population of the agricultural region east of the Elbe (the seven eastern provinces of Prussia, the two Mecklenburgs, and the grand duchy of Hesse) increased nearly ninety-one per cent, while that of industrial West and South Germany increased but little over twenty-three per cent; in the period between 1871 and 1900, on the contrary, these rôles were reversed and the increase in the agricultural

East was but twenty-six per cent against seventy-nine per cent[1] in the industrial West and South. This contrast points to a sharp distinction in the natural and cultural characteristics, which finds a clear expression also in the economic policies of the districts. In Italy, too, the industrial North is essentially distinct from the wine and fruit grow-ing South. In Austria-Hungary a common tariff system, in force for more than sixty years, has not been able to obliterate, and in fact has served rather to emphasize, the differences between the two halves of the monarchy; even in Austria alone, Galicia and Bukowina form a separate economic division in consequence of their territorial location, and their special situation is also taken into account in certain pro-tective measures, such as the law for the encouragement of manufactures and preferential deliveries.

The following table shows the classification of the territorial domain of the United States of America.

UNITED STATES DOMINIONS

	Area in square kilometres.	Population.
Mother Country	7,839,384	76,085,794
Colonies	1,755,878	9,812,493
Total	9,595,262	85,898,287

The most important colonial possession is formed by the Philippine Islands which have an area of 296,310 square kilometres and a population of 7,600,000. In accordance with their constitution of 1787, the United States pursue the policy of including every territorial accession in the single customs domain. This policy was followed even in the case of distant Alaska and the Hawaian Islands, which are treated in a political sense not as colonies but as territories, as well as with the colony of Porto Rico. Yet with regard to the Philippines, the Tariff of 1909 was forced to concede

[1] H. Pohle, *Die Entwicklung des deutschen Wirtschaftslebens im 19. Jahrhundert*, second edition, Leipsic, 1908, p. 27.

a customs position in some respects different from that of the rest of the country, and this notwithstanding the fact that the agreement entered into in the Treaty of Paris of 1899 obligating the United States to grant ' most favoured nation ' privileges for a period of ten years had expired. But in the mother country also, the Western States, separated geographically by the Rocky Mountains, the Southern States with their plantation economy, and the industrial Northern States, show quite different degrees of industrial development and have therefore different interests, and these have led to numerous disagreements in regard to commercial policy, the immigration question, &c.

In regard to China, Turkey, Brazil, and Argentina, any text-book in geography will show that they are by no means economically homogeneous political divisions.

Since the time of Colbert, it has been the aim of every statesman to secure the largest possible customs domain to the end of assuring a rich internal development and of enabling the state to exert outwardly great economic power. The success of this policy has always been remarkable where substantial economic homogeneity already obtained among the districts thus merged in their customs policy, and where the obliteration of customs lines involved the removal of only artificial obstacles to the external realization of unity. This was the case, for example, in France and Austria, and later in Germany and Italy. But it was a colossal blunder to conclude that economic homogeneity can be actually created as well as merely turned to account by the establishment of a common customs boundary. In consequence, the broad customs domains of the present day are a fiction of economic policy; they fall in fact into several economic divisions which have indeed common political interests, but in the economic field itself their interests conflict. And while with passing time these divisions may perhaps tend to increase in size as measured by population, they decrease in territorial extent; for economic wants are determined, not by the land, but by the character of the people who dwell upon it. Yet the assertion can by no means be made that every natural economic division must also be an independent customs domain. Side by side with the conflicting interests are others which are common, and the intensity of the two sets of interests must rather be investigated and compared in each particular case and the degree of economic rapprochement or separation determined accordingly. Customs lines are not so rigid as political boundaries and in the future will no doubt show more gradations from country to country than is at present the case, when we distinguish only between countries with customs unity, most-favoured nations, and those not in the most-favoured class.

2. The Small Economic Divisions

The Evolutionary Tendencies of the Small Economic Divisions. As there are political divisions and customs districts so large and so far from uniform that they cannot form unified economic spheres, so also there are states which are too small, and which in spite of their political independence are forced to lean upon other states or upon a larger participation in the world economy. Yet the normal size of an economic unit, to exceed which leads to subdivision, and to fall short of which means a shifting outward of the centre of gravity, is by no means definite and fixed. In the earlier stages it depends upon the character of the land, then with the progress of industrialization, more and more upon the density of the population, and further upon the conditions with respect to culture and the phases of economic development dominant at the time. It is smaller in the case of manufacturing than for agricultural countries, but increases in extent for the former with the growing requirement of industry toward specialization. For present-day Europe a territorial area of from one-fourth to one-half million square kilometres and a population of from thirty to fifty millions may be regarded as representing the normal size. The countries named in the table below might then be considered as of normal extent.

EUROPEAN ECONOMIC DIVISIONS OF 'NORMAL' SIZE

Country.	Area in square kilometres.	Population.	Year.
Germany	540,778	60,641,489	1905
Austria-Hungary	676,249	51,340,378	1910
France	536,464	39,601,509	1911
Great Britain	314,339	45,216,665	1911
Italy	286,682	34,686,683	1911
Spain	504,517	20,068,381	1909

It is of course no mere accident that the normal size has been so generally realized in Europe, for these states have secured the economic extent which answered to their needs in a long and varying historic development.

States notably under the normal size of an economic unit encounter no great difficulties under prevailing conditions of free trade; it was for this reason, too, that Belgium, Holland, Denmark, Sweden, and Norway remained longest true to that policy. With the general adoption of protectionism, different courses are open to the small countries. If they are altogether too small, their only recourse may be incorporation in a neighbouring larger economic sphere, which sometimes takes the shape of a formal tariff union as is the case with Luxemburg and Germany, Liechtenstein and Austria-Hungary, Monaco and France, San Marino and Italy. But even if independence in tariff policy is jealously guarded, economic dependence is unavoidable; Montenegro, for example, in spite of her repellent attitude, is economically dominated by her trade relations with the neighbouring Austria-Hungary. The following table gives the area and population of these tiny states.

SMALL STATES OF EUROPE

State.				Area in square kilometres.	Population.
Montenegro	.	.	.	9,080	228,000
Luxemburg	.	.	.	2,586	259,891
Liechtenstein	.	.	.	159	9,500
Monaco	.	.	.	21·6	15,600
Andorra	.	.	.	45·2	6,000
San Marino	.	.	.	61	11,000

Larger states than these will not be inclined to give up their national individuality by being merged in a neighbouring domain. They are likely either to seek to combine the preservation of their distinctive existence with the securing of a larger economic unit through a customs union with neighbouring states, based on equality of position, or else to endeavour to win for their national industry a larger influence in the field of foreign trade.

The Formation of Customs Unions.   During the nineteenth century endeavours toward the formation of customs unions among politically independent states were fairly active, but they were actuated by the most varied motives and directed toward quite different ends.   To convinced free-traders such unions seemed a step in the gradual abolition of all the tariff lines of all the nations of the earth.   They thought a great customs union would tend to draw in contiguous territory, and the customs lines would be farther and farther extended until the whole inhabited world would form one universal union in which no duties at all would be levied.[1] Further, the foundation of the German *Zollverein* in 1833, the forerunner of the establishment of the German Empire, produced a great effect on men's minds and incited to imitation.   France especially strove energetically to erect a counterpoise against the rapidly growing economic importance of Germany by uniting some of the West European countries.

[1] L. Bosc, *Zollalliancen und Zollunionen in ihrer Bedeutung für die Handelspolitik der Vergangenheit und Zukunft*, German translation by Dr. S. Schilder, Berlin, 1907, p. 38.

Among specific attempts of this sort the following may be named : negotiations of France with Belgium beginning in the year 1835 ; the proposals of Léon Faucher for the formation of a South European Customs Union (*union du midi*) consisting of France, Spain, Belgium, and Switzerland ; that of Leroy-Beaulieu in 1879 for a West European Customs Union (*union douanière occidentale*) including France, Belgium, Switzerland, and Italy ; that of M. Schwab in 1896 (in his book, *Le danger allemand*) for the formation of a Union between France, Spain, Greece, and Italy ; and G. de Contenson's proposal in 1903 to form a Latin Alliance (*alliance latine*) consisting of France, Italy, and Spain.[1] Finally, the building up of world empires by the United States of America, England, and Russia, and in particular the idea of a Pan-American Customs Union gave a great impetus to the movement for a Central European Union. The first proposal of this sort came from Molinari in the year 1878 (*union douanière de l'Europe centrale*) and has since been repeated in France and Germany with interminable variations.

The causes which blocked the realization of such a plan are identical with those which make the idea of incorporation so repellent to the small states, notwithstanding that the strongest interests of an economic character would urge to such a course. In the first place, the proposals were not free from political implications, or at least they were bound to be susceptible to such interpretation by the other party. Hence there arose a danger on the one hand for the political independence of the smaller nation and on the other for its neutrality, guaranteed by international treaties. Only within a political community is the political situation very favourable to the plan of a customs union. The customs unions in the English colonies owe their existence to this condition, namely, that of Australia resulting from the Constitution of 1900 and that of South Africa following the Treaty of Bloemfontein of March 24, 1903, and the Union

[1] Op. cit., pp. 134, 139, 150.

Constitution of 1909. Between foreign states the political barrier is the greater in proportion to the difference in political power. A further obstacle has been the fact that under the dominant influence of free-trade theories a customs union has always been taken to mean the complete obliteration of intermediate customs lines ; this would necessarily lead with progressive industrialization to continually more extensive differentiation in productive conditions, and hence to increasing certainty that crises originating in the one country would affect the other seriously. When people once think themselves into the realization that there is possible a whole series of intermediate stages between a mere commercial agreement and a complete customs union and that a line of sharp distinction can be drawn between the common and the dissimilar interests of two countries, then the prospect should be more hopeful for such a less intimate union as might be designated by the term customs league, customs agreement, customs alliance, or the like. A brief summary of the attitude of the neutral states of Europe on the subject of customs union promotion may confirm this view.

Soon after the establishment of the German Customs Union, Belgium was confronted with the French proposal for union, which apparently owed its genesis to the initiative of King Louis-Philippe. According to the plan worked out by the French Minister, Duchâtel, in 1836, Belgium was simply to adopt the French system of customs duties and consumption taxes and submit herself to the leadership of France in her whole commercial policy. This would not have been in fact a customs union, but rather a customs annexation after the manner of Monaco. The opposition of French industries, threatened by free trade for the Belgian manufactures, and in a much greater degree the intervention of the powers which had guaranteed the neutrality of Belgium in 1831, frustrated the plan.

In Holland also, after the separation of Belgium, the

question of a customs union was brought up, in connexion, in the first place, with the German Customs Union. The obstacles which manifested themselves were in part the political solicitude of the Dutch Government and in part also the high protective duties of the German Union, an application of which to Holland would lead, it was feared, to a falling off in its brisk transit trade. When in turn the wish for a customs union with Germany came to be expressed in Dutch commercial circles on the occasion of the drafting of the German Tariff of 1900, the port cities of North Germany opposed the step, fearing a loss of trade to the Dutch ports of Rotterdam and Amsterdam, which are more favourably situated for the industries of the Rhine country and Westphalia. The union of Holland with Belgium was also taken under consideration. The idea was first proposed in 1878 and was supported by the chambers of commerce, but on January 19, 1880, the Dutch Government declared against the move in the lower house of the parliament. The reason given referred to the great difference in the consumption taxes of the two countries, but the Government was, as a matter of fact, no doubt more influenced by political considerations. When the plan was again broached and came up for discussion in the Belgian lower house on March 27, 1903, the Government moved the order of the day.

Perhaps the keenest interest in the question of customs unions was felt in Switzerland, which in view of its geographical location was bound to experience the greatest inconvenience from the changing protective duties of the surrounding great nations. At first, and in fact as early as 1879, advances were made toward France, as Germany had gone over to protectionism in the new tariff law put in force about that time, while from France were emanating the liberal ideas of a commercial union of the Central European states. Opposition at once arose in Switzerland, based on the fear of loss of national independence. When France later denounced all her treaties for February 1, 1892, passed a high protective tariff, and adopted an attitude not at all friendly to such agreements, Switzerland turned again to Germany and was a party, as was Belgium also, to the Middle-European treaties of December 1891.

The idea of a Scandinavian customs union has also been frequently brought up. From the year 1874 to July 1, 1890, such a union subsisted between Sweden and Norway, but it was first modified by the so-called Inter-Dominion Law (*Zwischenreichsgesetz*) and finally entirely dissolved, along with the political union, on June 7, 1905. But the economic hopes which were entertained from the separation failed to be realized, and soon afterwards proposals were made looking to a customs union between Sweden, Norway, and Denmark. In the interests of this propaganda the ' Northern League ' was formed in Copenhagen in 1904.

The Middle-European December treaties of 1891, concluded after general negotiations by the three countries of the Triple Alliance (Germany, Austria-Hungary, and Italy) among themselves and with Belgium and Switzerland, are to be regarded as at least a movement in the direction of a commercial-policy alliance. By interlocking agreements the countries formed a unified whole, so that no commercial treaty could be terminated alone if the others were to remain in force. The outward expression of this interlocking took the form of an adaptation of the whole conventional tariff to each of these agreements in such a way that each contained not merely the special concessions granted to the particular party to the convention, but in addition the tariff modifications among all the co-operating states. In this way something approaching a common economic sphere for a population of 131,000,000 was assured for a period of twelve years. Later, the field of the treaties was widened by agreements affecting Russia and the Balkan countries —Roumania, Servia, and Bulgaria. Yet at the renewal of the treaties in 1905 and 1906 the original idea was again dropped, so that the final commercial treaties of these states are no longer formally different from other such agreements.

The Specialization of Industry with a View to Foreign Trade. More successful have been the efforts to make up for the inadequacy of domestic markets by capturing markets abroad. To this end the smaller countries have clung longer and with greater tenacity to the free-trade policy; even to-day the Netherlands, Belgium, Switzerland, and Denmark still belong to the countries with a minimum of protective tariff. They have also taken a more active part in all movements toward international unions and avoided national differentiation as far as possible. Belgium, for example, in her tariff law, automatically takes account of and reciprocates every concession granted by any foreign country; her system thus takes the form of a unified tariff while adapting itself constantly to the varying treatment accorded Belgian products in all other countries. The small countries have also bestowed especial care on their transit trade, which consequently amounts, in the case of Holland for example, to much more than the country's own commerce, while in Belgium and Switzerland it approaches the exports in the value of the goods involved.

The table which follows gives a general view of the customs districts of the world, arranged in order of their territorial extent, showing the density of their population and the amount of imports and exports reckoned on a per capita basis. The figures are taken from the official statistics of the countries for the year 1910, or the year nearest that date for which figures are available, other years being indicated in parentheses.

CUSTOMS DISTRICTS OF THE WORLD

A. EUROPEAN CUSTOMS DISTRICTS

Country.	Area in square kilo-metres.	Population.	Popula-tion per square kilo-metre.	Imports per capita. (Marks.)	Exports per capita. (Marks.)
1. European Russia . .	5,003,840	116,505,500 (1909)	23·3	25·7	18·0
2. Turkey . .	2,987,117	24,028,900	8·0 (1908–9)	2·4	1·4
3. Austria-Hun-gary . . .	676,249	51,340,378	75·9	48·0	41·4
4. Germany. .	540,778	64,925,993	120·0	137·6	115·2
5. France . .	536,464	39,601,509 (1911)	73·8	146·7	127·5
6. Spain. . .	504,517	19,503,068	38·7	41·4	39·7
7. Sweden . .	447,864	5,522,474	13·4	137·4	121·3
8. Finland . .	373,604	3,059,324 (1909)	9·2	101·7	76·8
9. Norway . .	322,909	2,357,790	7·6	204·5	147·6
10. Great Britain	315,725	45,216,665 (1911)	143·2	259·2	241·4
11. Italy . . .	286,682	34,686,683 (1911)	121·0	75·8	48·6
12. Roumania .	131,353	6,684,265 (1907)	50·9	48·9	73·6
13. Bulgaria . .	96,346	4,329,108	45·1	33·0	24·0
14. Portugal . .	91,943	5,423,132 (1900)	58·9	54·5	28·3
15. Greece . .	46,657	2,631,952 (1907)	40·7	49·4	42·8
16. Servia . .	48,303	2,911,701	61·1	—	—
17. Switzerland .	41,324	3,765,123	91·2	387·8	257·3
18. Denmark. .	38,969	2,757,076 (1911)	70·8	231·9	220·2
19. Netherlands .	33,079	5,858,175 (1909)	177·0	941·9	759 4
20. Belgium . .	29,455	7,423,784	251·7	437·1	360·8

B. Non-European Customs Districts

Country.	Area in square kilometres.	Population.	Population per square kilometre.	Imports per capita. (Marks.)	Exports per capita. (Marks.)
1. United States of America .	9,403,970	92,284,139	9·8	74·3	84·8
2. Brazil . .	8,061,260	23,070,969	2·8	42·1	56·0
3. Australian Commonwealth	97,713,910	4,449,493 (1911)	0·6	275·4	341·8
4. British India .	4,610,317	314,955,240	68·5	7·5	9·4
5. China (proper)	3,970,000	407,335,000	102·6	6·8	5·6
6. Canada . .	3,745,574	7,081,869 (1911)	1·9	219·3	165·7
7. Mexico . .	1,987,201	15,063,207	7·6	.28·6	40·8
8. Peru . . .	1,769,804	4,586,000	2·5	28·4	20·6
9. Persia . .	1,645,000	9,000,000	5·5	20·5	¦15·9
10. Bolivia . .	1,470,196	2,267,935 (1908)	1·5	24·9 (1909)	46·1
11. South African Union . .	1,225,547	5,958,499 (1911)	4·9	134·6	74·8
12. Colombia .	1,181,573	4,141,791 (1905)	3·5	11·8 (1905)	11·9
13. Venezuela .	1,020,400	2,685,440	2·3	112·0	135·6
14. Egypt . .	900,000	11,287,359 (1907)	12·5	43·8	53·9
15. Chile . . .	758,206	3,249,279 (1907)	4·2	142·2	157·2
16. Siam . . .	600,000	7,000,000	11·6	16·4	23·0
17. Japan, not including Korea	451,759	51,591,342 (1911)	114·5	18·8	18·6
18. Ecuador . .	307,243	1,500,000	4·9	.24·9 (1909)	27·4
19. Paraguay .	253,100	686,937 (1907)	2·7	37·8	29·0
20. Uruguay . .	186,915	1,042,686 (1908)	5·6	16·6	17·1
21. Nicaragua .	128,340	600,000 (1906)	4·7	19·9 (1908)	24·6
22. Honduras .	114,670	553,446	4·8	19·9	18·2
23. Cuba . . .	114,524	2,048,980 (1907)	17·9	217·7	316·6
24. Guatemala .	113,030	1,842,134 (1903)	16 3	11·7	22·4

B. Non-European Customs Districts—*contd.*

Country.	Area in square kilo- metres.	Population.	Popula- tion per square kilo- metre.	Imports per capita. (Marks.)	Exports per capita. (Marks.)
25. Panama . .	75,685	419,029 (1909)	5·5	100·4	17·7
26. Dominican Republic .	50,070	650,000 (1909)	13·0	28·2 (1909)	55·3
27. Costa Rica .	48,410	379,533	7·9	87·2	92·4
28. Salvador . .	34,126	1,133,000	33·3	13·4	26·1
29. Haiti . . .	28,676	2,029,700 (1909)	70·7	11·6 (1908–9)	6·9

It must, to be sure, be taken into account that the extent of participation of a country in the world's trade is influenced by various factors, such as the geographical location, the nature of the land, the political organization, &c. Further- more, the numbers given in the official commercial statistics are, as is generally known, not strictly comparable, on account of differences in the methods of collecting .the data. For example, in the case of Belgium, and in a still greater degree in that of Holland, the figures given in the table include in the imports and exports a considerable part of the transit trade of the countries and hence are higher than in fact they should be. It is none the less unmistakable that the smaller countries tend toward a greater density of population and a larger relative export trade. The following summary by rank will make this still clearer in the case of the European countries.

Country.	Area in millions of square kilometres.	Country.	Inhabitants per square kilometre.	Country.	Exports per capita in marks.
1. Russia	5·00	1. Belgium	251·7	1. Netherlands	759·4
2. Turkey	2·99	2. Netherlands	177·0	2. Belgium	360·8
3. Austria-Hungary	0·68	3. Great Britain	143·2	3. Switzerland	257·3
4. Germany	0·54	4. Italy	121·0	4. Great Britain	241·4
5. France	0·54	5. Germany	120·0	5. Denmark	220·2
6. Spain	0·50	6. Switzerland	91·2	6. Norway	147·6
7. Sweden	0·45	7. Austria-Hungary	75·9	7. France	127·5
8. Finland	0·37	8. France	73·8	8. Sweden	121·3
9. Norway	0·32	9. Denmark	70·8	9. Germany	115·2
10. Great Britain	0·32	10. Portugal	58·9	10. Finland	76·8
11. Italy	0·29	11. Servia	55·7	11. Roumania	73·6
12. Roumania	0·13	12. Roumania	50·9	12. Italy	48·6
13. Bulgaria	0·10	13. Bulgaria	42·0	13. Greece	42·8
14. Portugal	0·09	14. Greece	40·7	14. Austria-Hungary	41·4
15. Greece	0·06	15. Spain	39·8	15. Spain	38·9
16. Servia	0·05	16. Russia	23·3	16. Servia	29·6
17. Switzerland	0·04	17. Sweden	13·4	17. Portugal	28·3
18. Denmark	0·04	18. Finland	9·2	18. Bulgaria	24.0
19. Netherlands	0·03	19. Turkey	8·0	19. Russia	18·1
20. Belgium	0·03	20. Norway	7·6	20. Turkey	1·4

In cases where the amount of exports from non-European customs units appears surprisingly high in comparison with the European view of the difference in cultural advancement, it must be borne in mind that the composition of the exports is also a significant matter. The more advanced a nation becomes, the more diversified will be its industrial activities and the exports will embrace a continually widening range of articles. The more concentrated in a single field the exports of a country are, the greater will be the risks attending chance variations in the amount of the goods produced and the character of the market for them, which will correspondingly reduce the profits of the business as a whole. In the industrial states of Europe the most important single articles of export never make up more than from five to ten per cent of the total exports. With this proportion may be compared the figures given in the following table, which shows the fraction of the total exports of some non-industrial countries formed by certain special articles.

COMPOSITION OF EXPORTS OF NON-INDUSTRIAL LANDS

Country.	Article.	Per cent of Total Exports.
Russia	Grains	more than 60
Sweden	Timber	45
Roumania	Grains	more than 70
Bulgaria	Grains	50
Denmark	Animal products used as food (Butter, Meat)	76
Egypt	Cotton	84
Australia	{ Grains	50
	{ Animal products	42
Siam	Rice	88
Bolivia	{ Tin	46
	{ Rubber	34
Brazil	{ Coffee	41
	{ Caoutchouc	40
Chile	Saltpetre	72
Colombia	Coffee	40
Costa Rica	{ Bananas	50
	{ Coffee	30
Cuba	Cane sugar	74
Santo Domingo	{ Sugar	41
	{ Cacao	35
Ecuador	Cacao	71
Salvador	Coffee	70
Guatemala	Coffee	88
Honduras	Bananas	more than 50
Mexico	Precious metals	49
Nicaragua	Coffee	42
Panama	Bananas	52
Paraguay	Hides	48
Uruguay	{ Wool	37
	{ Hides	27
Venezuela	Coffee	45

3. Customs Districts Wholly or Partly Dependent

Colonies. The industrial divisions of the greater part of the inhabited surface of the earth are not fully autonomous in their economic policies, but dependent in a greater or less degree on the will of some other country. In this respect, further, there are to be distinguished two possible kinds of dependence. The economic division may belong to another and larger one in such a sense that it is to be regarded as a part of it, yet does not receive the same political and economic treatment; such districts are colonies. Or the industrial division in question may be bound by non-revokable political agreements and its political and economic interests subordinated to those of other states in such a way that, while it belongs to none of them, it is forced to remain entirely open to their commercial competition; it is then called an 'open-door' district. The following table shows the extent of the two categories of economic spheres according to their present standing.

DEPENDENT ECONOMIC DIVISIONS

	Area in millions of square kilometres.	Population in millions.
The earth as a whole	145·5	1,679·5
Colonies	53·7	535·0
Open-door lands (including open-door colonies)	44·1	626·0

Colonies, then, in the broadest sense, are territories which belong politically to a greater domain, the mother country, yet are not placed on an equality with the ruling part of it, but have their political and economic interests subordinated to those of the mother country. There may be a series of gradations in the condition, according to the standpoint from which they are judged. From the standpoint of civil and international law the distinction is usually made between true colonies, which are completely subject to the foreign power, protectorates, in which, while a separate political power continues to exist, yet the dominating influence is assumed to be that of the protecting state, and finally, spheres of interest, which are assigned to powers by international agreement.   In respect to the administration, each state prescribes the categories which seem best adapted to the accomplishment of its ends.   Thus the English separate on the one hand colonies with responsible government—the self-governing dominions, in which legislation is in the hands of an assembly representing the people, but in which the mother country, represented by a Governor-General, possesses a veto right which is almost never exercised.   These are Canada, the Commonwealth of Australia, New Zealand, and the South African Union.   On the other hand there are the crown colonies, where legislation and administration are in the hands of a Governor, in addition to whom, in the crown colonies proper (as distinguished from protectorates), there is also an advisory legislative council.   India occupies a special position, but one more nearly approaching that of the crown colonies. According to the economic organization, again, settlement colonies are distinguished from exploitation colonies.   The former lie in the Temperate Zones and hence are peopled to an increasing extent by white settlers, and advance toward industrialization; exploitation colonies, on the contrary, are given over to tropical agriculture and hence are chiefly worked by the native coloured population, over whom stand the resident whites as a relatively small, ruling and property-owning class.   The economic organization naturally exerts a decisive influence on the political constitution and administration, and the English exploitation colonies are uniformly crown colonies.   The history of colonial possessions is one of continual changes.   One cause of these is formed by the shiftings in political power.   At the beginning of the nineteenth century the English colonial possessions were only about one-third as extensive as those of Spain.   Since that time the Spanish colonial domain has almost completely fallen away, while the English has increased enormously. Of very recent date are the colonial possessions of Germany, Italy, Belgium, the United States of America, and Japan. But the changes affect not merely the ownership ; they relate as well to transformations in the colonial districts themselves. The exploitation colonies do not advance beyond the stage of subjection to the mother country, while the settlement colonies show a decided tendency to develop toward independence or union. A union, in such a sense that the colony becomes a province of the mother country on a plane of full equality, can be advantageously effected only when, in consequence of the geographical situation of the two population groups to be united, the relations between them are so intimate and the community of interests so great that a common legislative body is able to meet the requirements of both. In this way Algeria is a province of France like any other, electing, like the rest, her representatives to the French parliament. The attempt of Spain similarly to incorporate Cuba came to grief, however, because the peculiar needs of the island could not be satisfactorily filled by the three representatives sent to the Spanish Cortes. Otherwise the colonial districts settled by Europeans seem to approach with sufficient political and economic development toward a stage of complete independence. Thus the four great English self-governing dominions, Canada, Australia, New Zealand, and South Africa, stand at present in a relation only of rather loose alliance with the mother country. On the other hand, countries of the Torrid Zone can change from a position of independence to that of colonies, as happened, for example, with the Congo Free State in the year 1908 and at least in some degree with the republic of Liberia in 1910. Finally, it is to be pointed out that colonies may be at the same time open-door territories, as when the mother country is restricted by international agreements in its right to control the economic policy of the colony and especially in the determination of its customs duties.

The economic aims and means involved in colonial policies are also subject to considerable change.   In the seventeenth and eighteenth centuries colonies were treated as compulsory markets for the industrial products of the mother country ; all attempts at an independent industrial development were suppressed and importation and exportation were monopolized for the benefit of the mother country.   But the separation of the United States of America demonstrated how dangerous such measures of compulsion may become.   After that event the effort was to substitute positive methods for negative, actively encouraging the development of colonial production along lines in which competition with the mother country could not arise.   This policy met with the greatest success in the tropical colonies, where encouragement of the production of high-value raw materials such as cotton, jute, hemp, caoutchouc, coffee, tobacco, valuable woods, &c., not merely brought high profits to the colony, but also facilitated and secured the supply of raw materials for the industries of the mother country.   In the way of manufactures, the production of raw sugar, cotton-seed oil, and the like was permitted.   But with regard to these colonies, some restrictive measures are still kept in force.   For example, England keeps the duties on cotton manufactures at a very low rate in British India in the interest of her own cotton industry, in spite of the fact that since ancient times a famous cotton industry has had its seat in India.   The tariff now in force admits cotton yarns duty-free while cotton cloth is subjected to a tax of only three and one-half per cent *ad valorem.* Moreover, simultaneously with the introduction of this duty, the Cotton Duties Act of 1896 was passed, by the terms of which Indian manufactures must pay a consumption tax equal to the duty on the domestic product, so that in effect the imported goods are placed on complete equality with them. In Egypt also, after the establishment of two cotton-spinning mills in 1901, one of them in connexion with a weaving mill, the Egyptian Government immediately passed a regulation subjecting their product to a consumption tax of eight per cent ' as compensation for the loss of customs income '. But in the case of the colonies peopled with European settlers an increasing measure of liberty to determine their own commercial policy had to be granted. They frame their own tariff laws in accordance with their fiscal requirements and need of protection, and are obligated to the mother country only to the extent of granting her a most-favoured-nation position. The system of preferential duties, which was a feature of earlier commercial policy has been again brought into use. It was recommended in the English Colonial Conferences which have been taking place since 1887, and was carried into effect after the termination of interfering commercial treaties of England with Belgium and Germany. The first step was taken by Canada, where the law of June 13, 1898, granted a duty reduction of twenty-five per cent, which was increased on July 1, 1900, to thirty-three and one-third per cent, and specialized in the tariff law of November 30, 1906, into a detailed preferential tariff by individual articles. The South African Union, in the agreement of March 24, 1903, granted a tariff concession of twenty-five per cent and remits the duty altogether in cases where it does not exceed two and one-half per cent *ad valorem*. New Zealand, in the law of November 24, 1903, adopted a general increase in the duty rates applicable to other than English goods. The Australian Tariff of 1907 grants especially moderate rates to English goods. France, too, in the Tariff of January 11, 1892, amended by the law of March 29, 1910, granted duty reductions to her colonies, and receives in return a preferential treatment at the hands of the colonies of Tunis, Senegal, Guinea, the Ivory Coast, Dahomey, and French Congo. Similar preferential duties between mother country and colonies are found in Portugal, Spain, Italy, the United States of America, and Japan. The mutual preference may be carried to such a point that the colony is incorporated in the customs sphere of the mother country, and the products of the two will enjoy as a rule complete freedom from duty, though exceptions are made in special cases. Such a relation subsists between France and Algeria, as well as some other colonies (Gabun, Guadeloupe, Martinique, French Guiana, Réunion, Indo-China, St.-Pierre and Miquelon, New Caledonia, Mayotta and the Comoro Islands, Madagascar and dependencies); also between Spain and the Canary Islands, and between the United States of America and Porto Rico, the Hawaian Islands, Guam, and the Philippines, though the Payne Tariff of August 1909 excepts rice and limits the quantity of tobacco and sugar. Quite recently the more advanced colonies have been given the right to conclude independent commercial treaties with foreign countries. In England the commercial treaties of the mother country were formerly valid also for the colonies. Since the year 1880, India, Canada, Newfoundland, the Australian colonies, Cape Colony, and Natal have usually been excepted, though the right was reserved for them to join in the agreement within a period of two years after the signing of the treaty. In 1895, in a circular letter to the Governors-General of the self-governing colonies, England recognized the right of independently concluding treaties, but required that the negotiations should be carried on through England. The commercial treaty between Canada and France in 1907 was in fact directly concluded, the consent of the British Embassy in Paris being a mere empty formality.

Great Britain holds dominion over the largest colonial possessions and in consequence also feels the strongest reaction upon her foreign commerce. Of her total imports about twenty-five per cent come from her colonies, while thirty per cent of her exports are sent to them. The following tables give a general view of present conditions in the field of colonial possessions. They are based on the latest available statistical tables and include also countries under protectorates (designated by a letter ' P ' in parentheses).

I. COLONIES OF GREAT BRITAIN

A. European Colonies

Colony.	Area in square kilometres.	Population.
Gibraltar	5	19,596
Malta	303	228,442
Total, European Colonies	308	248,038

B. Asiatic Colonies

Cyprus	9,282	273,857
Aden (including Perim)	207	45,859
Socotra	3,579	12,000
Straits Settlements (including La-buan)	4,222	714,069
Ceylon	65,712	4,109,054
British India	4,592,298	314,955,240
Hongkong, with leased area, colonies, and Wei-hai-wei	1,787	583,108
Malay Protectorate States (P)	120,120	1,720,850
Bahrein and Kamaran Islands (P)	730	68,100
Borneo: Sarawak and Brunei (P)	204,782	660,000
Maldive Islands (P)	300	30,000
Total, Asiatic Colonies	5,003,019	323,172,137

C. African Colonies

South African Union :		
Natal	91,611	1,191,958
Cape Colony	717,417	2,563,024
Orange River Colony	130,515	526,906
Transvaal	286,003	1,676,611
Swaziland	16,928	99,959
Basutoland	30,344	405,832
Bechuanaland (P)	712,250	125,350
South Rhodesia	384,809	769,471
North Rhodesia	753,690	1,001,400
Nyassaland	103,085	970,430
Uganda	578,865	3,503,564
British East Africa	523,180	2,295,336
Zanzibar, with Pemba	2,640	245,000
Somaliland (P)	176,120	302,859
St. Helena and Ascension	210	3,877
North Nigeria	662,263	8,069,071
South Nigeria	206,889	7,836,189
Gold Coast	207,200	1,502,898
Sierra Leone	83,165	1,400,000
Gambia	9,373	160,807
Total, African Colonies	5,676,557	34,650,542

D. AMERICAN COLONIES

Colony.	Area in square kilometres.	Population.
Canada	9,659,822	7,081,869
Newfoundland	110,681	237,531
Labrador	310,800	4,076
West Indies	31,164	1,679,191
Bermuda Islands . . .	49	18,994
British Honduras . . .	22,269	40,510
British Guiana	234,395	296,041
Falkland Islands . . .	16,835	2.272
Total, American Colonies .	10,386,015	9,360,484

E. AUSTRALIA AND POLYNESIA

Australian Commonwealth . .	7,704,168	4,449,493
Territory of Papua . . .	234,450	400,000
New Zealand	271,304	1,008,468
Fiji Islands	20,047	139,541
Tonga Islands and other Pacific Islands	37,113	201,386
Total, Australian and Polynesian Colonies . . .	8,267,082	6,198,888

F. SUMMARY

Totals for Europe . . .	308	248,038
Asia . . .	5,003,019	323,172,137
Africa . . .	5,676,557	34,650,542
America . . .	10,386,015	9,360,484
Australia and Polynesia . . .	8,267,082	6,198,888
Grand Total . . .	29,332,981	373,630,089

II. COLONIES OF FRANCE

A. ASIATIC COLONIES

French India	513	277,723
Indo-China :		
Cochin-China	56,965	2,870,514
Cambodia (P)	175,450	1,193,534
Annam (P)	159,890	5,513,681
Tonkin	119,750	5,896,510
Laos	290,000	663,727
Kwang-chow-wan . . .	1,000	177,097
Total, Asiatic Colonies . .	803,568	16,592,786

B. AFRICAN COLONIES

Colony.	Area in square kilometres.	Population.
Algeria	505,769	5,231,850
Tunis (P)	120,000	1,804,002
Sahara	2,394,202	—
French West Africa :		
Senegal	191,640	393,945
Mauritania (P) . . .	893,696	223,000
Upper Senegal and Niger . .	782,736 }	
Military Territory of the Niger .	1,383,742 }	5,058,656
French Guinea . . .	238,988	1,497,770
Ivory Coast	325,228	899,479
Dahomey	97,220	748,999
French Congo (including portion ceded to Germany in 1911) :		
Gabun	312,812	4,000,000
Middle Congo	441,076	3,000,000
Onbanghi-Chari . . .	400,000	2,000,000
Tchad	580,000	1,000,000
Mayotta and Comoro (P) . .	2,168	96,314
Madagascar and Dependencies .	585,533	2,706,661
Réunion, St. Paul, Amsterdam .	2,500	177,677
Somali Coast (P) . . .	120,000	208,061
Total, African Colonies [1] .	9,377,310	29,036,414

C. AMERICAN COLONIES

St.-Pierre and Miquelon . .	241	6,482
Guadeloupe and Dependencies .	1,771	182,238
Martinique	987	182,024
French Guiana	88,240	39,117
Total, American Colonies .	91,239	409,861

D. OCEANIC COLONIES

New Caledonia and Dependencies	18,483	55,886
Tahiti, &c.	3,235	30,563
Total, Oceanic Colonies .	21,718	86,449

Totals for Asia . . .	803,568	16,592,786
Africa . . .	9,377,310	29,036,414
America . . .	91,239	409,861
Oceania . . .	21,718	86,449
Grand Total	10,293,835	46,125,510

[1] Exclusive of French Morocco with 417,000 sq. km. and 3,500,000 inhabitants.

III. COLONIES OF GERMANY
A. AFRICAN COLONIES

Colony.	Area in square kilometres.	Population.
German East Africa . . .	995,000	10,032,227
German South Africa . . .	835,100	95,747
Kamerun (without area ceded in 1911)	495,600	2,720,166
Togo	87,200	1,000,363
Total, African Colonies . .	2,412,900	13,848,503

B. OCEANIC COLONIES

New Guinea, old Protectorate (Bismarck Archipelago and Kaiser Wilhelmsland) . . .	240,000	531,510
New Guinea, new Protectorate (Caroline, Pelew, Ladrone, and Marshall Islands) . . .	2,476	55,285
Samoa	2,572	36,338
Total, Oceanic Colonies . .	245,048	623,133

C. ASIATIC COLONIES

Kiaochow	501	201,000
Totals for Africa . . .	2,412,900	13,848,503
Oceania . . .	245,048	623,133
Asia . . .	501	201,000
Grand Total . . . , .	2,658,449	14,672,636

IV. COLONIES OF THE NETHERLANDS

Dutch East Indies . . .	1,520,628	37,717,377
Dutch West Indies :		
Surinam	129,100	85,094
Curaçao	1,131	52,741
Dutch Guiana . . .	394,789	200,000
Total	2,045,648	38,055,212

V. COLONIES OF BELGIUM

Congo Colony	2,382,800	20,000,000

VI. COLONIES OF PORTUGAL
A. ASIATIC COLONIES

Goa, Daman, Diu . . .	3,658	531,798
Macao	12	63,991
Timor and Kambing . . .	16,248	200,000
Total, Asiatic Colonies . .	19,918	795,789

B. African Colonies (Portugal)

Colony.	Area in square kilometres.	Population.
Cape Verde Islands . . .	3,822	147,424
Madeira	815	150,574
Guinea	33,900	170,000
St. Thomas and Principe Islands .	939	42,103
Angola	1,270,200	3,800,000
Mozambique	761,100	2,300,000
Total, African Colonies . .	2,070,776	6,610,101
Totals for Asia	19,918	795,789
Africa . . .	2,070,776	6,610,101
Grand Total	2,090,694	7,405,890

VII. COLONIES OF SPAIN
A. African Colonies

	Area	Population
Canary Islands	7,624	358,564
North Morocco	21,350	400,000
Rio de Oro	189,540	12,000
Ifni and South Morocco . .	126,370	4,000
Spanish Guinea (with Fernando Po and Annobon) . . .	27,715	160,946
Total, African Colonies .	372,599	935,510

VIII. COLONIES OF ITALY
African Colonies

	Area	Population
Erythrea	118,610	279,551
Somaliland	371,500	400,000
Libya	1,051,000	1,000,000
Total	1,541,110	1,679,551

IX. COLONIES OF DENMARK

	Area	Population
Iceland	104,785	85,188
Greenland	120,589	11,893
Danish West Indies . . .	359	27,104
Total	225,733	124,185

X. COLONIES OF RUSSIA

	Area	Population
Khiva (P)	60,000	500,000
Bokhara (P)	205,000	1,500,000
Total	265,000	2,000,000

XI. COLONIES OF THE UNITED STATES OF AMERICA

	Area in square kilometres.	Population.
Alaska (1867)	1,430,390	64,356
Guam (1899)	544	10,000
Hawaian Islands (1898) . .	16,703	191,909
Panama Canal Zone (1904) . .	1,228	144,614
Philippine Islands (1899) . .	297,917	8,276,802
Porto Rico (1899) . . .	8,897	1,118,012
Tutuila Group (1900) . . .	199	6,800
Total	1,755,878	9,812,493

XII. JAPANESE COLONIES

Formosa	35,790	3,392,063
Japanese Sakhalin . . .	32,294	35,823
Kwantung (P)	3,311	462,399
Korea (P)	217,494	13,125,027
Total	288,889	17,015,312

'Open-Door' Districts.   The expression of the 'open door' came into use after the Peace of Shimonoseki of April 17, 1895, from certain emphatic utterances in connexion with the future commercial policy of the part of eastern Asia which was threatened by Japan.   Since that time it has happened with still greater frequency that countries which had previously stood open to the equal competition of the world have been brought into the sphere of influence of a particular state and in consequence more or less cut off from the free world market.   By regions of the open door are now understood more specifically such economic districts as through non-revocable political treaties are limited in their right of self-government with respect to their commercial policies to the extent that they must remain open to the free competition of all foreign countries.   According to Schilder, they are such countries 'as through international agreement are permanently limited in their freedom of action as to their commercial and customs policies and subjected to restrictions in their jurisdiction.   The main emphasis is to be laid on the permanent character of these limitations and restrictions, since both in form and in fact completely sovereign states are by the conclusion of commercial treaties often limited for relatively short intervals in their freedom of action as to their commercial and tariff policies and in other respects as well '. But the essential distinction lies rather in the fact that a modern commercial treaty, even when it does not specify a ' comparatively short interval ', is terminable, while the permanent restrictions laid on the open-door domain follow from international treaties which are political in character and therefore non-terminable. It happens, indeed, though seldom, with fully sovereign states also, that in their international political agreements they subject themselves to limitations of an economic character, but these never go so far as to annul the right of the states to determine their own commercial policy. The familiar article of the Frankfort Treaty of Peace of May 10, 1871, assures ' eternal ' mutual most-favoured treatment between France and Germany, but this has not hindered either state from carrying out a radical protective policy. The expression ' freedom of action ' says too little, for the open-door country may conclude commercial treaties, though it is not allowed to guard its own interests in its own way; ' commercial and tariff policy ', on the other hand, is an antiquated expression, coming down from the period when commercial treaties and tariff regulations were looked upon as matters opposed to each other and to be judged from different points of view, while to-day both are included under the title of commercial policy. Exterritoriality, or the freeing of foreigners from the jurisdiction of the country, and establishment of consular jurisdiction grew directly out of the imperfection and unreliability of the juridical institutions of oriental countries; the arrangement has, as a matter of fact, some incidental economic effects, but it is non-essential to the concept of the ' open door '.

The non-revocable political treaties which limit the freedom of action as to the commercial policy of an open-door country may be of different kinds. Formerly they were usually treaties which the country of the open door concluded with the various great powers. After the conclusion of an unsuccessful war the victorious power used its political ascendancy to secure for itself certain commercial advantages either in the treaty of peace itself or in a non-terminable commercial treaty based upon it. But the other great powers would immediately hasten to secure the right to share the same advantages. Thus, for example, the capitulations, which were granted by Turkey as early as the sixteenth century and which were later granted or confirmed by other oriental countries in connexion with peace treaties, arose from one-sided concessions by which the merchants of the European power which was a party to the treaty were placed on an equality with those of other European states, secured admission for their goods on payment of a small *ad valorem* duty, and received certain assurances as to consular protection, jurisdiction, the furnishing of aid in case of danger to their ships, replacement in case of plundering by pirates, &c. France, Austria, England, and Russia have been great rivals in this respect. After the Opium War, China was forced by England to sign the Treaty of Peace of Nanking of August 29, 1842; this document really represents the first commercial treaty of China, and its advantages were first extended to the United States of America and France in the commercial treaties of July 3 and October 23, 1844, and later to numerous other countries. In recent times two or more of the great powers conclude treaties among themselves by which they mutually guarantee the rights of the open door in a certain country which is not a party to the treaty. Thus the General Acts of the Berlin Congo Conference of April 19, 1886, decided the destiny, so far as commercial policy is concerned, of the Congo basin; thus too, Germany, Great Britain, and the United States came to an agreement in the Samoa Conference of July 14, 1889, concerning the commercial relations of the Samoan Islands, and in the same way the Algeciras Acts declared Morocco an open-door country, &c.

Two points are characteristic of such political agreements ; the first is the unification of one-sided most-favoured positions, and the other is the establishment of a uniform low *ad valorem* duty. In the old capitulations, as well as in the numerous treaties which were made about the middle of the nineteenth century by the countries of Europe and the United States of America with Turkey, Persia, China, Japan, Siam, &c., it was specified that these oriental nations should treat the European and American merchants and goods on a basis of complete equality, which, however, did not obtain in the opposite direction. The duty in the case of Turkey was originally only three per cent, which was gradually raised to eleven per cent ; Persia was allowed to collect only five per cent, Siam only three per cent, &c.

Open-door domains show a development in two different directions. Occasionally one of the foreign powers competing for the trade of the country will gain the political ascendancy and reduce the district to the position of a colony dependent upon that power ; this has happened in the case of the Hawaian Islands annexed by the United States of America, of Korea and Formosa annexed by Japan, of Tunis and Morocco annexed by France, of Tripoli annexed by Italy, &c. When such a change takes place, the colony frequently remains for some time in the open-door position, levying moderate *ad valorem* duties at a uniform rate on goods from all countries ; sooner or later, however, it goes without saying that it is bound as closely as possible to the mother country. The second possibility of development is that the open-door country or some part of it may make such progress in civilization that political independence and hence also control over its own commercial policy cannot be withheld from it. Japan, the Balkan States, and Egypt afford examples of the last-named course.

A general view may here be given of the situation as to open-door countries and the changes they have undergone. In Europe, Turkey has longest occupied this position. By the old capitulations, which were mainly agreed upon at the same time with treaties of peace, the import duties of Turkey were fixed at the uniform rate of three per cent *ad valorem*. In the years 1861 and 1862 real commercial treaties were concluded with most of the European States and in them the duty rate was raised to eight per cent. To these treaties special tariff conventions were added, in which was specified the commercial value of goods on which duties were to be collected. Many inconsistencies arose from differences in these conventions, and the Turkish Government laboured to increase the duties on imports. In 1882 it denounced all the commercial treaties, which in consequence expired at the beginning of the 'nineties. The only result of the subsequent negotiations was the new commercial treaty of August 26, 1890, with Germany; but the essential part of this agreement, namely, a treaty tariff built up of detailed schedules, could not go into effect so long as the other powers possessed claims to the old eight per cent *ad valorem* duty. The Turkish Government attempted independently to raise the import duty to eleven per cent on April 14, 1901, but was compelled by the unanimous protest of the European powers to refrain from carrying out the plan. In October 1904 the Government renewed the demand for a three per cent increase in the rates, on the ground of the financial necessities of the Macedonian reform work. The new *ad valorem* rate of eleven per cent did not take effect until June 25, 1907, after the promulgation of the General European Convention, April 25 of the same year. This convention was based on special agreements between Turkey and the various powers, and all the powers with the single exception of France joined in it. At present Turkey is striving to obtain a new increase to fifteen per cent. The explicit consent of Austria-Hungary and Italy has already been secured, the former in the

agreement of February 26, 1909, confirming the annexation
of Bosnia and Herzegovina, and the latter in the Treaty of
Peace of Lausanne of October 18, 1912.

Much more sweeping in its consequences, however, than
this liberalization of the restrictions, was the progressive
contraction of the open-door territory of Turkey which
resulted from the successful struggles for independence on
the part of Turkish provinces. On January 30, 1847, the
princes of Moldavia and Wallachia combined their territories
in a customs union, which proceeded in 1850 and 1866 to an
increase of import duties to first five and then seven and
one-half per cent, in spite of decided opposition to the step
on the part of Austria-Hungary, on the ground that it was
contrary to existing treaties. Then, when the newly formed
Roumania achieved its political autonomy, it naturally
acquired at the same time independent control of its own
commercial policy. As early as May 3, 1843, Servia published
a tariff of its own, but was obliged to withdraw it on account
of the protest of the Porte. Renewed efforts in the 'sixties
and 'seventies led finally to the recognition of the complete
independence of Servia in the Treaty of Berlin in 1878.
By Article 8 of the same agreement, Bulgaria was still bound
by the commercial treaties of Turkey, but in the circular
note of January 28, 1884, the new nation laid claim to the
right of concluding commercial treaties independently of
Turkey. A law of December 17, 1887, empowered the
Bulgarian Government to undertake direct treaty negotiations, and these led to the conclusion of treaties, first with
England in 1889 and later with the other powers. As
a result of the Balkan War of 1912–13 the whole European
possessions of Turkey up to Constantinople and its environs
were lost to that power. In consequence, Albania, the
Turkish territory in Thrace, and the little free state on
Mount Athos are the only open-door territory remaining of
the Turkish European dominions. The island of Crete,
which had been a separate customs district since May 18–22,

1899, fell to Greece, and changes have taken place in the sovereignty over the Aegean islands.

In Africa we come first to Egypt, which has remained an open-door country, despite the fact that through a firman of the Porte of August 7, 1879, it received confirmation of the right to conclude independent commercial conventions and that since that date it has actually concluded such agreements with several countries. The object specified in these treaties has been to raise the duty on imports to ten per cent *ad valorem* as soon as all the other powers should give their consent to the change. Since, however, this consent could not everywhere be obtained, the old eight-per-cent duty based on the commercial treaties formerly concluded by Turkey is still in force. The continuance of this condition down to the year 1934 is assured by the British-French Colonial Treaty of April 8, 1904.

By the Treaty of Peace of Lausanne, October 18, 1912, Turkey ceded Tripoli and Benghazi (Cyrenaica) to Italy. Italy has not obligated herself to maintain the open-door status in the newly organized colony of Libya, but has on economic grounds maintained existing conditions. By an edict of the Governor on December 10, 1912, a duty of eleven per cent on imports was imposed, but some important articles of consumption, such as hops, wheat, rice, flour, pastry products, cured fish, coffee, tea, and petroleum, pay only four per cent; in addition, some other articles were later placed on the free list.

Algeria is not merely a colony, but as early as 1848 it was proclaimed ' an immediate part of the French territory '. Tunis was placed under the protection of France by the treaty of May 12, 1881, but continued at first to be an open-door country, and was brought into the unqualified position of a colony in 1898 only on condition of certain concessions to the foreign powers. In regard to cotton manufactures, the treaty with Great Britain of September 18, 1897, prescribed the maintenance of the five per cent *ad valorem* duty down to the close of the year 1912.

The British-French Colonial Treaty of April 8, 1904, promised Morocco to France and Spain, under the condition that there, as in Egypt, the most-favoured-nation agreement should be confirmed for a period of thirty years. In the General Acts of Algeciras the powers in conference granted an increase in the Moroccan import duties from five and ten per cent to seven and one-half and twelve and one-half per cent. The principle of the open door was maintained in operation by the Franco-German Morocco-Congo Treaty of November 4, 1911. In consequence the open-door position will be continued, even though the Franco-Spanish agreement of November 27, 1912, has undertaken a sort of division of Morocco into a larger French and a smaller Spanish colony with internationalization of Tangier.

Abyssinia, or Ethiopia, has been pledged to the retention of the open-door principle by the non-revocable treaty of May 14, 1897, with Great Britain. When France, in the revocable commercial treaty of January 10, 1908, stipulated the levying of a general import duty of ten per cent and one of eight per cent on beverages, Great Britain, after the exchange of notes of April 13 and May 4 and 12, 1909, permitted the incorporation of this provision as a part of her own non-revocable treaty.

Free trade was determined to be the policy of the eastern and western Congo basins by the Berlin Congo Conference, which was in session from November 15, 1884, to February 26, 1885, and the Acts of which were signed April 19, 1886. The eastern Congo basin includes German East Africa, Nyassaland, British East Africa, Uganda, and the Benadir Coast; the western basin is occupied by the Congo Free State, which by the treaty of November 28, 1907, and the Belgian law of October 15, 1908, has become a Belgian colony; also the Portuguese possessions at the mouth of the Congo, the French Congo colony as far as the watershed of the Ogowe, the Shari, and the Nile, and a part of Kamerun, which was enlarged in the Franco-German Morocco-Congo Treaty. On financial grounds, the right to levy import duties up to ten per cent was granted by the Acts of the Brussels Conference of July 2, 1890. The duties actually levied were at first held somewhat lower on the basis of special agreements among the powers concerned, or at five per cent in the eastern basin and six per cent in the western, with arms and ammunition at a general rate of ten per cent ; later, however, an increase of all duties to ten per cent has come into effect. By mutual agreement of the powers concerned, the open-door principle has also been applied to the German, English, and French colonies of western Africa— Togo, Dahomey, Nigeria, the Gold Coast, and the Ivory Coast.

The West African negro republic of Liberia, established in 1847, is on the road to a colonial relation in consequence of the assumption of a quasi-protectorate by the United States of America in the year 1910. Nevertheless, the commercial policy of the country has been placed on an open-door footing by the loan treaty participated in by American, English, French, and German banking firms, which was concluded in December 1911 and published on December 31, 1912, and which established an international customs administration.

Zanzibar became a colony by the terms of the Anglo-German Colonial Treaty of July 1, 1890, but remained open-door territory, the import duties being fixed at seven and one-half per cent.

In Asia, China has been forced by the commercial treaties concluded after the Opium War or since 1842 to open the country to foreign trade and to content herself with a low import duty applying uniformly to all the provinces and in general not exceeding five per cent *ad valorem*. In the meantime, however, the Chinese customs domain has been greatly reduced in extent. By the Treaty of Aigun, May 28,

1858, and that of Peking, November 14, 1860, Russia received a territory of 855,000 square kilometres. China also lost Hongkong to England in 1842 with a considerable extent of territory in addition in 1898, Formosa to Japan in 1895, Kiaochow to Germany, Kwangtung with Port Arthur to Russia, and Wei-hai-wei to England in 1898. In addition, strong movements for independence are manifesting themselves in the outlying provinces. In 1912 Tibet drove out the Chinese troops and is likely to come under English control as a protectorate. The part of Mongolia ruled by the Kutuchta in Urga has also declared itself independent and by the treaty of November 3, 1912, placed itself under Russian protection. In Eastern Turkestan a similar movement is noticeable.

Japan was likewise an open-door country after it was thrown open by the United States of America in 1854. The import duties were low, foreigners enjoyed the right of consular jurisdiction, and the foreign treaty powers were accorded uncompensated most-favoured-nation status. But with the great progress of the country these special privileges came to be looked upon with an unfriendly eye. As early as the 'seventies, the Japanese Government was striving for a revision of the treaty relations, but for the time being, without success. Not until after 1894 did the Japanese succeed in carrying through new commercial treaties which did away with exterritoriality and placed the most-favoured-nation provisions on a mutual basis. The import tariff of March 30, 1906, transformed the *ad valorem* duties which had previously dominated the system into specific duties, and raised the rates. The tariff laws of April 15, 1910, and July 17, 1911, brought further increases in the duties, and with their advent Japan was definitely lifted out of the ranks of open-door domains.

Korea still remained an open-door country after the annexation by Japan on August 29, 1910, as the low *ad valorem* duties of but from eight to ten per cent and the special status of foreigners continue in force. This, however, is to be regarded as a transitional condition only.

Siam has been an open-door country since the conclusion of treaties to that effect about the middle of the nineteenth century. Its Government may collect duties of three per cent only on imports and must grant exterritoriality and other special privileges to foreigners.

Afghanistan has been placed under British influence by the terms of the British-Russian Treaty of August 31, 1907, but is, however, to be regarded as an open-door country in consequence of the equal treatment granted to Russia. Similar considerations apply to the central Asiatic khanates under Russian protectorate, Khiva, Bokhara, Khokand, Samarkand, and Tashkend.

By the treaty with Russia of February 10/22, 1828, Persia was bound to *ad valorem* duties of five per cent, which most-favoured-nation treaties made applicable to other countries as well. The English-Russian Treaty of Partition of August 31, 1907, by which Russia received preferential rights in the north and England in the south, left the commercial-policy relations unchanged. Oman, on the Persian Gulf, lies within the English sphere of influence, but as it levies only *ad valorem* duties of five per cent, it is an open-door section.

In Oceania the following political districts are still open-door territory : the Samoan Islands, on the basis of the General Acts of the Berlin Samoa Conference of June 14, 1889 ; the Tonga Islands (belonging to Great Britain), on the basis of the agreement of November 14, 1899, between Great Britain, Germany, and the United States of America ; and finally, the Caroline, Ladrone, and Pelew Islands, on the basis of the Spanish-German Treaty of February 12, 1899.

III

THE OBJECTS OF WORLD ECONOMY

1. WORLD COMMERCE

The Concept of Commerce. As soon as men learn to know each other on a peaceable footing their relations take on more and more an economic character. Each seeks to devote himself to that line of production in which he can attain the largest measure of economic success and so is thrown back upon his fellows both for the disposal of his products and for the satisfaction of his varied wants. Moreover, these wants themselves broaden and multiply, for contact with strange men stimulates to imitation and the sight of new goods incites a desire to possess them. Thus not merely individual persons, but also the composite economic units, the families, communities, and states, become centres of a progressively differentiating productive and consumptive activity. All mutual transactions between economic subjects constitute what we call *commerce.*

These mutual transactions are of various kinds. They are directed in part to the exchange of goods, because only by that means can the division of labour which brings such great benefits be effected. Out of the exchange of goods grow those multiplied transfers of value to accomplish which a universally recognized medium of exchange, money and its substitutes, is required. Men strive also to come into more intimate relations with one another personally, and to learn to know new lands and conditions, and in consequence the human interchange of travel often assumes an importance equalling or even surpassing that of the exchange of goods. Mutual understanding is brought about by the transmission of intelligence, either fixed in writing or expressed in conventional symbols or in recent times by actual word of mouth, as can now be done with greater promptness and ever-decreasing cost between the most widely separated points on the earth's surface. The interchange of goods, of persons, and of intelligence appear as the three great branches of commerce; and for them special transportation facilities, such as railroads, navigation lines, mail service, telegraph and telephone systems, must be provided.

Commerce, however, in this sense, does not serve economic ends exclusively, but the purposes of general culture as well. Goods are transferred not merely for the sake of making a profit, but unselfishly also, in the interest of the common good or that of other individuals. People travel and communicate with one another to transact business or to seek opportunities of work, but also for the purposes of recreation and of culture. These extra-economic relations have economic effects, in the first place because they help to bring about the creation and maintenance of institutions important for the production and exchange of goods, and further because the spiritual culture promotes the material, for it creates new wants and teaches the means of satisfying them.

International Commerce. Commerce, in the sense spoken of above, is essentially the same whether carried on within the borders of a single economic division or across and beyond such borders. But in view of the fact that in international commerce not only the private-economy units but the politically organized economic communities as well are opposed, not merely the economic facts as such come under consideration, but regard must also be had for the national-economy point of view, inasmuch as it is concerned with transfers of values which, at the same time that they affect individuals, are also added to one national economy and subtracted from the other. When a case of goods is carried out of Germany into France, the railroads must take account of the weight and the character of the goods (whether iron articles, textile manufactures or the like), since the transportation rates are based on these data. It is an economic consideration how much the railroads earn by the transfer, but the more important interest centres in the determination of the amount of power to satisfy human wants which is inherent in the goods. Human beings, also, in their passage from country to country, appear as bearers of economic values, in the first place because they decrease on the one hand and increase on the other the number of consumers, but often also because they similarly affect the amount of labour-power. The exchange of intelligence is only in part subservient to economic ends, but it is employed in value-transfers among other uses, as for example when an agricultural estate or a mining or manufacturing enterprise passes by letter or telegram into the possession of a foreigner.

Two important distinctions are still to be made in regard to goods. In the first place, it is not a matter of indifference whether the articles concerned in imports and exports are destined for final consumption or for use in further production, i.e. whether they are consumers' or producers' goods. Thus the national economy of a country is certainly more favourably affected when one hundred million marks are used to purchase raw cotton, which will be increased in value many fold in succeeding transformations by the industry of the country, than if the hundred millions had been expended for coffee which would be consumed at the same value. So when machinery, electrical apparatus, railway material, &c., are purchased, which find enduring application in the productive processes of the country, a different judgement must be passed on such a transaction from that which is applicable to the importation of fashionable articles of women's apparel, which are merely consumed and do not survive a single season. And in fact, every civilized state strives to encourage the importation of means of production through exemption of raw materials from duty, and measures for encouraging the purchase of machines which are only to be obtained abroad, &c. The view of the classical political-economy that only products and not the factors of production, labour and capital, can be internationally exchanged has turned out to be completely erroneous. America and Australia have shown in a surprising degree how by the help of European labour-power and European capital, branches of production can be called into life outside of Europe, which will furnish products (wool, chilled meats, butter, &c.) not merely for home consumption but for the European demand as well. In the intimate connexion between consumption and production, transfers of capital may also take place in the form of consumers' goods, for even the quantities of grain, meat, &c., necessary for the maintenance of labourers finally serve productive ends. Hence the extent of capital transfers cannot be computed with certainty from the quantity and character of the imports and exports of goods.

It is further to be emphasized that there is really no money in international commerce, since there is no way of forcing such a medium upon a foreigner, and all payments must therefore be made in goods. Gold coins are taken as gold only and notes only as representing gold. On this fact is based, for example, the gold-premium policy of the Bank of France, which supplies coins reduced by wear for sending into foreign countries, because it knows that in this way their foreign value will be decreased in comparison with the domestic. In a striking sense bills of exchange in the domestic economy are mere representatives of credit for goods, and in international commerce bills of exchange form the most important means of liquidation.

Thus among visible international value transfers the first place is taken by goods; these may be either products or means of production, hence capital. The second factor in production, labour-power, is also transferable, though in a lesser degree. It will therefore be best for our purpose to take up and consider in order, first the international exchange of goods in general, then international transfers of capital, and finally international migration.

The Causes of International Value Transfers. In international commerce the deciding factor, as already mentioned, is the value bound up in a material good or connected with a human individual. These values may be very different in different economic communities. The material things may come into the economic territorial units as finished products, or if these encounter too great obstacles in the form of customs duties, freight charges, &c., they may come as capital goods, and after their arrival may undergo processes adding to their value. In the case of human beings the same tendencies manifest themselves, but the obstacles will be greater, since labour-power is not separable from the person of the owner as is capital; also the geographical distinctions as to distance, climate, &c., the political, as to legal institutions, and the social, as to speech, religion, &c., will be much more formidable.

The cause of the variation in value, again, is to be sought in the fact that the value of a material good or of a given unit of labour-power is not an intrinsic characteristic, but is attributed to it by humanity. Every economic community has its separate give and take of supply and demand, and hence also its independent process of value building. In this respect the different economic groups resemble communicating vessels, in which, under conditions of free exchange, all economic value constantly seeks a uniform level, though never quite reaching it. Where this condition of free exchange is not present, as happens especially where it is interrupted by the operation of customs taxes and cartel agreements, artificial differences in the level of values will appear. Thus we find that manufactured goods are frequently exported from countries of higher values within the country to those of lower. In such cases the national-economy difference in level becomes inverted from the private-economy standpoint; the entrepreneur is compensated for failure to make a profit, or for actual loss incurred in exporting by higher profit on his domestic sales.

2. The International Exchange of Goods

The Development of World Commerce. Material goods form the most important as well as the most conspicuous object of world-economic dealings. The international exchange of goods is also relatively the easiest to gain an idea of, in view of the commercial statistics which are compiled by all nations. Errors and non-uniformities in the methods of keeping the statistics occur in plenty, to be sure, but so long as only round numbers are dealt with, these may be left out of account. But in computing the world commerce from the figures for the foreign trade of the different countries, it is incorrect to add together all imports and exports, as is so often done, as the exports of one country are the imports of another and hence each transaction would be counted twice. In a computation of such a nature the figures for imports will be more reliable than those for exports, and this for several reasons. In the first place, goods are generally subject to duty on importation, and much less frequently on exportation, and the fiscal interest involved naturally leads to greater accuracy in the statistical records. It is further to be taken into account that countries are chiefly separated by the ocean, which is international and on which also values originate and disappear. The ships themselves do not appear at all in the commercial statistics, as they are built outside the customs zone, and outside of it they perform their transportation services and pass out of existence. The earnings from shipbuilding must be given special consideration, as has in fact been done in the English commercial policy since 1898. Freight earnings may, however, appear embodied in the values of goods. In handling within a country, the value of the goods is increased by the cost of transportation to the frontier, and on crossing the border they are set down as exports in the one country and imports in the other at a value including this increase. If they are carried across an intervening country, this country receives its transportation charges from the difference in the import and export value of the goods so carried ; otherwise the computation is the same. But when the international ocean separates the exporting and importing country, the freight earnings accrue to the country under whose flag the goods are transported, and hence appear in the import but not in the export value. For example, if English goods are sent in English ships to America, the American commercial statistics will naturally show the full value, that is, the market price including cost of transportation to the landing-port; but not so the English statistics, which will take account only of the value at the time of lading and hence not including the cost of transportation at sea. Thus English exports would have to be increased, in so far as they are carried in English ships, by the addition of the ocean freight earnings of the shipping. The product of fisheries on the high seas forms another import to which there is no corresponding export from any other country, as this value also originates on the international waters.

If, now, the import values furnished by the commercial statistics of all countries are taken as a basis, a result is reached that places the total international exchange of goods at 15,000,000,000 marks for the year 1860 and at 70,000,000,000 for the year 1910, showing that the amount has increased nearly fivefold in a half-century. The growth was not at a uniform rate, to be sure, the influence of fortuitously varying circumstances being very marked ; the years 1873, 1882, 1891, 1900, and 1907 show the principal high points, followed in each case by more or less pronounced depressions. The greater uniformity of development in recent decades indicates that the community of interest among the more important economic groups is becoming increasingly potent. The most marked increase in export trade is shown by those countries, such as the United States of America, Germany, and Italy, which have entered the field of world economy comparatively late but with their powers fresh. In the older commercial states like England and

France, progress has been more moderate. The change has, moreover, already led to a shift in the order of rank. Great Britain still keeps the lead of all the commercial countries, with imports for 1910 of £574,500,000 (11,720,000,000 marks) and exports of £534,100,000 (10,896,000,000 marks). But at a much smaller distance in the rear than formerly follow Germany, with imports for 1910 of 8,929,900,000 marks and exports of 7,474,700,000 marks, and the United States, with imports for 1910 of $769,400,000 (3,231,500,000 marks) and exports of $1,864,500,000 (7,830,900,000 marks); France has fallen to fourth place, with imports for 1910 of 7,173,300,000 francs (5,810,400,000 marks) and exports of 6,233,800,000 francs (5,049,400,000 marks). A special type is furnished by those countries, such as Belgium, Holland, and Switzerland, which carry on a considerable indirect trade and hence secure a share of the progress of the neighbouring larger economic divisions. The extraordinary growth of imports as compared with exports in Austria-Hungary and Russia is a result of the progressive industrialization which increases the home consumption of the agricultural products of the country and also the demand for foreign productive agents, machinery and raw materials. The following tabulation shows the growth in foreign trade of the leading countries. In order to eliminate chance variations, the trade for five-year periods is taken as a basis of comparison, and the figures give the average annual imports and exports in millions for two such periods two decades apart, and the percentage of increase in each for the twenty years.

As the external senses of men tend to dominate their opinions at the expense of internal judgement, they are prone to bring the economic importance of a country into some sort of connexion with its territorial extent. This optical illusion is responsible for the general over-estimation of the importance of colonial possessions and oversea markets. In reality there is the greatest difference in the economic development of various sections of the earth, much the larger

GROWTH OF FOREIGN TRADE OF LEADING NATIONS

Country.	Average Annual Imports (Millions).		Average Annual Exports (Millions).		Per cent of Increase.	
	1886–90	1906–10	1886–90	1906–10	Imports.	Exports.
United States of America (Dollars)	717·2	1,379·7	738·4	1,813·4	92·4	145·6
Germany (Marks) .	3,583·3	8,311·8	3,257·4	6,732·4	132·2	107·0
Italy (Lire) . . .	1,389·6	2,928·8	954·4	1,905·2	110·8	99·6
Belgium (Francs) .	1,506·0	3,541·0	1,312·4	2,819·3	135·2	114·7
Great Britain (Pounds Sterling)	389·6	629·9	298·5	487·9	67·7	63·4
France (Francs) .	4,219·0	6,099·3	3,439·9	5,527·2	44·5	66·8
Russia (Roubles) .	364·9	898·5	634·4	1,132·4	146·2	78·5
Austria-Hungary (Kronen) . . .	1,136·3	2,768·1	1,451·0	2,366·0	143·6	62·3

part of it remaining very far behind the most advanced portions. World commerce is a product neither of physical nature nor of peoples in respect to their number and physical qualities, but of advanced civilization. The table below gives a comparison of the relative proportions of the total area, population, and commerce of the world made up by different geographical divisions. The West European countries, Great Britain, France, Germany, Belgium, Holland, Denmark, Sweden, Norway, Austria-Hungary, Italy, Spain, and Portugal, are grouped together, and this division compared with the United States of America, with the rest of the inhabited and with the uninhabited portions of the earth's surface.

DISTRIBUTION OF POPULATION AND WORLD TRADE

Division.	Per cent of Land Area of the Earth (Total 145,500,000 square kilometres).	Per cent of Population of Earth (Total 1,679,500,000).	Per cent of World's Commerce (Total 70,000,000,000 Marks).
Western Europe . .	2·6	16·9	60·0
United States of America .	6·7	6·1	4·6
Remainder of the Inhabited Earth , . . .	82·0	77·0	35·4
Uninhabited Regions .	8·7	—	—

Foreign and Domestic Trade. The question is now frequently raised as to the relative growth of inland and foreign
trade. It has been asserted by many writers that with all
the rapid progress of international commerce it does not
increase so rapidly as the exchange between domestic
markets, while other writers seek to prove that various
indications point to a relatively more rapid growth of the
external over internal exchange.[1] The statement of the
problem is misleading, as only similar quantities can be
compared. By foreign trade we mean the movement of
goods across a particular line, the boundary of the country
in question ; domestic trade, on the other hand, is the trade
carried on over a given area, the area inside the boundary
line ; these two processes can no more be numerically
compared than can measurements of distance with measurements of area. No better result is reached by taking as a basis
of the comparison the proportion of the products of the
country marketed at home and abroad, or again, the figures
for the different classes of business done by transportation
enterprises. Let us take for example the case of a quantity
of printed cotton fabric manufactured by an Austrian
cotton-printing establishment exclusively for exportation to
the Orient. The Austrian textile mills which provide the
printing establishment with the necessary cloth, and the
spinneries which supply these weaving mills with their yarns,
will report that their market is found in this case exclusively
within the country, even though the market is entirely
created by the export trade. Equally dependent upon the
export sale is the business of the dealers in food-stuffs,
the clothing manufacturers, &c., who supply the needs of
the entire group of people deriving their livelihood from the
preparation of the exported goods. The transportation of
the raw cotton from the frontier to the spinnery, of the yarn
from the spinnery to the weaving mill, of the cloth from

[1] Cf. Sigmund Schilder, *Entwicklungstendenzen der Weltwirtschaft,*
Berlin, 1912, vol. i.

this to the printing factory, and of the finished fabric to the frontier, all are distinct commercial processes which will be separately counted and treated as so many constituents of the domestic commerce. In short, in the value of an exported product are incorporated a whole series of commercial acts and business transactions which with respect to foreign trade are combined under one entry, but in inland trade are separated under numerous entries and multiplied many fold.

Relative Extent of Foreign Trade. In view of the great inequality as to area and population, the absolute figures for imports and exports do not afford a satisfactory index of the participation of the different peoples in the world trade. For this comparison a calculation of the *per capita* figures is better suited. It must be admitted, too, that the size of the economic division strongly influences the relation between the amounts of internal and external trade. Modern production, to remain effective, must be more and more specialized, and specialization, again, is possible only with corresponding expansion of the market. Hence, if a state is so small that it does not afford a domestic market of sufficient extent, numerous commercial transactions must take place across the border which could otherwise have been effected entirely inside the boundary. A relatively greater proportion of raw material and food-stuffs must be imported, and in turn the country will devote itself to the production of special articles in which it can command an advantage in the world market. Examples are offered by the manu-factures of watches and clocks and of lace in Switzerland, and of arms in Belgium, and by the butter and pork produc-tion of Denmark. In this process production largely takes on the form of elaboration industry, raw materials being drawn from foreign countries and the wares made from them again exported. This is true even of agriculture, in Denmark, for example, where oil-cake, soy beans, &c., are imported for feed and large quantities of animal products exported. For this reason, as explained, the *per capita* share of the small states is very large, and it has, moreover, notably increased in the last twenty years.   This is made clear in the following table, which shows the annual average foreign trade *per capita* for typical European countries for two five-year periods twenty years apart.

EXPORTS PER CAPITA OF POPULATION

Country.			*Average Exports per capita.* 1886–90.	1906–10.	*Increase per cent.*
Belgium (Francs)	.	.	.	213·9	381·0	78·1
Italy (Lire)	.	.	.	31·4	55·2	75·8
France (Francs)	.	.	.	89·7	140·8	68·0
Germany (Marks)	.	.	.	65·8	103·7	57·6
Switzerland (Francs)	.	.	220·0	308·9	44·5
Austria-Hungary (Kronen)	.	.	33·6	47·5	41·4
Great Britain (Pounds Sterling)	.	7·88	10·83	37·4

In Great Britain the imports *per capita* of population rose rather steadily from £5 10s. 2d. in 1854 to £11 11s. 2d. in 1873, near which point they remained fairly constant; in 1900 a temporary culmination was reached at £12 14s. 3d., and then, after a brief falling-off, they resumed their upward trend, reaching £15 11s. 4d. in 1911.   The exports of British products amounted in 1854 to £3 10s. 3d. *per capita* of population, then rose to £8 1s. 0d. in 1872, when they fell back and only in very recent years again reached that amount; the year 1911 shows a figure of £10 1s.

The Currents of World Trade.   The most important fact in this connexion, and one which in spite of its susceptibility to statistical demonstration is continually overlooked in every-day life, is that the international exchange of goods not merely proceeds in the main from the industrial nations, but that it is also chiefly directed toward the same class of countries, while the enormously more numerous agricultural and colonial domains play a very subordinate rôle.   In the first group we must reckon Great Britain, Germany, France, Belgium, Switzerland, Austria-Hungary, and Italy of the European countries, and among countries outside of Europe, the United States of America and Japan.   Under colonial domains we will include only the colonies of the same countries named, including, however, their protectorates. The following table will then show the distribution of the exports for the year 1910 of each of the countries named among the three groups. (The countries of the industrial group form 8·8 per cent of the area and contain 24·8 per cent of the population of the earth.)

DISTRIBUTION OF EXPORTS

Country.	Per cent to countries of the Industrial Group.	Per cent to countries of Agricultural Group.	Per cent to countries of the Colonial Group.
Great Britain	39 0	31·5	29·5
Germany	58·3	40·6	1·1
France	69·4	30·6	
Belgium	67·2	32·74	0·06
Switzerland	80·3	19·7	—
Italy	68·3	31·7	—
Austria-Hungary	72·0	28·0	—
United States of America	56·8	42·2	1·0
Japan	54·3	35·7	10·0

The Causes and Effects of the International Exchange of Goods. Viewed from the side of the importing country, the higher value of goods is what induces their importation from a country where their value is lower. This difference in value may indeed be lessened or obliterated by the costs of handling and transportation connected with trade, but as a matter of fact these costs diminish with the progress of commerce and the simplification of intermediate handling, so that new latent differences in value constantly make themselves manifest. A difference in value will arise when in one economic domain a demand backed up by purchasing power exists for certain goods, which however are not produced domestically at all or not in sufficient quantities, and when domestic production cannot be extended as in the case of some other economic domain. More frequently, however, it is the situation in the exporting country which forms the incentive to international exchange of goods. This is the case when natural conditions lead inevitably to over-production, or when by extending the scale of production its cost can be materially reduced. In such cases the foreign price need not be higher than the domestic, and under some circumstances may even be held at a lower figure when the cost, of a return shipment prevents the return of the goods, or when the methods of economic protectionism (to be taken up later) are brought to bear on the situation. The lower value in the foreign country may then offer a means of securing higher profits.

The effect of importation on production depends on the character of the goods and the conditions affecting domestic production. The bringing in of goods ready for consumption which cannot be produced at home, such as spices in Europe, can only influence domestic production when it turns out goods which might be substituted for those imported. Raw materials and productive agents will be an advantage to domestic industry when the latter is capable of development. The importation of manufactured goods will diminish home industries, because it will oppress the domestic establishments operating only at a higher cost, or may destroy them entirely if none are able to meet the competition. It is true that such importation may under some circumstances spur on the domestic industry to become able to meet the competition when it was not so before. Thus the free-trade period in Austria-Hungary caused the transformation of brewing from a hand-work to a manufacturing industry, and brought about the transfer of silk-weaving from Vienna to the provinces. It must always be borne in mind that production costs are not fixed quantities, but are subject to change under competitive conditions. This transformation, however, assumes the extension of consumption as well as the successful retention of the home market with the reduction in production costs, and this result may be much more definitely assured by a policy of protection than by free competition.

The effect of importation on consumption will in general be favourable, since the stronger competition will lower prices. But whether this price reduction will be permanent or not depends upon the maintenance of domestic production and upon the rôle played by the particular country in the total market of the foreign production in question. If the domestic production is suppressed, it may be possible for the victorious foreign competitor to recoup himself by later advance in prices for the sacrifice undergone in the period of competitive struggle. But again, if the foreign industry is producing for the world market, it will hardly be in a position to pursue a policy of price discrimination in its different market territories. Such a policy will be practicable only in cases where the market is a one-sided one and the purchasing country is dependent in a high degree, as, for example, the market of Germany for potassium salts in the United States of America.

Questionable as is the proposition that importation reduces the production of the importing state and reduces its prices, the opposite proposition, that exportation increases production and raises domestic prices in the exporting country, though often maintained, is still more questionable.[1] An increase of production will in fact be the rule, even though it may not at all keep pace with the growth of exportation. Exports of cattle from Austria-Hungary to Germany have increased, in consequence of the high prices prevailing in the market country, while production has not increased. The increased exportation was made possible only by decreased consumption at home. Quite erroneous, however, is the proposition that an increase in production, whether to supply the home market or for exportation, necessarily involves utilization of less favourable production situations and therefore an increase in productive costs. The normal case in modern industry is a decrease in costs with increase in the size of plants. In agriculture, even, the tendency is in the same direction in consequence of the progressive substitution of machinery for hand work. A rise in prices is likely to occur

---

[1] Richard Schüller, *Schutzzoll und Freihandel*, Vienna, 1905, pp. 212 ff.

only in case the value of the goods in the foreign market is considerably higher than their value in the producing country, when the producer will not be inclined to part with the goods at home at a price lower than that which he can secure for them abroad. But when, as is to-day more and more frequently the case, exportation operates to distribute the fixed costs of production over a greater amount of product and hence to lessen the cost of each unit produced, the domestic consumption itself must profit by the trade.

3. INTERNATIONAL TRANSFERS OF CAPITAL

The Essential Nature of International Capital Transfers. In view of the vagueness of the significance of the capital concept in economic theory, an understanding on the subject is the first consideration for the present discussion. Each individual economic unit has command over a certain quantity of economic value. This quantity of value may either have been given a material embodiment in land, buildings, machinery, raw materials, manufactured articles, or the like, and so take the form of so-called ' goods ', or it may lack such an embodiment, as when it takes the form of rights to services or other considerations, rights to the use of natural agents, relations such as those of a merchant to his customers, of a periodical to its subscribers and advertisers, and the like. The economic value is thus an abstraction from certain relations of the economic individual to the outer environment. It does not depend upon the thing which appears as its bearer, and hence may vary independently of any change in it. An article of luxury, for example, may rise and fall in value with the greatest rapidity without undergoing the slightest physical change.

The totality of economic value, material and immaterial, is thus made up of potentiality, which in turn falls into two parts. These are respectively the potentiality of enjoyment which is destined for personal use and hence is consumed, and the potentiality of production which is to serve for the creation of new economic values and is increased only to this end. This productive power is capital in the private-economy sense only ; capital from the national-economy point of view is only that part of private capital which serves the purpose of creating new economic values in the way of production of goods as distinguished from the creation of value through the transfer of goods from one economic individual to another. Capital consists therefore of a mass of economic values, which may be embodied in material things, but are not necessarily so embodied, and whose embodiment, moreover, is extremely mutable. It may consist of money, goods, machinery, railways, ships, buildings, plots of ground, claims, &c., or may change from the form of money into that of goods, buildings, &c., and vice versa.

We possess little information in regard to transfers of capital from one country to another, as statistics on the subject do not exist and would be very difficult to collect. One is thrown back upon the estimates of the specialists in the different countries for the material for an approximately accurate picture of movements of capital. The beginnings for such statistics have been made by the International Statistical Institute, before which body Alfred Neymarck has laid a compilation of the amounts of European transferable securities (*valeurs mobilières*) handled in the countries of issue and in foreign countries.[1] The distribution of capital, however, does not correspond with that of effective possession. In the first place, large masses of capital may be transferred which do not appear in notes, bonds, shares, &c. Furthermore, securities may pass into the possession of foreigners and still remain in the country of issue ; they may be purchased by foreign capitalists and deposited in the country of issue, as is often done from fear of political complications

---

[1] *Bulletin de l'Institut international de statistique*, vols. ix (1895), xi (1897), xii (1899), xiii (1901), xiv (1903), xv (1905), xvi (1907), and xvii (1909).

or with a view to avoiding high property, income, or inheritance taxes.

In England, Sir Edgar Speyer, in a lecture given before the Liberal Colonial Club in May 1911, estimated the capital investments in foreign countries at 3,500,000,000 pounds sterling and the annual income in the form of interest at £180,000,000. He supposed the English capital invested abroad to be about equally divided between the colonies and foreign countries.

France occupies the position of the Banker of Europe, as it has financed half, if not two-thirds, of that continent and a large part of the world. Paul Leroy-Beaulieu estimates the annual accumulations of the country at 3,000,000,000 francs, of which scarcely one-third can be employed at a moderate yield within the country, so two-thirds must be exported.[1] French ownership of commercial securities was estimated for the year 1908 at from 105,000,000,000 to 110,000,000,000 francs, of which from 35,000,000,000 to 40,000,000,000 represented foreign paper.[2] In the ten years from 1902 to 1911 nearly thirty billions are thought to have been taken up by foreign issues, while in the same time French loans consumed only eight and one-half billions.[3]

Germany, according to data furnished by the Imperial Marine Office (Reichsmarine-Amt), has about sixteen billion marks in foreign securities and in addition from eight to nine billions invested in oversea enterprises.[4]

Belgian capital is also active in foreign countries to a large extent. According to the Russian Ministry in Brussels, Belgian enterprises in different countries at the end of the nineteenth century were operating with a capitalization as

[1] *L'Économiste français* for August 13, 1910.
[2] Alfred Neymarck, *Finances contemporaines*, tome vi. *L'Épargne française et les valeurs mobilières*, Paris, 1911, p. 12.
[3] Victor Augagneur, ' Französisches Kapital im Ausland ' in *Die Zeit* for May 11, 1913.
[4] *Die Entwicklung der deutschen Seeinteressen im letzten Jahrzehnt*, supplementary volume of the *Marine-Rundschau*, 1905.

follows: in Russia, 340,000,000 francs; in Germany, 20,000,000; France, 23,000,000; Portugal, 43,000,000; Italy, 66,000,000; Austria-Hungary, 52,000,000; and Spain 86,000,000.[1]

Capital investments by the United States of America go chiefly to the other American countries. The Bureau of American Republics in Washington has published the following figures for the different countries (in millions of dollars): Mexico 700, Costa Rica 7, Guatemala 20, Peru 20, Honduras 2, Nicaragua 1·5, Salvador 1·5, Panama (outside the Canal Zone) 1, Hayti 1, Argentina 30, Bolivia 19, Chile 19, Brazil 50, Colombia 2, Ecuador 3, Venezuela 3, Dominican Republic 3, Cuba 135; total, one billion dollars. Aside from loans to governments, the amounts represent chiefly railway stocks and bonds, also the founding of banks, mining enterprises, and industrial corporations. Considerable transfers of capital also take place from Europe to the United States, through speculation on the American stock exchanges by English, Dutch, Germans, and Frenchmen. It is asserted in Dutch exchange circles that in the forty-five years since American securities were first offered in Europe, 1,100,000,000 Dutch gulden have been lost in them in the Netherlands alone.

Among debtor nations of Europe, Russia, Austria-Hungary, and the Balkan States deserve especial notice. In Russia France has invested sums estimated in the year 1907 at from nine to ten billion francs.[2] In Austria-Hungary the foreign ownership of securities was asserted on the ground of calculations based on the cashing in, renewal, and cancellation of coupons, to amount to 9,809,000,000 kronen at the end of the year 1903. Of this sum 4,653,000;000 kronen represented German-owned and 3,270,000,000 kronen French-owned securities.[3]

---

[1] Josef Grunzel, *System der Handelspolitik*, second edition, Leipsic, 1906, p. 584.

[2] A. Sartorius, Freiherr von Waltershausen, *Das volkswirtschaftliche System der Kapitalanlage im Auslande*, Berlin, 1907, p. 48.

[3] *Tabellen zur Währungsstatistik. Verfasst im k.-k. Finanzministerium. Daten zur Zahlungsbilanz.* Vienna, 1904.

China has become an enormous field for investment, though confessedly a very uncertain one as to its risks. According to an official account published by the Chinese press, the public debt of China, including the Boxer indemnity, amounted on June 30, 1912, to 1,359,000,000 taels in round numbers, or 3,737,000,000 marks; in the year 1911 this indebtedness required payments totalling 55,400,000 taels (152,350,000 marks) to foreign countries as interest. The field of mining exerted an especially strong attraction on foreign capital, as China is among the richest in coal of all countries of the world. The most important concessions to foreigners were granted in the reform year of 1898 and since that time. There were founded in particular several British enterprises, such as the Chinese Engineering and Mining Company with coal-mines in K'aip'ing Chih-li, and the Peking Syndicate (1898) with concessions in Honan and Chansi, also the British-French Yunnan Syndicate (1902), the German Shantung Mining Corporation with mining privileges within a zone extending sixteen kilometres on each side of the Shantung railway, and finally the South Manchurian Railway Company, now in Japanese hands, with coal-mines in Manchuria. In view of the strong current of hostility to foreigners, the formation of mixed syndicates composed of Chinese and foreigners was next resorted to. Conspicuous among these are the German-Chinese companies, Ching Hsing in the south-west part of the province Chih-li and Chung Hsieng in Shantung. Since 1908, purely Chinese enterprises have also been given concessions, and their number has rapidly increased. In many cases, too, the concessions already granted to foreigners were repurchased, frequently at no inconsiderable sacrifice, the necessary capital being raised in part through national subscriptions. The convulsions of the revolutionary year, however, brought the purely Chinese enterprises into an especially dangerous situation, so that they were compelled to seek security in foreign support. The result has been that a form of co-operation has developed, in which the technical and commercial direction is in the hands of foreigners, and the Chinese are assured complete equality as to the use of capital and share pf profits, being represented in the organization by the Chinese Government.   In Chinese industry, foreign capital is the more dominant in proportion as the branch in question is widely removed from agriculture.   Participation of domestic capital is also discouraged by the fact that in times of political unrest it is often required to be sacrificed to the national cause, and hence its existence is kept secret from prudential motives.   Of the forty-six cotton-spinning mills with 932,506 spindles, which were counted in China at the close of the year 1911, six, with 289,000 spindles, are in European and six, with 150,000 spindles, in Japanese hands.   The two greatest sugar refineries belong one to an English and one to a German-Chinese company ; the two beer breweries are German ; of three iron and steel works, one is English ; of twenty ship-building establishments fifteen are European ; of eight leather-goods factories, five are European, &c.   In earlier years a lively competition for railway concessions had also arisen among the foreigners until a strong agitation in favour of nationalization set in ; finally the edict of May 9, 1911, for the transfer of railways to the state was promulgated, which formed the immediate cause of the Revolution as it stimulated into open conflict the opposition between provincial particu-larism and governmental centralization.   A statement of the participation up to the present of European capital in Chinese railway projects asserts that £32,500,000 has been so invested.[1] This was distributed among the different countries as follows :   England £16,700,000 ;   Germany, £6,800,000; France, £5,600,000; France-Belgium, £1,600,000; United States of America £1,500,000 ; and Japan, £250,000. By the new railway loans of the year 1912 the amount is increased by over £23,000,000.   Foreign banks are also active

---

[1] Annual Reports of the Imperial and Royal Austro-Hungarian Consular Offices, 1912. Annual Report of the Imperial and Royal General Consulate in Shanghai for 1911, p. 150.

in China, including three British and Japanese establishments with a capital stock of about £34,000,000.

In Japan, according to a statement of the Ministry of Finance in 1911, foreign obligations were as shown in the following tables:

FOREIGN INDEBTEDNESS OF JAPAN

Obligation.	Amount (in Yen).	Interest (in Yen).
National Debt	1,437,449,203	62,711,242
Local Loans	176,313,875	8,859,617
Corporation Securities	151,250,000	7,266,250
Total	1,765,013,078	78,837,109

These figures, however, do not include the paper representing internal Japanese loans which are in the hands of foreigners. When these are included, the amount of interest passing annually into foreign hands is increased to approximately 80,000,000 yen. Foreign capital invested in stock-company and partnership enterprises amounted at the close of December, 1910, to 32,925,000 yen. According to a statement of the Ministry of Commerce and Agriculture this was distributed as follows:

FOREIGN INVESTMENTS IN JAPAN

	Total Foreign Capital (Yen).	New in 1911 (Yen).
1. Japanese and part Japanese Enterprises:		
Stock Companies	21,850,126	471,304
Partnerships	642,000	223,500
2. Foreign Enterprises:		
Stock Companies	6,743,663	50,000
Partnerships	3,689,210	206,250

In Canada, according to the *Monetary Times of Canada*, at least $1,750,000,000 of foreign capital are invested. The share of Great Britain in this amount is given at $1,050,000,000 and that of the United States at $500,000,000. In Mexico, a statement by the president of the Canadian Commercial Bank before a stock-holders' meeting of the bank is authority for the assertion that the capital interests of the United

States in Mexico amount to approximately $1,000,000,000; of this amount thirty-five per cent is invested in railways and forty-five per cent in mining enterprises. The investments of England are $700,000,000, of which sixty per cent is in railways, fifteen per cent in mines, and twenty-five per cent in agriculture and miscellaneous industries. Capital investments of the other European nations (France, Germany, Belgium, Holland and Spain) were estimated at $300,000,000, which is placed chiefly in the banking business and in wholesale and retail trade.

For Argentina, the foreign investments of capital are stated for the close of the year 1910 at around 9,000,000,000 marks,[1] distributed as follows:

FOREIGN INVESTMENTS IN ARGENTINA

Enterprises.	Amount (Gold Piastres).
Loans and various Argentine securities	691,831,000
Railways	804,413,000
Banks	37,511,000
Harbour improvements	22,163,900
Street railways	91,576,270
Meat refrigeration plants	8,391,500
Gas and Electric companies, Water-works and Sanitation	58,035,015
Land and Mortgage companies	160,799,285
Miscellaneous corporations	41,650,100
Mortgages and property ownership	150,000,000
Trade and credit	200,000,000
Total	2,266,371,070

The figures given indicate merely that international transfers of capital are very large and that certain countries are creditors and others debtors. In regard to the extent of the movements of capital year by year, to the important relation in which the domestic investment of any country stands to its investment in foreign countries, and to the relative part played by the several countries in investment in

[1] Albert B. Martinez and Dr. Maurice Lewandowski, *Argentina in the Twentieth Century*, German translation from the fourth French edition, Gotha, 1912.

the various borrowing states, we have as yet no adequate information.

The Form of International Capital Transfers. As capital may appear in the form of any kind of economic values, it seeks in case of transfer to take on the form best adapted to the purpose. From this fact follows a distinction between transfers which take place in commerce within a state and in that between different states. Within a state, money capital is preferred for all acts of transfer except in so far as its use may be avoided through the agency of a common value depository, a bank, by mere exchange of signatures. This is due to the fact that money is most easily converted into any other form of capital and as a result of the relatively short period of time required for the transfer, the loss in interest is inconsiderable. The creditor usually loans his capital in the form of the money prescribed by law, and the debtor repays it in the same form. But between different states only capital goods can be transferred, since in international commerce there is no legal money. Gold coins and gold bars are usually accepted, since in most countries the privilege of free coinage is assured, but they pass only as goods according to their metal content and are used only in case of necessity on account of the cost of transportation and loss of interest. Bank notes are treated as gold certificates only and hence are rejected whenever redemption by the issuing bank is not entirely beyond question.

But capital in the form of goods is not so readily convertible as capital in the form of money. A country may export capital in the form of wool to a country which can utilize capital only in the form of railway construction material. The difficulties of conversion of capital goods are overcome by means of purchase and sale of foreign exchange which, like money, divides primitive exchange of goods into two acts ; the first set of goods are sold for bills of exchange and the second set are bought with these bills of exchange. To a striking degree the bill of exchange has achieved a dominant position in those countries, such as England and the United States, which have shown the greatest preference for the cheque as a money-saving medium of domestic trade. Foreign exchange is hence, from the private economy point of view, the first and most important form of international transfer of capital; but on the national economy plane there must take place the interchange of goods whose representative the bill is, and in this connexion the exchange of goods may take place between other countries than those concerned in the capital transfer. Let us assume an example: France wishes to send capital to Greece; this might take place by France transporting to Greece railroad construction material to the value of the amount in question, but it may also be effected by means of the exportation of sugar exchange on London. With this exchange received from France as a transmission of capital, Greece may finally purchase the railway material from Germany. Thus the transfer of capital takes place from France to Greece but is based on shipments of goods by several countries among themselves, somewhat according to the following diagram:

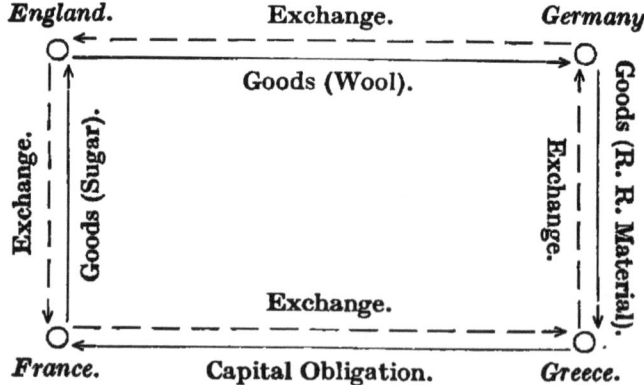

Thus goods play a double rôle in international commerce: they may be objects of international trade or they may be a medium for the transfer of capital. In the first case they are sold; in the second case they are merely loaned according to their capital value. But it makes no difference in respect to the goods whether they serve one purpose or the other. The locomotives which Greece orders from France may be paid for with Greek money or with French money which has been raised by Greece through a loan floated in Paris.

Securities may, however, be judged from quite other points of view than either that of goods or that of exchange media. They may be regarded, that is, as evidences of property rights destined to permanent capital investment, such as government bonds, notes, debentures, shares, &c. From a private economy viewpoint, such capital certificates are looked upon as goods and are bought and sold as such. But from the standpoint of national economy, no new economic value is produced by them, but the transfer of already existing economic values merely facilitated. Yet even from the national economy point of view, the acquisition of such securities represents an enrichment of the country. The rights evidenced by the securities will not always be based upon or fulfilled by a transmission of economic values, since one-sided transfers also take place through gifts, inheritances, &c. On the other hand, not all the claims of one country against another are represented by securities, since by sales, agreements, and other legal transactions a mass of undocumented claims arises. Finally, the claims against a foreign country may increase without new capital transfers taking place, for the earnings of capital invested in the foreign country—interest, dividends, and the like—may not be drawn by the creditor country but may be invested as new capital in the debtor country or some other foreign land.

The Causes of International Transfers of Capital. Capital sums may become objects of international transfer on economic and also on other grounds. In an economic sense the decisive factor is the difference in the earnings of capital, which operates in a manner similar to a difference in level in water. This is explained by the fact that each economic division forms an independent market for capital, with peculiar conditions of supply and demand. A complete equilibrium is however never reached, in spite of the ease of transfer, because certain hindering factors work against it.

In the first place, a single capital market is not unified, but is composed of two different yet mutually interacting groups of buyers and sellers. The one group is concerned with loan capital, in the placing of which an ultimate loan risk but no business or entrepreneur risk is assumed. Such loans are therefore made on the basis of a uniform rate of interest, determined in advance; of this character are government loans, promissory notes, debentures, mortgage loans, bank and savings deposits, &c. The second group, on the other hand, is concerned with entrepreneurs' capital; in investments of this character the assumption of the risk of the business by the investor is the essential point, and such investments therefore yield a variable return in the form of dividends and the like. They are represented by corporation stocks, business shares, &c. The two groups stand in an intimate mutual relation. In a period of improving business conditions the second group will predominate; in times of business depression, on the other hand, the first. Hence the low prices of government securities and the high prices of dividend paper in 1912 were at least in part a quite logical result of economic development, which after the crisis of 1907 has taken on the character of a more and more rapid upward movement. It goes without saying that the fixed interest must normally be lower than the earnings on capital in the form of dividends, since in the latter case the return includes also compensation for the assumption of entrepreneur's risk. Interest is also, to be sure, a return on capital but only from the standpoint of the lender, as from the standpoint of the entrepreneur it is reckoned as a cost. Occasionally, indeed, the income computed on the market value of dividend-yielding stocks may fall below the income from the safest interest-bearing paper. In Austria, in 1912, for example, the public securities yielded a higher rate than many corporation stocks. This is possible in cases where purchasers anticipate quick speculative gains through dealings on the exchange and hence have little regard to the dividends. In general, a higher yield of capital will bring in its wake a higher rate of interest, and a falling yield of capital will depress interest rates. Yet not every change will produce a similar and proportionate result in this respect. Production is stimulated less by the absolute rate of return on capital than it is by the momentary difference between that return and interest, since production works with borrowed capital, or at least bases its calculations on the amount which the invested capital would yield if merely loaned, which is to say without the assumption of the entrepreneur risk. This difference may be very small even when the return on capital is high, especially when banks of issue precipitately raise their discount rates in order to protect their gold reserves.

The market for loan capital is influenced on the side of supply, in the first instance, by the amount of capital available. But in this connexion not merely the creation of capital in the economic division in question comes into consideration, but also the importation of foreign capital. But foreign capital will only move into a country when and so long as the rate of interest in that country is higher than in its original home, and in fact the difference, under otherwise similar conditions of investment, must be great enough to offer a compensation for the inconveniences and dangers which are always connected with any investment of capital in a foreign country. Such obstacles grow out of the greater difficulties in controlling the economic and political situation in a foreign country, out of differences in standards of value, out of the less ready saleability of foreign securities, and the like. Of the capital present in the country, only that part will be effective on the market which is expressly designated to be loaned. This designation, however, depends on the personal views and the circumstances of life of the owners of the capital. In France, the typical country of small bond-owners who prefer a small but sure income to a greater, more uncertain one, the supply of loan capital is so large that it irresistibly seeks foreign markets. The determining factor in the demand for loan capital is in the first place the loan needs of the state and other public corporations. This demand has risen to an extraordinary degree in recent years, as governmental expenditures have increased, and military preparations in particular have directly and indirectly consumed enormous sums, and also because the great cities have been forced to borrow large amounts for the municipalization of their street railways, gas and electric plants, &c. Private enterprises also, with the increasing extent of their operations, find more and more favourable opportunities for issuing bonds instead of additional stock obligations, as in this way earnings beyond the amount necessary to pay interest go to increase the yield on the stock previously issued. It is true that here also the total demand for loans does not press upon the market but only that part of it which in fact requires to be covered. Since, for example, in the United States of America the bank-note circulation is not covered, as in Europe, by discounted paper but by public securities, United States bonds, which must be deposited in the national treasury, more than half of this government paper serves, not as investment, but as a basis of note issues. As a result of this situation the market value of these bonds is relatively very high ; in 1912 bonds bearing interest at two per cent reached the price of 109. Needless to say, the organization of the market is also significant, for credit requires special organized agencies, banks, savings institutions, trust companies, &c. The number and character of such institutions, their distribution by branches over the country, the principles of their business policy and their influence over the people are decisive on many points. The difference in the customary rate of interest in different countries is a result of the inequality in the loan risk which, it is needless to say, is less in the capital-producing than in the capital-consuming countries, and

differs sharply in the latter also according to their political
and economical development. Within a given economic
division the interest rate is again graduated according to the
risk associated with the various loan seekers, according to
the duration of the loan, the method of repayment (payment
by instalments, &c.).

In the market for entrepreneurs' capital, the demand is
determined by that portion of native and foreign capital
which seeks not a fixed interest but the highest possible
yield. It is very elastic, since it can readily increase and
decrease at the expense of the portion that would ordinarily
serve as loan capital. The flow of domestic capital into
enterprises may be obstructed by various circumstances.
In the first place, mortgage loans offer a field of investment
with so high a yield and so little accessible to foreigners that
the dividends from industrial operations may offer little
attraction. In Roumania, for example, students of the subject
have pointed out that the wished-for nationalization of
Roumanian industry cannot be carried out because money
brings eight per cent in mortgages without any risk, and hence
the usual dividends of five or six per cent attract not Roumanian but English capital, which receives only two and a half
or three per cent when invested in English paper. Similar
situations obtain in many countries. In Canada, the rate
of interest for safe mortgages is from seven to eight per
cent, in Argentina from ten to eleven per cent. Still other
influences make themselves felt. Chinese capitalists, for
example, avoid industrial activities because in this way they
declare their property and then can be compelled to contribute
to more or less voluntary national subscriptions. The inflow
of foreign capital into enterprises is opposed in the first
place by the circumstance that in the countries of surplus
capital especially, fixed interest paper is preferred. Many
undertakings, as especially banks, large industrial corporations, &c., strive to adapt themselves to this preference by
a conservative dividend policy ; they fix the rates of dividends

and accumulate a surplus in prosperous years in order not to have to lower them in bad years. Demand in this field depends on the spirit of enterprise in the population, but also on the given conditions under which it must operate. Among these given conditions are included first of all the politico-economic guaranties which a country offers to production in its various branches. Under this head fall especially the questions of tariff protection and other economic protective measures, legislation affecting industry, and the conditions of the association of capital, the organization of trade and transportation (particularly the possibility of cheap freights by water), efficiency of institutions for the protection and insurance of working-men, and the burdens of taxation and other payments. It is frequently the case that a manufacturing enterprise erects a branch factory in one of its foreign markets, when for any reason manufacture in the foreign country appears more advantageous than exportation thither. Occasionally the introduction of a high protective tariff compels such action. Thus, for example, the McKinley Bill of 1890 and the Dingley Bill of 1897 in the United States of America, the Russian Tariff Laws of 1891 and 1903, the French Tariff of 1892, and the Austro-Hungarian of 1906, have been extremely favourable to the establishment of foreign branches. That, none the less, tariff protection is not the sole decisive factor is shown by the fact that even in free-trade England in recent years, numerous American and German branch factories have been established. The general and permanent favouring conditions must be further supplemented by the temporary stimulus of a favourable business situation. But in times of rapid business improvement the demand for capital for production is increased by the added demand for speculative purposes, dividend-yielding paper being bought not for the purpose of investment but as a means to quick gains through market fluctuations. The return to be expected on the capital, the dividends, must exceed the customary rate of interest in the country by an amount sufficient to compensate for the entrepreneur risk assumed, this risk depending, not like the loan risk on the personal ability to pay of the borrower, but on the actual chances of the undertaking. Ricardo[1] derives the difference in the return on capital from the differences in ground-rents in the various countries. According to his view the natural limitations of the amount of land gives the possessor a monopoly which compels the owner of capital to renounce in favour of the land monopolist an ever-increasing share of his profits as industrial development proceeds. The land monopoly can exert its power on the industrial enterprises, which in advanced countries represent the larger part of production, in two ways: by increase in the value of sites or through a rise in the cost of the necessaries of life for the labour force. But the cost of the site is for modern large-scale production so small in comparison with the other capital expenditures that it could seldom be decisive. The costs of the necessities of life, moreover, are no longer, and for a long time have not been, determined by the conditions in any particular country but by those in the world market, though this world influence may, to be sure, be more or less effectively warded off by the economic policy of a country. The view of Ricardo is therefore untenable; still less tenable is that of Sartorius[2] according to which modern trusts and combinations also form monopolies which, 'in so far as they use their monopolistic power to put up prices, likewise become reducers of the general profits, for which competition is carried on, as much as are the land monopolists.' In the first place, combinations and trusts are not monopolies, because they do not exclude competition. Least of all, in view of the high mobility of capital, are they in a position to lay a special tribute upon that of any particular country.

---

[1] David Ricardo, *Principles of Political Economy and Taxation*, chap. ii.

[2] A. Sartorius, Freiherr von Waltershausen, *Das volkswirtschaftlhche System der Kapitalanlage im Auslande*, Berlin, 1907, p. 31.

But the economic basis of the difference in the earnings of capital may be strengthened or weakened by various extra-economic forces. Such causes originate in the first instance from the relation between the capital and the person of the entrepreneur. Capital may go anywhere but it is only called for where business enterprises are undertaken and flourish. Now the entrepreneur as an individual is not influenced exclusively in his choice of a location for his establishment by the rate of profit to be expected. He is seeking before all a home, and only a considerable pressure on the side of industrial conditions will induce him to emigrate. And in the choice between different foreign economic fields, various personal motives may prove decisive. Kinship in nationality, or at least a common speech, will always operate as an attraction. Thus, for example, the relations between Spain and South America since the dissolution of the colonial domination have not merely continued but in recent times have shown new life. An agreeable climate may under some circumstances play a very important rôle. An example is offered by Egypt, which has a strong immigration of foreign business enterprisers for the reason in part that it offers the prospect of restoration of enfeebled health, while on the other hand Brazil has suffered from the fear of the yellow fever. Too great a difference in the culture level of the population is a hindering influence; thus, of all the European merchants, only the Greek will consent to settle under purely Arabic surroundings. People who have once established themselves in a foreign country continue to attract thither others from their own country, sometimes through relations of kinship or friendship but often also by the mere example, so that very frequently a preference not otherwise to be accounted for may be observed on the part of certain foreign merchants for a particular economic field.

Uncertainty of law enforcement and oppressive taxation may strongly favour the migration of capital. In countries rich in capital, to be sure, the potent consideration is less likely to be uncertainty in law enforcement than a momentary fear of political complications. Still more persistent may be the influence of oppressive taxation, as has especially been the case in France, where on grounds of social policy legislation has endeavoured to subject property incomes to heavier taxation than labour incomes, which are less secure and less easily concealed, and has also introduced strong progression in the inheritance taxes. The effect of these measures, however, has been that savings have been accumulated to a larger and larger extent in foreign banks, which have not been slow to take advantage of the opportunities.[1]

The direction of international transfers of capital is further influenced by political considerations. Political amity favours the flow of capital out of the richer country into the one which is poorer or more enterprising. The indebtedness of Russia to France and of Italy to Germany has not indeed been caused by the political alliances but has in any case been increased on that account. Capital also smooths the course for the political expansion of the mother country by working fields which are later to be won as colonies, protectorates or the like. It hopes in this way to secure for itself an especially active support and later a preferential position on the part of the home government. In this way French capital in Tunis and Morocco, and Italian in Tripoli, has prepared the way for political power. The United States of America is similarly pressing forward with the power of its capital in other American countries in order to extend the influence of its pan-American ideas.

The Effects of International Transfers of Capital. The quantity of capital is not inherent in the economic values which are sent as capital from one country to another. The exported capital is added to the property of the other

[1] Alfred Neymarck, *Finances contemporaines*, tome vi ; *L'Épargne française et les valeurs mobilières*, Paris, 1911, pp. 131, 163.

economic division and may there as well be employed as
consumers' goods as invested in the form of capital. When
a country floats foreign loans in order to establish unproduc-
tive official positions, or when it becomes the field of foreign
enterprises. which merely satisfy the demands for pleasure
on the part of the local population, it is behaving no differently
from the individual human being who procures for himself an
agreeable present income at the expense of his future income.

Capital is really fruitful for the country into which it
goes only when it remains capital, that is, when it is devoted
to the creation of new economic values. In this respect,
again, a distinction must be drawn between entrepreneurs'
capital and loan capital. The most favourable case is that
in which domestic entrepreneurs' capital is increased by
foreign loan capital and in this way made more productive,
just as in private business. The man who buys a house with
100,000 kronen of his own money receives an income of
5,000 kronen if the net yield is five per cent, while the man
who uses only 40,000 kronen of his own money and borrows
the other 60,000 from a savings bank at four per cent has,
if the total return is the same, to give up 2,400 kronen of
the 5,000 in interest to the savings bank but the remaining
2,600 are to be credited to a capital of his own of only
40,000 kronen and so raise its yield to six and a half per cent.
But the attraction of foreign entrepreneurs' capital may be
profitable even when not in the same degree as that of
impersonal loan capital. The establishment of branch
factories by foreign enterprises stimulates the native productive force and creates opportunities for work. In addition, such branch establishments presuppose a nationalizing
process which amounts in the end to an actual gain in capital.
The disadvantages may easily predominate when there are
connected with the enterprises economic interests of the
community which cannot be so effectually safeguarded in
foreign hands, as in the case of railways, harbour improvements, gas and electric works, &c.

The effect of exportation of capital on the exporting country is likely to be disadvantageous. The country rich in capital is prone to prefer loaning its capital to a foreign country at a high rate of interest to employing it in enterprises of its own. In consequence, the spirit of enterprise in the loaning country is killed, and in addition the rising competition of the newly founded enterprises abroad, based on capital borrowed from the country in question, must be met. When in addition to these circumstances the dissemination of material welfare through the broader strata of the population leads to the loss of the incentive to rise from the lower to the upper classes, the country becomes a ' nation of bond-holders '. France has passed through this transformation and England is well along the same road. In most cases, however, cause and effect will in this connexion be interchanged. The spirit of enterprise is not weak because the exportation of capital is large, but rather the reverse ; capital must leave the country because, as a matter of experience, the activity of saving develops in inverse ratio to the spirit of enterprise. French industry does not lack for capital, but it may truly be said that French capital suffers from the lack of industries.

A political disadvantage must be placed beside the economic disadvantage already discussed. The flotation of public loans in the country may be rendered difficult when foreign nations compete and offer better terms of investment. These loans of capital may quite possibly serve to strengthen the political opponent in some future struggle, for they may even be used for the purchase of military supplies. Such a disadvantage can hardly be avoided and attaches to all international value transfers. Every industrial nation is ready and glad to sell ordnance and any other munitions of war, even in the face of the danger that the purchasing country may become a political opponent, since in case of refusal the business would merely be lost and the other country could not be prevented from securing the material.

An important advantage of exportation of capital may be achieved in case it is used to promote the exportation of goods. Loans to foreign countries are often granted under the condition, expressed or implied, that the creditor country is to receive the contracts for railroad or highway construction, harbour improvements, and the like, or for munitions of war, or is to be granted concessions for railways or mining enterprises or for other undertakings affecting its economic interests, depending upon the purpose to which the loan is applied. This condition may in part enforce itself automatically, because of the fact that modern banks, which mediate the foreign loans, form at the same time the financial supports of the manufacturing enterprises interested in the exportation of the goods. It is also more directly imposed because the government of the creditor country must be initiated into the foreign loan proceedings and will seize the opportunity to exert its influence on behalf of domestic industry. Thus, in the year 1906, Servia refused to recognize the demand of Austria-Hungary to be treated on a basis of equality in regard to the impending purchases of arms because the acceptance of the necessary loan in France had been conditioned on the granting of the contracts to French manufacturers. In Brazil the circumstance that the railways are in the hands of English and North Americans is decisive in the awarding of contracts for locomotives, cars, &c., and even for the appointment of officials and engineers.

In the English financial press the existence of an equalizing mechanism between the exportation of capital and of goods is even assumed, similar to that which political economy earlier constructed between the exportation of goods and the rate of foreign exchange. When, according to the theory, in a country such as England, rich in capital and active in exports, the exportation of goods is reduced, the possibility of capital investments in the country is also decreased; in consequence, the exportation of capital increases, which fact, however, revives the exportation of goods through its alleged close connexion with commerce.   But the better employment of export industries fixes again increased masses of capital, while finding its own outlet in foreign countries, &c. This assumption, however, is incorrect.   In the first place, the revivifying effect of capital exportation extends to only a portion of the exports of goods, and hence may be more than compensated in the final result to be shown in the commercial statistics by a reverse change in other classes of goods. Investments of capital in foreign countries may promote the export trade of cannon factories and shipyards, but in a less degree or not at all that of textile mills.   Then, too, the course of business in goods which are produced in large quantities depends less upon the production conditions of a particular country than upon the general business situation.   If this general business situation is bad there will be a decrease, not merely in exports of goods, but also in exports of capital, because a greater supply of capital corresponds to a lessened demand ; furthermore, in view of the sharp competition between owners of capital, the debtor countries will be less inclined to consent to the prescription of the condition that in their purchases of goods they must grant a preference to the creditor country.   If the course of business were bad in England alone, this would be a proof only of the diminished competitive power of the country.   The prospect of increasing exports of goods through investments of capital in foreign countries would be the less hopeful since the higher price of the goods to be ordered would be figured into the cost of the loan by the debtor country, and in consequence, other conditions being equal (rate of interest and the transfer price), the English money market would be avoided or drawn upon only indirectly through the medium of other countries. Thus, in the year 1910, Brazil borrowed money in France and, in spite of the press campaign carried on against the procedure, purchased her war material in Germany because it was cheaper there.   Least of all can the existence of such a compensating mechanism as that referred to be proved by the fact that according to the English commercial statistics an increase in the excess of imports can be brought into relation with a decrease in the exportation of capital and vice versa.[1] This is impossible, in the first place because an excess of imports may result not merely from a decrease in exports, but also from a greater increase in imports, with exports remaining constant or even increasing. Thus, for example, in the years 1884–90, foreign investments of capital were extraordinarily large—larger than ever before or since, yet exports sank from 242,000,000 pounds sterling in 1882 to 213,000,000 in the year 1886, not surpassing the earlier high-water mark until the years 1889–91, and then but temporarily. Imports followed a quite similar course. Nothing at all can be proved by the English commercial statistics except the successive changes in business conditions, which have also left distinct traces in the commercial policy of other countries.

Finally, large capital resources extend the field of labour. They have also a high political value, since the country possessing such resources is in a position to procure and retain political friendships by granting generous credit conditions, and also to punish political opponents by the withholding of credit. Thus the political alliance between Russia and France has a very material support in the Russian demand for credit, while Italy, on her entry into the Triple Alliance, has had to suffer keenly from the unfriendly attitude of the French money market.

4. International Migrations

The Essential Features of International Migrations. Just as in case of the transportation of a good, so with every change in the abode of a human being from one economic division to another, a shift in economic relations takes place.

---

[1] Sigmund Schilder, *Entwicklungstendenzen der Weltwirtschaft*, Berlin, 1913, vol. i, p. 377.

But, while the movement of goods is controlled by purely economic motives, in accordance with which an advantage ordinarily accrues to the country of departure as well as to the receiving country, the case is very different in the migrations of human beings. Numerous considerations, personal, political, national, and religious, influence such movements, which accordingly may, economically speaking, be a disadvantage for one country or for the other, or for both. Furthermore, the double economic rôle of the human being here stands sharply forth. On the one hand, as a bearer of labour power, he embodies one of the two factors of production ; on the other, however, as a consuming unit, he represents the final goal of economic activity in general. Now it is an important distinction whether the individual seeking entrance into another economic division comes more as a producing or as a consuming force, whether he is seeking opportunity to make profits or merely an agreeable sojourn. In the first case he is a factor of foreign commerce, while in the latter he is a factor of emigration.

The foreigner who moves, merely as a consumer, to a new economic division may have in view a permanent or merely temporary stay. In the event of permanent residence, the case is one of the settlement of a person who lives on an income and is connected with the question of capital transfers already discussed. A result quite similar to that of a capital transfer is achieved even when the individual in question leaves his capital in his previous abode and consumes in the foreign country only the income derived from it. When, for example, an Englishman removes to France and leaves the capital on which he lives invested in an English bank, this capital is from an economic standpoint no longer English, but is French capital invested in England ; it has been denationalized even when the Englishman retains his nationality after his change of residence. Even the pensioner who takes up a permanent residence in a foreign country creates a demand on the part of that country against the country which is obligated to pay the pension. The pensioning of English officials who have returned to England after a short period of service in British India thus forms a steady source of Indian foreign indebtedness.

The foreigner who comes into another economic division merely as a consumer, but makes there only a temporary sojourn, does not occasion international transfers of capital, but rather international payments which for the most part add to the consumption goods of the national economy, and hence do not come into consideration from the standpoint of capital formation. Foreign travel affects chiefly those countries which exert some special attraction in the form of beauty of landscape, climatic advantages, healing springs, historical monuments, social gratifications, and the like. The richest and most varied tourist traffic is that of France, where Paris especially, as the centre of an old culture and as a world-renowned pleasure resort, forms throughout practically the entire year an objective point for foreigners, not merely from European countries but from other parts of the world as well, and where further the Riviera in winter, by its combination of desirable climatic and social features, attracts an international public of large purchasing power. After France rank Italy, which from old time has enjoyed wide repute on account of its art treasures and historical monuments, and Switzerland, which has shown great skill in the commercial utilization of its attractive landscapes by means of a shrewdly managed hotel industry. Austria-Hungary exerts considerable attractive force by means of its healing springs. In recent years the Scandinavian countries have also come into vogue with their distinctive beauties. Of countries outside of Europe, Egypt should be especially named as a preferred winter resort for the English and Americans.

The emigrant enters the foreign economic division in the first instance as a producer, for his consumption is only the cost element in the utilization of his productive power.

The emigration laws of the various states have met with the difficulty of fixing a definition of an emigrant in terms of external characteristics, the inner motive not being accessible. Most of the laws have on this account given up a general definition.   The Hungarian law (Statute II, 1909, section 1) designates as an emigrant any one ' who betakes himself into a foreign country with the object of continued engagement in productive activity' and leaves to the administrative officers the determination of this purpose of earning money. Some laws fix upon the outer circumstances of the journey, such as the low-class passage or the low cost of the ticket, indirectly concluding from these that the purpose is that of earning money.   Thus the Italian law of January 31, 1901 (Article 6), and the Spanish law of December 21, 1907 (Article 2), designate as emigrants persons travelling to oversea regions in the third class or a class declared to be equivalent thereto.   The French decree of March 9, 1861 (Article 7), designates as an emigrant every passenger ' who does not eat at the captain's or officer's mess and who pays for his passage, including quarters and meals, in the case of sailing ships less than forty francs, or in the case of steamships less than eighty francs, per week of the expected or usual duration of the voyage '.

Two important distinctions are combined in the concept of emigration, one temporal and the other geographical, both with economic reactions.   On the one hand we have permanent emigration, which, indeed, may not exclude a purpose of ultimate return, but still is undertaken with a view to engagement in productive pursuits for an indeterminate period in the foreign country ; on the other hand there is temporary emigration or seasonal migration, in which residence is taken up in the foreign country merely for the period of a work season or for an even shorter time.   Geographically speaking, three important migrational movements are to be observed, the intra-European, that from Europe to oversea regions, and the East-Asiatic.

The intra-European migration proceeds from many widely separated points. The most important is Italy,[1] which annually sends out in the spring to other European countries numbers of people from the northern provinces; these emigrants find employment in agricultural and construction work, and return in the late autumn with their savings. The following table shows the number of these temporary emigrants to Europe and Mediterranean countries:

ITALIAN SEASONAL EMIGRATION

Date.	To France.	To Switzerland.	To Austria-Hungary.	To Germany.	Total.[2]
1906	62,497	80,019	39,521	68,295	276,042
1907	63,105	83,026	41,953	75,885	288,774
1908	57,702	76,708	36,998	59,780	248,101
1909	56,863	66,931	30,989	53,391	226,355
1910	60,956	79,843	36,233	53,648	248,696

Belgium is a country which shows a predominantly temporary emigration; according to the official statistics the number of immigrants is actually greater as a rule than that of the emigrants. The migratory movement takes place chiefly between Belgium and the neighbouring countries, France, Germany, and Holland, the share of the oversea regions falling quite into insignificance in comparison. The following table of emigration to and immigration from various countries brings out the proportions:

BELGIUM EMIGRATION AND IMMIGRATION

Country or District.	Emigration.		Immigration.	
	1908.	1909.	1908.	1909.
France	17,411	20,025	16,296	16,090
Germany	4,739	4,432	7,092	8,329
Holland	4,497	4,485	6,956	7,133
All Europe[2] . . .	29,767	32,282	36,118	38,090
Countries outside of Europe	2,527	2,908	2,037	1,398
Total . . .	32,294	35,190	38,155	39,488

A much greater centre of seasonal migration is Austria,

[1] Fr. Nagri, *L'Emigrazione temporanea*, Rome, 1911.
[2] The totals include further details not given in this table.

especially Galicia, Dalmatia and parts of southern Tyrol. From Galicia proceed the Slavic migratory labourers (*Sachsen-gänger*), who find employment in sugar-beet culture and other agricultural work in various countries of Europe. The number of these wandering seasonal labourers has risen to an enormous extent and is already estimated at 450,000 annually. At least 400,000 go to Germany alone, although in that country the requirement of identification (*Legitimationszwang*), according to which every labourer must sacrifice time and money in procuring an identification card, works against this form of immigration, as do also the Prussian special regulations against foreign Slavs. In France 5,000 Austrian seasonal labourers on the average are employed, in Denmark 8,000, in Sweden 5,000, in Switzerland 2,000, and in Roumania from 12,000 to 15,000. Russian Poland is another region with considerable emigration. Among the countries of immigration, Denmark keeps exact statistics. According to these figures, in the year 1911, 10,320 labourers entered the country, of whom 2,128 were men, 8,115 women, and 77 children ; classified by country of origin, 8,101 came from Galicia and 1,828 from Russian Poland.

European emigration to oversea countries has developed to a remarkable extent since the introduction of steamship service. Characteristic changes have taken place in the predominating countries both of origin and of destination of the emigrants, and these changes lead to important conclusions as to the real causes of trans-oceanic migration. In spite of great deficiencies in the statistical records of various countries,[1] these clearly show that a stronger emigration movement sets in in the second quarter of the nineteenth century and is fed almost exclusively by Great Britain and Germany for nearly half a century. A particularly high wave was occasioned by the discovery of the rich California gold-deposits and the no less profitable workings in Australia, about the

---

[1] Eugen von Philippovitsch, article 'Auswanderung' in *Handwörterbuch der Staatswissenschaften*, third edition, Jena, 1909, vol. ii.

middle of the century.   At the beginning of the ' fifties ' the
annual emigration from Europe surpassed in any case the
number of half a million human beings. .Variations in
the outflow since that time have followed, chiefly from the
rise and fall of business conditions.   That the attractions of
the flourishing new economic fields exerted their first effect on
England and Germany in particular is to be explained, in the
first place, by the fact that these countries, in view of their
location on the Atlantic ocean, earliest received information in
regard to conditions in oversea countries and the opportunity
of reaching them.   On the other hand, these two countries
were so unequally developed economically that in particular
districts the desire for better opportunities of production
became especially strong.   In the years of the high tide of
emigration, that is from 1846 to 1855, seventy per cent of the
British emigration of 2,700,000 persons came from Ireland
alone.   In Germany, also, the eastern districts, already thinly
settled on account of the unfavourable conditions of land
ownership, have always furnished the largest contingents.
In the last quarter of the nineteenth century, Italy and
Austria-Hungary have taken their place at the head of the
list of emigration countries, and here again the thinly
populated districts with predominantly agricultural industry
furnish most of the emigrants.

The following table shows the course of emigration from
Austria-Hungary in recent years :

Year.	Austria.	Hungary.
1906	136,354	178,170
1907	177,354	209,169
1908	57,734	49,365
1909	129,808	129,337
1910	138,867	119,901

Nearly two-thirds of the Austrian and more than half of the
Hungarian emigration goes by way of German ports, and the
share of the Italian commercial fleet in the transportation of
the emigrants is also greater than that of the Austrian and

Hungarian. Approximately nine-tenths of these emigrants go to the United States of America and the rest almost exclusively to Argentina and Canada.

While the Italian seasonal migration to European countries originates principally in the northern part of the country, that is to say, in Piedmont, Lombardy, and Venetia, the oversea emigration, on the other hand, is recruited almost exclusively from central and southern Italy, or, more specifically, from the provinces of Salerno, Avellino, Campobasso, Caserta, Potenza, Cosenza, Apulia, Calabria, &c. Though most of these emigrants permanently leave their homes, and hence sell houses and ground plots, an increasing proportion of the total emigration none the less takes on the character of periodicity, as agricultural and day-labourers go to South America for a work season only, the harvest there falling in the European winter season. The last high point was reached by Italy in 1906, when 414,719 emigrants were recorded; since then a decrease has taken place. Of the 212,500 emigrants of the year 1911, 155,835 went to the United States of America, 37,666 to the La Plata valley, 18,011 to Brazil, 559 to Central America, 114 to Australia, &c. The number of Italian citizens living abroad was officially stated in 1910 as follows : Europe, 900,562 ; Africa, 191,919 ; Asia, 12,500 ; America, 4,445,056, and Australia, 7,709.

In the last few decades the emigration of Russia, as well as that of Spain and other Mediterranean countries, has notably increased; Spanish emigration is temporary in a higher degree even than that of Italy, as the relations between Spain and South America are rather intimate. England still shows a large number of emigrants, though it is partly balanced by a considerable compensating back-flow. The migrational movement takes place chiefly between Great Britain and the British possessions and the United States of America. Its extent is shown in the following table :

BRITISH EMIGRATION AND IMMIGRATION

| | Emigration. | | Immigration. | |
Year.	Citizens of Great Britain.	Citizens of Foreign Countries.	Citizens of Great Britain.	Citizens of Foreign Countries.
1907	395,680	239,269	160,588	133,045
1908	263,199	123,212	172,043	170,879
1909	288,761	185,617	149,068	112,257
1910	397,848	221,011	164,139	134,640

The emigration from Germany has fallen off sharply in consequence of the rapid industrialization of the country. In the record year for emigration, namely, 1907, 31,696 German citizens left the country; in the year 1911 only 22,690. North America continues to exert the greatest attractive force.

Among the countries of destination for European emigration the United States of America continues to occupy the leading place. According to the report of the Congressional Immigration Commission, 27,818,710 persons migrated to the United States in the period between July 1, 1819, and the end of the fiscal year 1909–10. This number is approximately equal to the total population of Austria, and the immigrants are chiefly drawn from the male population at the most productive age of from fourteen to forty-five years. The year 1907 was the record year of American immigration. The following table shows the movement since that time and indicates the age and sex distribution:

AMERICAN IMMIGRATION SINCE 1907

Year.	Number of Immigrants.	Number of Males.	Number between 14 and 45 years of age.	Excluded from landing.
1907	1,285,349	929,976	1,100,771	13,064
1908	782,870	506,912	630,671	10,902
1909	751,786	519,969	624,876	10,411
1910	1,041,570	736,038	868,310	24,270
1911	878,587	570,057	714,709	22,349

A great change has taken place in the nationalities of American immigrants. While in the decade of 1861 to 1870 forty-five per cent of the immigration was still British and thirty-four per cent German, in the record year of 1907 on the other hand, eighty-one and one-tenth per cent came from the countries of southern and eastern Europe, and only seventeen and seven-tenths per cent from those of northern and western Europe.   In the fiscal year 1911 the share of Europe represented ninety-one and four-tenths per cent of the total immigration, and that of south-eastern Europe sixty-five and four-tenths per cent ; the states most strongly represented are now Italy (190,020 in 1911), Austria-Hungary (161,283), Russia (160,970), and Great Britain (118,896).   But in other respects, also, important changes have taken place.   In the earlier period, the new arrivals were principally agriculturists with a fair degree of education, and settled permanently.   At the present time the percentage of illiterates is rising, and the new immigrants are pressing, not into the agricultural southern states but in a much greater degree into the North Atlantic states predominating in mining and manufactures, and especially into the great metropolis, New York city. Further, they have in view not permanent settlement, but a temporary period of acquisition, so that the number who later return to their native countries steadily increases.

The agricultural emigrants go chiefly to South America, and especially to Argentina, from which country many, however, turn aside to Brazil.   In the period from 1857 to 1909, 3,409,540 persons have immigrated into Argentina ; of these 1,892,721 were Italians, 882,271 Spaniards, 192,436 French, 93,349 Russians, 64,252 Austrians, 60,359 Syrians, &c.   In recent years the emigration of Russians and Syrians has risen with especial rapidity.   The Italians and Spaniards come in part for a work season only, so that the immigration is largely offset by a strong back-flow.   The following table gives a general view of the situation and development :

ARGENTINE IMMIGRATION AND BACK-FLOW

Years.	Immigration.	Emigration.
1857–1860	20,000	—
1861–1865	46,874	—
1866–1870	112,696	
1871–1875	148,422	
1876–1880	112,191	—
1881–1885	255,185	—
1886–1890	511,383	76,863
1891–1895	236,252	169,312
1896–1900	412,074	159,140
1901–1905	526,030	215,700
1906	252,536	60,124
1907	209,103	90,190
1908	255,710	85,412
1909	231,084	94,644
1910	289,640	97,854

Brazil shows a sharp increase in the immigration figures, and again principally in arrivals from southern Europe and Russia. In the year 1911, 135,976 persons entered the country, of whom 99,311 were agricultural labourers. The number who came at their own expense was 78,021 while the remaining 55,595 had their passage paid by the Brazilian Government. The immigration in recent years has been distributed among the more important nationalities as shown in the following table :

RECENT BRAZILIAN IMMIGRATION

Nationality.	1908.	1909.	1910.	1911.
Portuguese	37,628	30,577	30,857	47,493
Spaniards	14,862	16,219	20,843	27,141
Italians .	13,873	13,668	14,163	22,914
Russians	5,781	5,663	2,462	14,013
Turks	3,170	4,027	5,257	6,319
Germans	2,931	5,413	3,902	4,251
Austrians and Hungarians	5,362	4,065	3,930	4,132
Others .	11,378	5,778	8,150	13,705
Total	94,985	85,410	89,564	139,968

During the first decade of the twentieth century, Canadian immigration has been soaring rapidly, a result which has been chiefly due to the deliberate co-operation of the English and

Canadian Governments to this end. The migration to Canada of small farmers has been encouraged in every possible way. The total number of immigrants has increased to 311,084 in the fiscal year 1910–11 (as against 208,794 for the preceding year). Of this total number, 185,198 were men, 71,038 women, and 54,848 children. The increasing number of women is explained by the growth in the immigration of female domestic servants, and also by the fact that immigrants send home for their families as soon as they have secured a sufficient means of livelihood in the new country. The largest share of the immigrants is that of Great Britain, with 123,013; 121,451 came from the United States of America; but these are in large part Europeans who have continued their migration after a temporary residence in the Union. Of the countries of continental Europe, Austria-Hungary has furnished the largest number of immigrants (17,598 in 1911); then follow Russia, with 13,762 (Jews, Finns, and Poles); Italy, with 8,359, &c. The strongest current of immigration is directed toward the north-western grain-producing provinces of Manitoba, Saskatchewan, Alberta, and British Columbia, but of late Ontario has been exerting a stronger attraction by virtue of its industrial development.

Immigration into the British colonies in South Africa and Australia is regulated by the legislation of these countries, so that it is restricted more and more to new comers from the mother country. The following table shows the movement in recent years:

IMMIGRATION INTO AND EMIGRATION FROM CAPE COLONY

| | Immigrants. | | Emigrants. | |
Year.	Total.	From Great Britain.	Total.	To Great Britain.
1907	29,767	19,250	39,550	23,054
1908	27,498	17,525	32,929	19,517
1909	30,445	19,550	29,697	15,961
1910	31,281	23,814	26,913	16,095

IMMIGRATION INTO AND EMIGRATION FROM NATAL

| Year. | Immigrants. | | Emigrants. |
	Total.	East Indian Labourers.	Total.
1905	58,592	7,917	21,470
1906	41,609	11,641	24,460
1907	21,964	6,486	40,055
1908	18,403	3,174	46,026
1909	22,378	2,487	29,961
1910	30,340	7,935	20,332

IMMIGRATION INTO AND EMIGRATION FROM THE AUSTRALIAN COMMONWEALTH

| Year. | Immigrants. | | Emigrants. | |
	Total.	From Great Britain.	Total.	To Great Britain.
1907	68,638	17,194	56,124	10,484
1908	72,208	21,416	59,058	12,086
1909	83,609	29,959	54,676	12,490
1910	95,692	39,902	58,145	14,513

The emigration from eastern Asia includes Chinese and Japanese. The older and more important movement is that from the Chinese provinces of Fukien and Kwantung. From these districts traders and labourers have been going to Siam and the Malay Peninsula, to the southern archipelago, and in recent years even to America and Australia. But in recent years also a strong return current has set in, so that it is estimated that a compensating return flow of perhaps 250,000 should be opposed to the annual emigration of from 300,000 to 400,000. Japanese emigration began in the year 1868 with the transportation of large numbers of sugar plantation labourers to the Hawaian Islands and was soon after directed to the Pacific coast of the United States of America. The emigration to California has grown to such an extent that in the year 1908, 60,780 Japanese were living in San Francisco alone. The majority of these emigrants, however, engage in agriculture, especially fruit and vegetable growing. In recent years Japanese emigration has been directed also to South America.

The Causes of International Migrations. The incentive to

migrate into a foreign economic division may be very different in different cases; it is frequently of a personal nature but it is also often to be found in the political, national, or religious situation. At the present time, however, the underlying causes of mass movements can as a rule be economic only, as the non-economic motives are no longer strong enough outside of exceptional cases. Examples of emigration from non-economic motives are furnished by the so-called 'Muhad-schirs' (fugitives); these are Mohammedans who emigrate from portions of the former Turkish dominions which have fallen under foreign rule, such as Bulgaria, Bosnia, southern Russia and Crete, and settle in the Turkish territory of Asia Minor, where the government sets aside colonies or districts for their occupation. The German and Jewish agricultural colonies in Palestine also belong under this head. In 1868, several colonies were founded by a religious society of Württemberg calling itself the 'German Temple'. After an initial period of difficulties these groups reached quite a flourishing state; one is located near Jaffa, another on the plain of Sharon three kilometres from the same town, another one kilometre to the south of Jerusalem, and a fourth is on the narrow coastal plain between Mount Carmel and the bay of Haifa. The total number of these Templars perhaps amounts to about two thousand. The *Alliance Israélite* has also formed, with Jews emigrated from Russia, several agricultural colonies in the region between Jaffa and Jerusalem, on the belt of coast between Haifa and Jaffa and near the lake of Merom.

There is no doubt that the ocean steamship companies, for whom the immigration traffic has proven the best source of income, as well as their scattered agencies, have in addition to the above influences an active commercial one. In many countries with inadequate governmental regulation, these people have not hesitated at the use of discreditable methods, such for example as the payment to agents of commissions per head; as a result it is not incorrect to speak of a white-slave trade, especially in the Mediterranean region. Another lucrative source of gain is formed by the so-called ' prepaids ', that is, Europeans whose passage to America is paid in advance by friends or relatives who have preceded them on the journey. It is asserted in the United States that something near one half of the immigration to that country consists of such ' prepaids '. Commercial activity of this sort gives especial promise of success among the classes of population with a low cultural development. A further special inducement to emigration is temporarily afforded by an extraordinary reduction in the cost of ocean passage as a result of rate-wars between steamship companies. Thus in the past decade keen rate-cutting competitions have arisen between the North Atlantic shipping pool and the outside independent companies, in particular the Cunard Line, which had concluded separate agreements with the English and European Governments and later with the Italian navigation interests. In the course of the latter struggle, the price of a steerage journey from New York to Naples fell to thirty-two marks. Again, in 1913 the war with the Canadian Pacific Railway which, on the basis of an agreement with the Austrian Government, had established a steamship line of its own from Trieste to Canada, led to a reduction in the third-class passenger rates from North Atlantic ports to North America from 140 and 160 to 90 marks (from May 1, 1913, on). These various considerations may strengthen and favour the migratory movement, but they cannot in the last analysis call it forth. The real cause is finally economic in character and is to be found in the tendency toward equalization in the differences in the level of incomes and in standards of living in the different countries. Persons who either permanently, as possessors of adequate means, or temporarily, as pleasure seekers or tourists, enjoy an income without personal exertion, will, other conditions being equal, prefer countries in which the cost of living is lower than in the country from which they derive their labourless income. In this wise they come into a position to satisfy more wants and also to raise their social position.   Thus the movement of English people to southern Italy is partly due, among other causes, to the fact that foreigners can live more cheaply and so more richly in that section.   Switzerland, similarly, derives advantage from the skill with which the people have adapted every condition to the satisfaction of the needs of foreigners and so have kept down the cost of their entertainment.   In Austria, on the contrary, all efforts at increasing the tourist traffic must remain fruitless, so long as the foreigner does not have the feeling that more is offered to him for less money than elsewhere, and especially that a higher standard of living than that enjoyed by the natives is not being artificially created for him by means of special prices imposed upon foreigners.   Persons with a high level of income therefore gravitate toward countries with a relatively lower standard of living.   But it must be conceded that in this respect especially the economic tendency is interfered with by non-economic motives.   Certain classes seek only the highest-priced watering-places and summer resorts because they consider that their social position requires it.   In other cases, the expensive resort is chosen with a view to professional gain, and the expenses involved are to be set down to business outlay.

The conditions are reversed in the case of permanent or temporary emigration whose object is not an agreeable pastime but rather improved earning power.   Here the movement is from regions with a customarily lower standard of living to regions in which on account of the customarily higher standard the level of income is also higher.   Such emigrants take with them the more moderate demands of their former habits of life and hence can save something from the higher income.   The temporary emigrants accumulate these savings in order later to procure for themselves a more comfortable existence in the home country, as illustrated by the Italians.   The permanent emigrants use their savings to support members of the family who have remained at home, and finally retire in the possession of a small capital. A re-adjustment to the higher standard of living of the new home also takes place, it is true, but only gradually, probably not becoming complete until in the later generations of the emigrants.

The Effects of International Migrations. The advantages which give the decisive impulse to international migrations are of a purely economic character. The principal object of investigation in this connexion is the effect on the national economy, for only on account of such results will the governmental economic policy find itself constrained to interfere either to restrict or to further the movements.

The emigration of persons living upon an income and of pleasure seekers means a loss for the country which they leave and a gain to the country into which they go. Entirely apart from a probable simultaneous movement of capital, the consuming force of the country of immigration is increased to the advantage of the production already present in it. The country of emigration may also, it is true, gain a slight advantage, in so far as those persons who seek health or recreation abroad have their labour power increased and frequently get the range of their ideas broadened as well. In recent times repeated efforts have been made to make a quantitative estimate of the gain from tourist traffic to different countries. Among Swiss experts the number of travellers is stated at from 350,000 to 450,000 annually, and their average hotel bill at a minimum of twelve francs, making the total expenditure for this item alone 150,000,000 francs. To this sum must be added at least 50,000,000 francs for travel mementoes, post-cards, souvenir jewellery, &c. In the case of the Austrian tourist districts the total number of days of sojourn of foreigners has been estimated on the basis of a careful investigation by the Austrian Ministry of Finance at 5,070,000. Assuming an average daily expenditure of fifteen kronen, these travellers have left in the country no less than 85,000,000 kronen. The income of

Italy derived from foreign pleasure-seekers was estimated as long ago as 1897 at 300,000,000 lire, and by 1908 it had increased to 427,000,000 lire. The amount annually expended by foreigners on the French Riviera is given as more than 300,000,000 francs. The number of tourists who visited Norway in 1908 was estimated at 85,000, who, on the assumption that each spent 500 kronen while there, left in the country 42,500,000 kronen. The Americans who travel for pleasure in Europe also bring astounding sums to the countries they visit. Their total number is estimated by the trans-oceanic steam-ship lines at 150,000 yearly. On the assumption that each traveller spends $1,000, of which nearly a third goes for the cost of passage, we reach the result that $150,000,000 are brought to Europe each year through the American tourist traffic. The expenditures of the foreigners who annually visit France are estimated, according to the *Bulletin statistique*, as 350,000,000 francs.

While the tourist traffic is justly regarded as an important source of income for a country, yet the undesirable secondary effects which may also follow under some circumstances from a large influx of foreigners must not be overlooked. The higher standard of living of the foreigners may bring about a rise in the cost of the means of life and of labour-power, which may cause an increase in the costs of production in the region affected, and so a curtailment of its competitive efficiency. In countries with a low stage of culture the effect may be actually demoralizing, as the population may prefer to make their living by occasional services for the foreigners, or even by begging, rather than by its customary activities. The representative of the English Government in Egypt, for example, has officially requested the foreigners who visit Upper Egypt not to destroy the disposition to work on the part of the native population through too great generosity.

In the emigration of people in search of industrial

opportunities the country of emigration always suffers a loss through the fact that it is deprived of human beings in the productive period of life, for whose education and nourishment state, community, and family have made sacrifices. Attempts have even been made by various methods to compute the economic value of the emigrant, but every such attempt must fail because the decisive factor in valuation is not the cost expense. Values depend upon those considerations that are ordinarily included under the general designations of supply and demand.[1] Economic value does not inhere in the person or the thing in which it appears embodied, but is attached by outer circumstances to the thing which functions as its object, and hence varies with the market. The emigrant who leaves a country suffering under unfavourable industrial conditions in quest of a home with better opportunities of earning is raised in value economically by the change of habitat. The loss sustained by the country of departure is smaller than the gain to the country into which he goes.

It is only a lessening of this loss and this gain when the emigrants send back to their home-country savings out of their earnings, however great the amounts may be in an absolute sense. According to a report laid before the Congress at Washington by the Immigration Commission, $270,000,000 are annually sent from the United States to their home-countries by immigrants. This sum is distributed among the different countries concerned as follows: Italy, $85,000,000; Austria-Hungary, $75,000,000; Russia, including Finland, $25,000,000; Great Britain, $25,000,000; Norway, Sweden, and Denmark, $25,000,000; Germany, $15,000,000; Greece, $5,000,000; other Balkan States, $5,000,000; Japan, $5,000,000; China, $5,000,000. In Austria, the money sent home by emigrants for the years 1903–10 was estimated on the basis of the drafts of domestic

---

[1] Josef Grunzel, *Grundriss der Wirtschaftspolitik*, second edition, Vienna, 1913, vol. i, p. 55.

and foreign banks and the money-order traffic of the post-offices at 1,997,000,000 kronen, or an average of 250,000,000 per year.   To this should be added the savings brought back by the returning emigrants in person, which are estimated for the average number of 40,000 returning emigrants yearly at a minimum of 2,000 kronen *per capita* or a total of 80,000,000 kronen. Italy receives from her oversea emigrants about 350,000,000 fr. annually, to which is to be added another 150,000,000 fr., representing the savings of European migratory labourers. The income derived from this migratory movement thus amounts to more than a quarter of the total sum brought into the country by the exportation of merchandise. An item to be deducted in these cases, however, is the money sums which emigrants carry abroad with them or cause to be sent to them after departure. But even disregarding these deductions the amounts sent home form a very modest interest on the human capital thus loaned abroad. Even if the industrial conditions in the home-land are so extremely unfavourable that a large part of this human capital would be forced to lie idle if emigration were prohibited, it must still be assumed that the struggle for existence would have led finally to a change in the economic policy of the country and so to an improvement in those industrial conditions. Emigration helps only the individual person in a private economy sense ; from the national economy standpoint the poor country remains poor. It must be granted that a prohibition has never made emigration impossible, but decisive improve-ments in economic conditions can automatically cut off its sources, as is shown in a striking manner by a comparison between Germany and Austria-Hungary. It is therefore a theoretical error to assert that the seasonal migration of Slavic labourers is a disadvantage to Germany. The owner of a German manorial estate who pays 10,000 marks to Polish labourers who, by renouncing the wants characteristic of the German labourer, are enabled to carry home 5,000 marks of this sum, deprive the German national economy of this amount of value.[1] But against this loss must be credited a much larger gain in productive labour-power which would not have been procurable in Germany at all, or only at a much higher cost. Hence German agriculture is more correct in its instinctive feelings when it looks forward with increasing uneasiness to the time when internal reforms in Russia will make migration to Germany no longer seem desirable to the Polish labourer.

A favourable influence of emigration on the exports of merchandise is also traceable under certain circumstances. The emigrants take their habits of life with them into the new country and hence prefer as far as possible goods made in the home-land. In cases where they settle in considerable groups and retain a strong feeling of connexion with the home country, a noticeable stimulus to the exports of the latter may result. The Italian exports to South America are largely the effect of emigration.

Again, we must not underestimate the spiritual gain which the country of emigration experiences through the returning emigrants, who are often raised in culture and have their personal powers increased by their stay in the foreign land. An Italian economist writes as follows: [2] 'Emigration has stimulated the transfer of land-ownership in southern Italy from the hands of the old possessors into those of new emigrants who have returned from oversea countries with capital and with proven productive efficiency. It has also helped to combat the intellectual canker of southern Italy, illiteracy, as the emigrants learn from bitter experience the defenceless position in which they stand as long as they fail to acquire an elementary education. Even the humiliations to which the Italians were subjected in foreign countries

---

[1] A. Pohlman-Hohenaspe, *Laienbrevier der Nationalökonomie*, Leipsic, 1912.

[2] Emanuel Sella, *Der Wandel des Besitzes*, German translation by J. Bluwstein, Munich and Leipsic, 1912, p. 81.

worked to their advantage because it brought them to a realizing sense of their human worth.'

For the country of immigration, on the other hand, foreign labourers are an advantage only so long as there is in the country a lack of labour-power which cannot be supplied by other means, as, for example, by the use of machinery. A disadvantage ensues when native working-men are at hand, who, on the basis of their higher wages have established themselves at a higher standard of living and who therefore spend again in the country the money which they earn, while the foreign labourers take it in part out of the country. In every economic division a certain equilibrium is gradually brought about between the wages of labour, the product of labour, and the needs of life, and this balance is sharply disturbed by the introduction of immigrants with a lower standard of living, since their adaptation to existing conditions is a matter of slow transition, and in case of marked distinctions in nationality and race does not occur at all.

PART II.

THE DIRECTIONS ASSUMED BY ECONOMIC PROTECTIONISM

I

THE ECONOMIC PROTECTIVE POLICY IN GENERAL

I. THE ESSENCE OF ECONOMIC PROTECTIONISM

The Limits of the Concept. The economic policy known as Protectionism we have previously designated as the totality of those measures by which the national economy seeks to promote its interests in the world economy field. The essence of the concept includes an interrelation between national economy and world economy, between home production and the home market on the one hand, and foreign production and the foreign market on the other. It is only a part of productive policy as a whole, namely that part which turns to account the world economy relations of production itself. The promotion of production is not in itself a protective policy, because this is possible even without foreign trade, and in fact enjoys then the most favourable field of activity. Protection can be spoken of only when an attack is impending, and such an attack can come only from another national economy, hence from the world economy.

In the literature of the subject the concept of economic protection has occasionally been unduly extended. Lavison, for example, says : ' *La protection, d'une manière générale, c'est l'État intervenant pour défendre une industrie menacée par la concurrence étrangère,*' but he later avers that any support or encouragement of industry constitutes a protective policy. Thus : ' *Les tarifs différentiels, les exemptions d'impôt, les monopoles, les surtaxes, les distinctions honorifiques, les encouragements et appuis quels qu'ils soient, donnés par l'État à l'industrie privée, forment tous autant de variétés de la protection.*'[1] He asserts that in every struggle, and hence also in economic competition, there are two sorts of supports; either the foreign antagonists may be weakened by hostile acts, or the home combatants may be strengthened and encouraged. Lavison, in this connexion, overlooks the fact that the furthering of production is not always designed as a support in a struggle with foreign competition, but pursues primarily another object, namely, the development of the productive powers within a country; thus the influencing of relations to foreign countries appears as only an incidental result. When, for example, Australia, in the Bounties' Act of 1907, places a premium on the cultivation of cotton, rice, coffee, tobacco, &c., the authorities have in mind not at all a competitive struggle with foreign countries, but seek rather, as can clearly be seen from the conditions upon which bounties are granted, to provide a paying employment for white labourers. Bounties on exports belong then to a protective policy, but bounties on production only in so far as they extend their influence into the relations with foreign countries by means of a graduation of the bounty rates according to the use of domestic or foreign materials.

Systematic General View of Protective Measures. The policy of economic protectionism has for its object the promotion of domestic production. This may be accomplished either on the one hand through negative measures, excluding foreign influence, such as import duties, prohibitions of the live-stock trade by public health regulations, obstructing formalities and the like, or on the other hand through positive measures, utilizing relations with foreign countries for the ends of home production by means of bounties on exports, ship subsidies, investment of capital in foreign countries, encouragement to the immigration of foreign capital and labour force, &c. Positive measures have again in recent times achieved greater significance as a result of the circumstance that it was found to be no longer possible to make

[1] A. de Lavison, *La Protection par les primes*, Paris, 1900, pp. 7, 25.

progress with the negative measures on account of the commercial treaties concluded in the free-trade period. For example, on account of the fact that the principle of equal treatment of the flags of different nations which had been incorporated into commercial treaties, rendered impossible the promotion of a country's shipping by means of higher dues imposed on foreign ships or additional duties on goods imported in such vessels, the method of granting ship subsidies was resorted to.

The protective policy, it is true, relates in the first instance to the material embodiment of economic activity, the result of modern production, i. e. to commodities; but it seeks also, as soon as such means become inapplicable, to attract the two factors of production, labour and capital. This may be schematically represented by the following diagram :—

ECONOMIC PROTECTIONISM.

Affecting Commodities.	Affecting the Productive Factors.	
	CAPITAL.	LABOUR.
1. Negative measures (protective duties, differential transportation charges, administrative protection, protection by concerted popular action).	1. Negative measures (discouragement of foreign enterprisers, discouragement of capital exportation, discouragement of denationalization of capital).	1. Negative measures (discouragement of emigration, discouragement of immigration).
2. Positive measures (bounties on exports, transportation concessions, navigation concessions, inducements to shipping, bounties encouraging exportation, &c.).	2. Positive measures (encouragement of importation of capital, encouragement of exportation of capital).	2. Positive measures (encouragement of emigration and encouragement of immigration).

2. THE THEORETICAL BASIS OF ECONOMIC PROTECTIONISM.

Protective Theories hitherto Current. The theory of protectionism has hitherto occupied itself only with protective duties, that is to say, with the most important part of the protection with reference to commodities, and this is still the principal subject for discussion. **But** the decisive **arguments** may be extended to form a general theory of economic protection. The old but ever renewed opposition between tariff protection and free trade is thus given an interpretation corresponding to modern commercial conditions. The essential argument of the free-trade theory consists in the contention that the international exchange of goods is of benefit to all the countries concerned, including those which are unfavourably situated in regard to production, since each country will devote itself to those branches of production in which it has at least relatively the lowest costs. For the international exchange of goods, this view regards as valid the theory of comparative values which was first advanced by John Stuart Mill as the law of comparative costs, and later worked out by Bastable [1] with a special view to international trade, and which has recently been advocated by Fontana-Russo [2] as the very quintessence of modern commercial policy. In this connexion the fact is supposed to be decisive that the value of a commodity is determined not by cost of production but by the acquisition cost, that is, by the sacrifice which is connected with the commodity given in exchange for it. The imports of a country must then be measured by its exports. If, in Italy, Lombardy is better adapted to the production of cotton goods, and Sicily to the production of wines, then each province will reap an advantage by applying itself to its special line. If the natural conditions were favourable to some other branch of production, capital and labour would, it is argued, immediately redistribute themselves and bring about the most effective balance. But it is asserted that such a readjustment on the international plane is impossible, or (according to Fontana-Russo) at least difficult. The cost of production of the same article may therefore

---

[1] C. F. Bastable, *The Theory of International Trade*, second edition, London, 1897.

[2] Luigi Fontana-Russo, *Grundzüge der Handelspolitik*, German translation from the Italian, Leipsic, 1911.

be permanently different in different countries. For the purposes of international exchange, therefore, comparison is to be made, not between the costs of the goods exchanged, but between the costs of one and the same article in the several countries carrying on international exchange. If France can produce at the same cost ten cwt. of wheat or twenty cwt. of iron, while Italy produces at the same cost ten cwt. of wheat and fifteen cwt. of iron, then France will produce iron and import wheat, and Italy, conversely, will produce wheat and import iron. It is true that France is subject in the case assumed to the same costs as Italy for the production of wheat. But on account of its greater efficiency in the iron industry, it can more advantageously procure the wheat from Italy. If each country were to produce both classes of goods, the total production of the two would be twenty cwt. of wheat and thirty-five cwt. of iron. But when the desirable division of labour is effected, the product is twenty cwt. of wheat and forty cwt. of iron; that is, there is a resulting gain of five cwt. of iron. By the addition of new articles in additional countries greater complication is introduced. Let it be assumed that France, Switzerland, and Italy produce grain, iron, and wine at different costs as follows :—

	Grain.	Iron.	Wine.
France	10	15	20
Switzerland	8	20	15
Italy	15	30	60

It will be seen that Italy produces all the articles at the highest cost, and hence will find it advantageous to cultivate grain and draw its supply of iron from France and of wine from Switzerland, because in this way it obtains the goods more cheaply than it could produce them at home. Furthermore, France and Switzerland could make no unreasonable demands as to price because they would be hindered by their mutual competition. The division of the advantage gained

K

among the exchanging countries would depend upon the intensity of the demand.

Beside this argument is to be placed a second one, namely, that with due allowance for the other elements in the international balance of payments, the exports of a country must pay for its imports, and hence that an increase of imports must lead to an increase of exports. Eventually the equalization is brought about through the effect on the value of money, for with a continuing debit-balance, money would flow abroad, and as a result the value of money in the country would increase in relation to the value of goods, and the consequence of this, again, would be an increase in the exportation of commodities.

The basic error of this view, aside from the fact that neither the costs of production nor the costs of acquisition determine value, lies in treating the production and consumption of a country as fixed quantities which may be influenced by foreign commerce in their proportional combination but not in their total amount. As a matter of fact, production may not merely be increased by importation, due to the increased employment of idle capital or labour force, or to the better utilization of those already employed through the acquisition of raw materials, but may also be reduced in quantity if it has not developed to the point of meeting foreign competition. In the examples cited above, Italy would be impelled to sacrifice its grain production also to foreign competition, as it could then obtain all its goods more cheaply from abroad; but then it would no longer have the means to purchase them. Every national economy has two possibilities in the creation and destruction of economic values, one in the way of the inner economic balance consisting of production and consumption within the country, and one in the way of outward economic balance consisting of importation from and exportation to foreign countries. When an amount equal to or exceeding that which is gained in foreign trade is lost through the restriction of home production, then there is no gain, but eventually a loss is suffered. Importation and exportation do not stand in a relation of direct communication, but are separated from each other by production and consumption, and hence a continuously favourable inner economic balance may be able to offset an unfavourable outward economic balance. In the case assumed, Italy will do better to increase its iron production, even on the basis of twenty cwt. per unit of cost, rather than sacrifice it to the cultivation of wheat. The production of a country should permit the greatest possible utilization of the productive forces at hand. If Italy wished to cultivate only wheat it would soon be at the end of these resources, while France with the aid of foreign iron ores (which incidentally play an increasingly important rôle in the European iron-industry) might provide the whole world with iron.

In the field of protectionistic efforts we need only mention in this general connexion the attempt of Schüller to formulate a theoretical basis. He takes into account the influence of imports on production, and holds that protective measures are justifiable and advantageous when the increased production resulting from them is greater than the additional burden placed upon consumption. Customs duties seem to him the single practicable means of securing protection, and he investigates the basis for determining such duties by a method which will later be taken up. His minutely detailed calculations lead him finally to the advocacy of public regulation of economic life as a whole, and of commercial policy in particular.[1] With production controlled by private enterprisers, duties can only be roughly determined, but with public control, duties could be replaced ' by definite regulations fixing the kinds and amounts of goods to be brought in from abroad or to be produced within the country '. The original costs of all goods are supposed to be exactly known; the expense of the whole customs administration

[1] Richard Schüller, *Schutzzoll und Freihandel*, Vienna, 1905, p. 136.

would be saved, commercial treaties would give place to international contracts for the delivery of goods, and with such a national economic organization and policy, the general interests of the nation would, it is argued, be more effectively subserved than under a system of private enterprise. But if we pass by such Utopian schemes and view as a difficulty only, and not as a disadvantage, the continued existence side by side of private and national economic interests, we cannot impose upon the state any precise protective calculations for each kind of commodity, or devise a rule to fit every case, but must rather seek to formulate a general policy, as is done in other fields of political action.

The New Theory of Protectionism. Economic protectionism is directed to no other end than the securing of the domestic market to the business of a country by political means. Such a guarantee is necessary because any branch of production needs the largest possible stable market, and needs it the more urgently the more capital is invested in that branch and the more it strives toward specialization and reduction of costs. It is not necessary to set forth that the characteristic tendency in the growth of modern production is toward freeing itself from dependence upon nature and toward the saving of labour power, which ends can be accomplished only by attracting larger and larger amounts of capital. It goes without saying, too, that such artificial guarantees are justified only when they facilitate the establishment or make possible the continued existence of a branch of production without laying upon other branches, or upon consumption, burdens greater than the advantage gained. Such guarantees are directed against the disadvantageous influence of the world economy, i.e. against the admission from foreign markets of such goods or productive factors as might affect in an unfavourable manner the relations between production and consumption in the home market. The home market is not pre-empted because a market in foreign countries is despised, but for the simple reason that it is subject to political control. In so far as it is possible to secure foreign markets, the conclusion of commercial treaties with other states serves this end. The protective policy has not, therefore, as free traders have assumed, shown itself hostile to such treaties, but has even given an additional incentive to the extension of the treaty policy. Among the instruments of political power, customs duties occupy the first rank and their protective character is publicly manifest and generally recognized. In recent times a large number of other means have been seized upon, but these appear in many cases as evasions of the principles of international trade, and are likely to call forth reprisals on the part of the foreign market against which they are aimed.

The security of the market is, however, to be understood in a qualitative as well as quantitative sense, for the issue relates not merely to the quantity and value of the goods excluded or admitted, but also to their character. In the commercial statistics it makes no difference whether a country brings in coffee or cotton to the value of a given sum, but from the standpoint of the national economy it is not a matter of indifference whether the imports consist of finished goods which will be consumed at the value shown in the importation statistics, or of raw materials whose value will be increased manifold by domestic productive processes; or again, of means of production (machinery) which are to be put to permanent productive use. Furthermore, importation and exportation are connected, not directly, but through the intermediary of domestic production and consumption, and should therefore be so regulated that they will favourably influence the inner economic balance. The negotiations over commercial treaties in which emphasis is always laid on the possibility of increasing the value of imported goods through domestic production, show clearly that this object, not recognized by theory, is taken account of in practice; it is shown also in the autonomous-tariff policy which lays fiscal duties on articles of consumption, but avoids as far as possible taxes on raw materials, which offers for duties on wheat quite other motives than for those on cotton yarn, and which in fixing industrial duties takes account less of the absolute value of the goods and more of the margin of value between raw materials, part manufactures, and manufactured goods.

PROTECTION AFFECTING COMMODITIES BY NEGATIVE MEASURES

1. PROTECTION BY CUSTOMS DUTIES

The Genesis of Protective Duties. It is true that tariff duties no longer form the sole means of carrying out an economic protective policy, but they continue to form the most important of such means, and therefore, also, the one in connexion with which causes and effects are most easily traceable. It is often pointed out that the application of differential freight-tariffs, police measures affecting industry, &c., for the purposes of commercial policy, is a diversion of these powers from their original intention, and is hence a misapplication; but it must be remarked that customs duties also have undergone a transformation, as a result of which they now manifest a twofold character. Such charges were originally a form of commercial toll for the use of roads, bridges, or harbour improvements, or a compensation for the granting of protection and escort for goods and persons. The amount of the charge was determined by financial interests exclusively, no distinction being made between importation and exportation, and it was collected, not at the frontier, but at important commercial cities and trading points in the interior of the country. Customs duties were first separated from the tolls and excises, previously treated in the same way, by statesmen under the influence of mercantilism, who also transferred the point of collection to the frontier of the country.[1] Since that time, duties have served two purposes, the fiscal needs of the state and the

---

[1] Josef Grunzel, *System der Handelspolitik*, second edition (Leipsic, 1906), p. 340.

protective requirements of domestic production. The line of distinction, however, is by no means sharp. If a particular article is not produced in the country, a duty laid upon it will fall under the head of revenue duties, though a protective object will usually be added to the financial one when some other article destined to a similar application is produced in the country. Thus, in North European countries the interest of the domestic grain-production is a factor in determining the duty on rice, and similarly in the case of the interest of domestic horticulture and the tariff on tropical fruits. On the other hand, a silent but important ally of the protective tariff interests has been found in all countries in the Department of Finance, as the receipts from protective duties form an item difficult to replace in the national budget.

If, now, we survey the development of the commercial policies of the civilized countries since the beginning of mercantilism, which is to say since the origin of the present-day concept of national economy, we are struck always and everywhere by a remarkable inconsistency. In practice the tendency to protective duties has never yielded ground, while in theory the idea of complete prohibition and that of complete free trade alternately gained the upper hand. When world-economy considerations conflicted with those of the national economy, the interests affected have always striven for a compromise, in spite of the fact that economic science at one time urged complete separation from the world economy and at another time a merging in it. The prohibitive system and free trade failed in practical application, while the protective system lacked a theoretical formulation.

The mercantilistic theory advocated an exploitation of the world market in favour of the home country, and hence demanded not merely restrictions through duties upon the importation of manufactured goods and the exportation of the means of life and of raw materials, but prohibitions upon imports or exports, in aid of the national manufacturing industry. In the seventeenth and eighteenth centuries we find the prohibitive system laid down as the guiding principle of tariff legislation in many countries, but in practice it was always widely departed from, and generally employed only as a retributive measure against particular countries whose competition seemed dangerous at the time. Thus in England the East India Company was granted the right to export specie, which otherwise was forbidden. The extraordinarily strict Navigation Act of October 9, 1651, was directed almost exclusively against Holland, but even its Draconian penalties were unable to prevent the smuggling trade in Dutch goods, especially spirits. Trade with France likewise continued, in spite of prohibitions on both sides, until it led to the conclusion of the commercial treaty of September 26, 1786, containing mutual tariff-concessions. Trade with the Iberian peninsula was placed on a favourable basis by the famous Methuen Treaty of December 27, 1703, with Portugal, and by treaties with Spain. According to available statistical data, moreover, the imports of England in the eighteenth century increased at least as rapidly as the exports ; according to MacCulloch, the former rose in the period from 1698–1701 to 1784–92 from an annual average of £5,600,000 sterling to £17,700,000, the latter from £6,400,000 to £18,500,000.

In France, Colbert increased the protection in many cases through the introduction of prohibitions, but the latter were directed almost exclusively against the industrially more-advanced England, and were unable to check importation even from that country. According to Levasseur,[1] the imports of France from European countries increased in the period of 1716–87 from 71,000,000 to 379,900,000 francs, and exports from 105,700,000 to 424,400,000 francs. In Austria, the first import prohibition (which affected woollen goods) was contained in a decree of June 11, 1749, and in the tariff schedules of March 24, 1764, and September 26, 1774, the number of such prohibitions was increased. In the

[1] *Histoire des classes ouvrières depuis 1789*, vol. ii, p. 380.

schedules of August 27, 1784, and January 2, 1788, the prohibitive system was extended in principle to all goods which domestic industry was at all in a position to produce in sufficient quantity and of satisfactory quality. At the same time, however, the prohibitive principle was greatly modified by the provision that such foreign goods were not unconditionally excluded, but were merely ' removed from commerce ', which meant that they could not be bought and sold in the country, but might still be imported by private individuals for their own use on the payment of a duty. This example makes it particularly clear that the prohibitive system at the most flourishing period of its history was only a theoretical principle which in reality was subject to extensive qualifications.

It is still easier to show that absolute free trade similarly proved itself practically untenable, as in this case the demonstration may be limited to a single country, i. e. England. No other country ever accepted complete absence of tariff duties even as a theoretical principle. The English customs tariff which remained after the Cobden Treaty of January 23, 1860, is treated as a purely revenue tariff, but features aiming at incidental protection were by no means wanting in it. For example, the treaty stipulated that upon goods which were subject to indirect taxation in England, there should be levied when they were imported from abroad, not merely a duty corresponding to this tax, but a somewhat higher rate to compensate the English producers for the increasing costs which they encountered as a result of the collection of the tax. But when we note that in the case of distilled liquors, which were subject to an excise of eight shillings per gallon, this extra duty was placed in the treaty itself at two shillings, but in a supplementary article at five shillings, we must by no means assume that the English Government made so considerable an error in its cost computations. Similarly in the case of malt and chicory ; the extra duty made the tariff on foreign goods higher than the excise on the domestic product. Hardly had the Cobden Treaty been concluded when the agitation began on the express basis of this disparity for compensatory duties against foreign bounties on sugar. Even professed free traders supported these claims, asserting that duties are reprehensible solely when they seek to neutralize natural differences in situation and not when they seek to neutralize artificial ones. These theorists were not at all abashed at the paradoxical conclusion that in such a case free trade itself requires protective duties.[1] As compensation for the hall-marking fees, foreign gold and silver articles were subjected to a duty of seventeen shillings per ounce, and the repeal of this provision was not decided upon until 1890, after India had been burdened with the duty for many years. In 1888, again, the duty on bottled wines was temporarily increased for the purpose of encouraging the domestic wine-trade. England also made the first move toward increasing the stringency of the veterinary supervision regulations, a device which was later to become on the Continent one of the most effective means of protecting agricultural products. Nor were protectionistic motives absent when in 1901 a duty on sugar was introduced, making the rates higher for refined than for raw sugar, nor yet in case of the export duty on coal (which, however, was quickly dropped), though the fiscal needs which arose in connexion with the South African War must be regarded as the principal incentive for the imposition of this duty. Important substitutes for protection were introduced by England in the trade-mark law of 1887 and in the patent law of 1907. Further, the building up of the British Imperial Customs Union, with preferential duties for the mother-country, in the colonies brought to naught one of the most important achievements of the free trade period, viz. the elimination of differential duties. Finally, in May 1903, Joseph Chamberlain launched the tariff-reform movement ; with a view to forming an

[1] Carl Johannes Fuchs, *Die Handelspolitik Englands und seiner Kolonien. Schriften des Vereines für Sozialpolitik*, vol. lvii, no. 4, p. 74.

Imperial Customs Union between the mother-country and the colonies, the levying of the following moderate protective duties was advocated : ten per cent on manufactured goods, two shillings per quarter on wheat (the average annual quotations in London for 1912 were thirty-six shillings and thirty-five shillings and tenpence for wheat), and of five per cent on other necessities of life. The Unionist party decided in January 1913, after excited debates, to eliminate the question of a tariff on necessities from the campaign programme and to submit it to the electorate for decision on the occasion of a new election, since the general rise in prices of necessities interfered with the immediate carrying out of the project. Thus the English free trade of the past half-century is nothing but a continuous struggle between theory and practice, while the principle itself has been respected only because it was hoped that the example of England would affect the policy of foreign countries.

Another characteristic point is the metamorphosis which the free-trade doctrine itself underwent, under the influence of the still more emphatic demands of practical exigencies, when it was transferred from England to the European continent. The historical school of economics took its theoretical foundation from the classic school, but was compelled to effect a transformation of an especially fundamental character in the case of the free-trade theory. The verdict of the historical school was that, in deciding upon free trade or tariff protection, the question is not one of principle but one of the circumstances and the object in view ; that is to say, that in deciding the question of a raising or lowering of the tariff level we have to deal with the concrete conditions of the country, the varying factors of its development and the goal toward which it is striving. The practical issue is not as to whether duties should be introduced, but whether they should be lowered or raised. In the ' free-trade ' party in this sense we are therefore to include those who advocate the retention of existing duties, or, perhaps,

the modification of certain duties, in opposition to the
' protectionists ' who advocate the increase or, as the case
may be, the retention of certain duties opposed by the 'free
traders' as too high.[1] But in reality there lies in this conception a denial of the principle, as the distinction between
the free-trade idea and that of protection is not one
of degree but of kind. If the historical school recognizes the
validity of all the arguments of the classicists in favour of
the freedom of international exchange of goods, they cannot
look upon tariff protection as necessary, and restrict themselves to the framing of the issue as to whether this protection
is to be high or low. It is also a misunderstanding of all
movements for protection to ascribe to them the advocacy
of a steady increase in all protective duties, for often enough
the advantage of a protective tariff on one article may be
more than offset by protection on another. Hence this
opportunist point of view, which permits the theory to be
transformed in practice into its opposite, is untenable ; as
a matter of fact, the opposition is one of principle—that
between the national-economy and world-economy stand-
points.

Theories of Protective Duties. Complete as has become the
victory of the protective-tariff idea in economic policy, its
theoretical basis was, and has remained, wholly inadequate.
The deepest cause of this strange phenomenon lies in the
division in post-classical political economy, which on the one
hand was forced to yield to nationalist demands, and on the
other was dominated by the conception of a world economy
abstracted from all political boundaries and consisting merely
of economic individuals and not of great economic organizations. In this connexion we may distinguish between three
groups of theories, the developmental theories, the compensatory theories, and defensive theories. The developmental
theories look upon world economy as an ideal, but as one
which cannot be reached immediately, but only by way of

[1] Rudolf Kobatsch, *Internationale Wirtschaftspolitik*, Vienna, 1907, p. 196.

a transitional stage of development through protective duties. The compensatory theories seek a solution of the conflicts which arise from the existence side by side of national economy and world economy without concerning themselves with the question of the ultimate goal of the development. The defensive theories, finally, see in national economy itself the permanent form of organization which on political and economic grounds must defend itself against injurious tendencies originating in the world-economy sphere. According to the last view, the national economy is an organism, while the world economy is merely a community of commercial relations serving the interests of this organism; hence it is merely in an objective sense that the domestic market can be distinguished from the world market which supplements it, while in a subjective sense the control of both is to be effected from the unified standpoint of national economy. On the basis of this view, protection exists exclusively for the purpose of securing the domestic market. This might be called the market theory, and in any case it is to be numbered among defensive theories.

The accredited founder of the developmental theory is Friedrich List, though numerous anticipations of the viewpoint are found among the members of the classical school itself. Adam Smith repudiated developmental duties explicitly, because, while they might further a branch of industry, they could not increase the national income, since the industry of the country would in this way merely be diverted from a more advantageous to a less advantageous employment.[1] John Stuart Mill, however, regards protective duties, levied for the purpose of overcoming a momentary advantage held by a foreign country, as justifiable though only under the three following conditions: (1) they must be merely temporary; (2) they must be limited to the so-called marginal industries which are on the border of ability to meet competition, and would have to suffer extremely under the

---

[1] Adam Smith, *The Wealth of Nations*, book IV, chap. ii.

variations of world commerce ; and (3) the rate of the duty must afford no profit.[1] The greatest representative of classical doctrines on the continent, J. B. Say, also attempted to justify developmental duties in case a branch of industry promises in a few years to become so profitable as no longer to need the protection.[2] This idea received a special emphasis and more elaborate development at the hands of Friedrich List. According to his view, also, protective duties should be of a temporary nature only, though by no means limited to a period of a few years, as Mill proposed. Furthermore, the protection was not to be for the advantage merely of certain specified industries, since in a suitably situated country almost any branch of industry may be made profitable. List does, however, lay down an important limitation in that he recommends the protective system only for the countries of the temperate zone, since tropical countries must remain agricultural countries, and even among the former nations he regards as adapted to this policy only those which have command over a considerable extent of territory, a dense population, varied natural resources, and a fairly high degree of culture. The danger of monopoly would be eliminated by increasing internal competition.[3] The American economist, Carey, also argued along similar lines. Among more recent writers on commercial policy, Fontana-Russo represents the same theory, and in general stands upon the same ground as the classical political economy.[4] To the frankly agricultural state, as well as to the highly developed industrial state, unrestricted free trade must appear as theoretically the most desirable and practically the best system of commercial policy ; but in the period of transition from the agricultural to the industrial state, tariff protection would be indispensable to offset the temporary lead of the older industrial

[1] John Stuart Mill, *Principles of Political Economy*, book v, chap. x.
[2] J. B. Say, *Traité d'économie politique*.
[3] Friedrich List, *Nationales System der politischen Oekonomie*, chap. xxvi.
[4] Luigi Fontana-Russo, *Grundzüge der Handelspolitik*, German translation, Leipsic, 1911.

countries. The evolutionary and historical standpoint upon which Kobatsch takes his stand leads to a similar conclusion. In his view, duties are not an economic but merely a historical category, and under specified conditions they form a suitable means of guarding the interests of a particular national economy; they are 'a necessary evil of historic origin which will disappear as it has come when it has lived its day'.[1]

But the most extensive recognition has been obtained by the compensatory theories. A certain opposition soon developed between the pure free-trade principle and its practical application. The theory demanded the removal of all restrictions, so that each country might devote itself to those branches of production for which it possessed the best natural conditions; in this manner the way would be opened to an international division of labour which should prove no less fruitful than the technical division of labour in a modern factory. But practice soon found many cases in which the unrestricted application of the free-trade principle would have been a manifest disadvantage to the national economy. Such free-trade theorists as Mill, Cairnes, and the French economists, get over the difficulty by distinguishing between science and economic policy. The duty of the latter, in their view, is not the blind application of the doctrine recognized as correct by the science, which can only furnish the guiding principle, and cannot be the practical guide, but rather a careful consideration of the complicated human relations involved. Free trade should be the rule, which would be only proven by the exceptions in the way of tariff protection. If protection were the rule, every branch of production would from the beginning have a right to claim it, while in the other case the validity of any claim to protection will have first to be demonstrated.[2]

[1] Rudolph Kobatsch, op. cit., p. 239.
[2] Cf. A. de Lavison, *La Protection par les primes* (Paris, 1900), pp. 7 ff. ; Augier et Angel Marvaux, *La Politique douanière de la France* (Paris, 1912), p. 354.

Such exceptional cases were recognized in certain branches of production, as for example, that of food products and that of means of defence or other articles which are so important to the interests of the community that a country cannot rely upon commercial sources, and in such instances must prevent the process of development toward international division of labour. The cultivation of wheat, shipbuilding, the iron industry, and the merchant marine, have been repeatedly designated as such branches of production. Cauwès, for example, says: *Nous croyons qu'il existe un assez grand nombre d'industries qu'on peut appeler nécessaires parce qu'une nation ne pourrait impunément être pour elles tributaire de l'étranger. On avouera bien qu'il y a quelque différence à faire, par exemple, entre la bimbeloterie et la marine marchande, ou entre toiles cirées et l'agriculture. Parmi les industries vraiment nationales, il en est qui se rattachent à la puissance militaire, ainsi la marine, la métallurgie; d'autres, fournissant à des besoins absolus de consommation, doivent avoir leur siège principal sur le territoire afin de ne pas manquer au pays lors des interruptions de commerce produites par les crises politiques ou par les guerres.*[1]

Furthermore, the business maxim deduced from the free-trade doctrine, viz. that one should buy in the cheapest market and sell in the dearest, came into conflict with the doctrine itself. That is, it soon became apparent that the naturally most favourable market is not always the cheapest, since the natural conditions of production may be extensively modified through cultural agencies. This truth was very early manifest in England itself when the beet-sugar of the Continent, encouraged by export bounties, deprived the English sugar refineries of their means of subsistence. According to the free-trade business maxim it should have been exclusively an occasion for rejoicing that the European countries which produced sugar should tax themselves in

[1] Paul Cauwès, *Cours d'économie politique* (third edition, Paris, 1893), vol. ii, p. 485.

order to furnish their product to Englishmen at an especially low price; but according to the pure free-trade theory the export bounties constituted an artificial alteration of the price based upon the natural costs of production. It was the latter view of the case which led to an agitation in England, beginning in the year 1880, for the introduction of a compensatory duty on sugar exported under a bounty. The English government, it is true, rejected the proposal on the ground of the most-favoured-nation treaties which were in force, but the idea was later realized in the tariff legislation of the United States of America (beginning with 1894) and of British India (since 1897).

The inequalities in the tax rates of different countries have repeatedly been pointed out. Inequalities in the consumption taxes may be made up by the simple method of levying upon the imported product also, in the form of a duty or super-duty, a tax equivalent to that to which the domestic goods are subject. But when the basis of the tax is not the product but the productive enterprise, as is the case with many production taxes, the difference in the tax burden can be equalized only through the operation of a general protective tariff. It is in this sense that Lorenz von Stein has conceived of protective duties.[1]

The compensatory theory has further been recognized as applicable in cases where a country is very advanced in its legislation for the protection of the working-classes, and on that very account finds itself hampered in its ability to compete with foreign countries. The most important example is found in the history of the commercial policy of Australia. As early as 1865 the state of Victoria was forced to adopt protective duties because, with the discovery of the gold-fields, wages had risen so sharply that the continued existence of her young industries was threatened. The protective policy was continued in the tariff laws of the Commonwealth of October 3, 1901, August 8, 1907, and June 3, 1908,

---

[1] L. von Stein, *Lehrbuch der Finanzwissenschaft* (Leipsic, 1886), p. 373.

and found its most ardent advocates in the labour parties themselves.[1] The attempt was even made to procure for the workers a direct share in the advantages of the tariff protection by laying upon certain branches of industry a production tax equal to half the rate of the duty, with the provision that the enterpriser could be freed from the tax on condition that the wages committee should certify that he paid just and adequate wages. In the United States, also, the labour unions have frequently joined forces with the trusts in advocating an increase in the tariff protection.

The desire to ward off the effects of sweeping increases in the tariff rates of foreign countries is a further ground which has led to the adoption of compensatory duties. When some of the countries which have previously constituted the principal market for a line of goods produced for international exchange suddenly impose sharp restrictions on importation, the producing countries cannot, on account of the extent of vested interests affected, reduce their production—the procedure which the classical school represented as unavoidable —but will throw themselves with so much the greater avidity upon the markets remaining open. As a result, the prices will there be so reduced by the extraordinarily keen competition, that the existence of the established enterprises will be threatened. A compensatory duty is designed to prevent or at least materially to mitigate such a disaster, borne in upon the national economy from the world economy sphere. The history of the beet-sugar industry affords an example of this character. When in the interest of their sugar-producing districts, the United States of America excluded European beet-sugar by the Wilson Bill of 1894 and the Dingley Bill of 1897, the product was thrown with so much the greater force upon England and especially upon British India, where in consequence a crisis in raw sugar production ensued. When British India in turn imposed super-duties

[1] Robert Schachner, *Australien in Politik, Wirtschaft und Kultur* (Jena, 1909), vol. i, pp. 192 ff.

in 1899 as a defensive measure, the raw sugar poured into Eastern Asia and especially into Japan.

Not merely the political measures of the state, however, but the actions of private parties as well may force a foreign country to retaliation, in case they result in extensive exportation at cut prices. As early as the first decades of the nineteenth century, English industries were employing the expedient of selling in foreign markets large quantities of their manufactured products at prices below the cost to themselves in order to nip in the bud a similar industry developing in the country of import. Under present circumstances, solicitude for the domestic market leads to price-cutting exportation more frequently than does concern for markets abroad. Under two sets of circumstances particularly, modern industrial combinations resort to a reduction of prices in foreign markets below those obtaining at home. In the first instance, the trust-controlled goods are frequently sold at a reduced price to industries which further elaborate them in the home country in case the finished product is to be exported, when otherwise the elaborating industry would not be able to meet the competition in the export trade. In the second instance, the goods themselves are sold at a lower price abroad, when by so doing pressure can be removed from the domestic market, and hence the domestic price be raised to approximate equivalence with the sum of the world-market price, the freight and the duty. The establishment of such a reduced price abroad does not in itself signify sale at a sacrifice, for there is a corresponding gain through the higher domestic prices that are rendered possible by the lightening of the domestic market and the protective duties. Advantage will be taken of this policy whenever the domestic price under high tariff protection is so profitable that its maintenance will reward a sacrifice in exportation. In this case we have an example of the so-called ' dumping system ' later to be discussed. According to Fontana-Russo,[1] the

---

[1] Fontana-Russo, op. cit., p. 195.

protective tariff is justifiable in such cases because it neutralizes an artificial cause of competition, and hence the usual reproach of disturbing the natural development of economic forces cannot be brought against it. The proposal introduced into the English parliament by Joseph Chamberlain on May 28, 1903, for the imposition of protective duties ('Tariff Reform') was principally motived by reference to the cut-price exportations of German and American industries. Canada, in the tariff law of August 10, 1904, has introduced a special duty on goods whose contemporaneous market-price in the country of production is higher than the actual selling-price in Canada. By the terms of the law of April 12, 1907, now in force, this special duty is to be gauged according to the difference in price up to a maximum of fifteen per cent *ad valorem*. Australia has proceeded along the same general lines, while in British South Africa a commission appointed in the fall of 1912 in connexion with a revision of the tariff has made a similar recommendation. Finally, in the draft of the new American tariff law (Underwood Tariff Bill, 1913) a clause was contained according to which, in addition to the duties otherwise fixed, a special tax or 'dumping duty', equal to the difference between the export price of goods and their market value for domestic consumption in the country of origin is to be collected. This special duty was not to exceed fifteen per cent *ad valorem*, and in addition goods already subject to a duty of fifty per cent *ad valorem* are to be exempt from it.

According to the theories so far discussed, protective duties would still be only an exception to the rule of free trade, and hence would not occur as a permanent and general institution. The actual commercial policies of the countries of continental Europe, on the other hand, very early disregarded the fundamental position of the classical school that the international exchange of commodities equalizes differences in production costs. Instead, they made these very differences the basis of protective tariff systems, untroubled by the question as to whether the differences were to be traced to natural conditions (mineral wealth, geographical position, &c.) or to the institutions of the country (means of communication, taxation systems, &c.). The most recent tariff discussions have been replete with such calculations. From motives not difficult to fathom, the most favourably situated competing country and the domestic production district operating under least favourable conditions were preferably chosen as a basis of comparison. These figures, to be sure, were not used for an exact computation of the rates of duties, but only as illustrative examples. Richard Schüller has attempted to give a scientific foundation for this practice by means of a more careful investigation of production costs.[1] He maintains that the law that costs are increased by extending the scope of production is valid not merely for agriculture but for manufactures as well. In cases where in fact a reduction in costs ensues, it should be attributed to the progress of industrial technique by means of which production could have been cheapened even on the old scale. This position is quite untenable, as advances in industrial technique are usually the result of the extension of the market and of the scale of production ; nor would the rapid growth in the concentration of industries in combines, trade agreements, trusts, &c., be possible if an increase in production involved higher costs. So much only is true, that the costs do not decrease uniformly but may also suffer temporary reactions. Production-costs of the different commodities—Schüller further argues—are also very unequal within a country on account of the differences in conditions as to soil, freight, labour, and capital, and the variation between the highest and lowest costs is considerable. He would regard a country as in a position to export when the highest costs to be undergone in covering its needs are lower than the highest costs involved in producing in the import country a supply sufficient for its total consumption. If the

[1] Richard Schüller, *Schutzzoll und Freihandel*, Vienna and Leipsic, 1905.

difference between the highest and lowest costs in a country is large, this would signify that production could be extended under unfavourable conditions only, and hence a duty would work the more advantageously in proportion as this difference were less. The other factor to be considered would be the so-called ' superiority ' of the foreign country, which is regarded as being greater the farther its price rests below the domestic level, and the greater the foreign production. But it is erroneous to assert that an extension of production must be at costs which are higher the greater the variation in cost already present. The greater the production, the more strongly will capital be attracted, which, as Schüller himself admits, produces its first effect in equalizing the variations in productive conditions. In practice such theories fail because production costs cannot be controlled or even exactly computed. The significant question relates, not to the costs involved in turning out a unit of product (consumption of material, wages of labour, &c.), but in an ever increasing degree to the general costs which must be incurred in maintaining and conducting the enterprise (mechanical power, light, expenditures for officials and supervision, laboratories, interest, depreciation of invested capital, taxes, insurance premiums, &c.), as well as in marketing the finished goods (sales, warehouses, commercial travellers, advertising, &c.), and which only by means of a rather arbitrary estimate can be reckoned against a particular unit of the product. In the case of agriculture any attempt at such a computation must be abandoned in view of the great variations in yields, the interconnexion brought about by crop rotation between the costs of different crops (e.g. legumes as fertilizing agencies) the dependence of grain culture on stock-breeding, &c.

The developmental theories regarded the economic individual, disassociated from his political allegiance, as the ultimate end and the political state as a means of access to him, and an obstacle which could be overcome ; the compensatory theories concerned themselves not with the final

goal of development, but only with the friction surfaces of
the two kinds of interacting economic units. The defensive
theories in turn view the politico-economic state as the final
and permanent organization to which world-economy considerations must be subordinated to the extent even that
under certain circumstances they may be restricted by
protective tariff measures. The classical school, it is true,
was correct in the assertion that in the international interchange, individual men and not peoples or states carry on
commercial transactions, but it completely overlooked the
fact that commerce must be carried on across political
boundaries under conditions essentially different from those
obtaining within such lines, as the individual is influenced in
his economic activity also by the political community. In
a scientific sense these theories are still very incompletely
worked out. Attempts in this direction developed out of the
controversy carried on about the end of the century in regard
to the agricultural versus the manufacturing state (*Agrarstaat
und Industriestaat*). It was averred that the international
division of labour had led to a dangerous one-sidedness in
the economic character of the state, and to a separation
between raw material producing and manufacturing countries.
This condition was regarded as placing the latter in a dan-
gerously dependent condition, since the raw material countries
will naturally become industrialized, and hence be able to
purchase smaller and smaller quantities of manufactured
goods, and furnish to other countries smaller quantities of
the means of life. On this account the agriculture of western
Europe should, it was claimed, be rendered more efficient
by the levying of ' maintenance duties '. This reasoning led,
however, to an extreme position, the error of which has
already been pointed out. The political motive is emphasized
by Eugen von Philippovitch, who sees the decisive factor in
all commercial policy in the fact—' that it represents the
co-ordination of the economic forces of a community which
strives to assert and maintain itself as a political unit '.

The *staatlich-politische Moment* is in his view the most important ' since from the economic standpoint the distinction between Triest and Bodenbach is greater than that between Bodenbach and Dresden '.[1]

Our own view is derived from a criticism of the foregoing theories. The national economy being in our conception the highest organization, and that to which world-economy relations must continue to be subordinate, the developmental theories at once fall to the ground. The condition of an economic world community, independent of political boundaries to which developmental duties would look forward, is neither possible nor desirable. Compensatory theories, however, which aim to offset differences in production costs or in some elements of such costs at home and abroad, are likewise incorrect. If the differences are the product of political policy, as, for example, the taxation system, they can at least in the course of a somewhat lengthy period of adaptation be likewise artificially done away with. Natural distinctions based on location, character of the soil, &c., are found also among domestic establishments ; hardly two enterprises operate under equally favourable conditions, and in this way we should be forced to advocate the levying of duties within a country. From this theory would also follow the fatal error that protection should be extended to every branch of production in any degree possible within the country, in spite of the fact that the encouragement of many industries would do far more harm than good on account of the immoderate increase in the costs of the partly manu-factured material to be improved and finished. Our conception leads, therefore, immediately to the defensive theories, though of these latter we must at once reject those which advocate shutting out all world-economy influences. Philippovitch occupies the correct middle ground, but alongside the political moment which he emphasizes must be placed

[1] Book review in *Zeitschrift für Volkswirtschaft, Sozialpolitik und Verwaltung* (Vienna, 1905), vol. xiv, no. 4.

an additional economic one. The political boundary will increase not merely the political but also the economic differences between places as compared with equally widely separated ones within a country. On crossing a frontier the market for every kind of goods changes, even disregarding the duty, under the influence of different transportation and commercial institutions, different taxation, legal system, &c. The aim of modern tariff protection, as already explained in the case of economic protective policy in general, is to use the political power as a means of securing to a particular national economy its own domestic market.

Import Duties. Of by far the greatest importance for the protective policy are duties on imports. Leaving out of account revenue duties levied on purely fiscal grounds, these fall into two groups, agrarian duties on agricultural products, and industrial duties on manufactured goods.

In the early history of the protective policy, agricultural duties were expressly repudiated, since they would only have impeded the desired industrialization of the country by increasing the cost of living to the population, and hence raising industrial production-costs. Besides, agriculture, in the days of primitive means of communication, already enjoyed a sufficient degree of natural protection in the form of freight charges. But the rapid growth of American competition in grain in the decade of the 'seventies in the nineteenth century, forced the countries of continental Europe to take defensive measures, and the result was the imposition of protective duties on live-stock and animal products. But in the manipulation of the veterinary police regulations a weapon was soon found so convenient and so effective that the live-stock duties presently sank to a position of merely nominal significance. In this connexion an opposition made itself manifest, though at first in only a moderate degree, between small farming, which looked for its profit chiefly to stock raising, and even frequently enough appeared as a purchaser of grain, and the large landowners specializing more in grain production. In the course of the further development, wines and also various garden and truck products were successively included in the protective group, as it became evident that in these cases also we have to do with intensive cultivation.

The highest duties on grains are found in Portugal and Spain, after which follow in order Italy, France, Germany, and Austria-Hungary. The duty on wheat may be taken as representative of this class of imposts, and is shown for the different European countries in the following table :

DUTY ON WHEAT (RATE PRESCRIBED IN TREATIES) IN MARKS PER HUNDRED KILOGRAMS

Country.	Rate.
Portugal	Amount to be imported limited, duty adjusted from time to time.
Spain	6·48 (With occasional temporary reduction)
Italy	6 08
France	5·66 (With occasional temporary suspension)
Germany . . .	5·50
Austria-Hungary . .	5·35
Norway	4·86
Sweden	4·16
Serbia	4·05
Bulgaria . . .	0·40
Switzerland . . .	0·24
Roumania . . .	0·04
Russia	free
Denmark	,,
Belgium	,,
Great Britain . . .	,,
Netherlands . . .	,,
United States of America . .	3·95
Japan	2·68

The cotton and iron industries afford the best indication of the amount of industrial duties, since their products are staple articles of world trade, and are found present in almost every country at the beginning of industrial development.

In order, however, to make comparison possible, in view of the multitudinous character of the products, certain specified typical articles have been chosen and traced through all the tariff schedules. The following tables show the duties on the goods indicated in the different countries, computed in marks per hundred kilograms. The rates are prescribed by treaties with almost universal uniformity.

TABLE I

DUTY ON COTTON YARN, NO. 36 ENGLISH. SINGLE, UNBLEACHED

Spain	. . .	140·0
Russia	. . .	108·13
Portugal	. . .	68·04
Greece	. . .	48·60
Serbia	. . .	40·50
Bulgaria	. . .	32·40
Austria-Hungary	.	28·05
Italy	. . .	26·73
Sweden	. . .	22·50
Germany	. . .	18·0
Switzerland	. .	16·20
France	. . .	14·99
Norway	. . .	13·50
Belgium	. . .	12·15
Denmark	. . .	7 04
Roumania	. . .	4·05
Turkey	.	11% (ad valorem)
Netherlands	. .	free
Great Britain	. .	free
United States of America		67·20
Japan	. . .	22 28

TABLE II

DUTY ON COTTON FABRIC, SMOOTH, UNBLEACHED, of a weight of 10 kilograms per hundred square metres, made from No. 50 yarn, counting 38 threads to five millimetres square.

Russia	. . .	1,161·0
Spain	. . .	352·35
Serbia	. . .	105·30
Portugal	. . .	92·99
France	. . .	86·67
Germany	. . .	70·0
Greece	. . .	64·80
Belgium	. . .	64·80
Italy	. . .	63·18
Denmark	. . .	56·80
Roumania	. . .	56·70
Sweden	. . .	56 25
Bulgaria	. . .	32·40
Norway	. . .	28·13
Switzerland	. .	8·10
Netherlands	.	5% (ad valorem)
Great Britain	. .	free
United States of America		51·87
Japan	. . .	62·70

TABLE III

DUTY ON COTTON FABRIC, same as in Table II except printed in three colours

Russia	. . .	1,404·0	Greece . . .	97·20
Portugal .	. .	362·88	Belgium . . .	81·0
Spain	. . .	299·70	Roumania . .	68·04
France	. . .	152·28	Bulgaria . . .	60·75
Denmark	. .	151·68	Switzerland . .	48·60
Italy	. . .	129·68	Turkey . 11% (ad valorem)	
Sweden	. .	123·75	Netherlands 5% (ad valorem)	
Norway	. .	123·75	Great Britain . . free	
Austria-Hungary	.	121·55	United States of America 103·74	
Germany	. .	120·0	Japan . . .	87·14
Serbia	. .	105·30		

TABLE IV

DUTY ON LACES, MACHINE-MADE, UNBLEACHED, of a weight of 25 kilograms per hundred square metres

Russia	. .	2,539·0	Roumania . . .	328·0
Spain	. .	1,093·50	Bulgaria . . .	283·50
Portugal .	.	816·48	Denmark . . .	227·50
Norway .	.	674·50	Switzerland . .	81·00
Austria-Hungary	.	561·0	Belgium . 15% (ad valorem)	
Serbia	. .	486·0	Turkey . 11% (ad valorem)	
Sweden	. .	450·0	Netherlands 5% (ad valorem)	
Italy	. .	405·0	Great Britain . . free	
France	. .	405·0	United States of America	
Greece	. .	379·65	45% (ad valorem)	
Germany .	.	350·0	Japan . . .	69·60

TABLE V

DUTY ON BAR IRON, UNFASHIONED

Russia .	. .	9·89	Portugal . . .	0·68
France	. .	6·07	Switzerland . .	0·24
Spain .	. .	5·18	Turkey . 11% (ad valorem)	
Italy .	. .	4·86	Netherlands 5% (ad valorem)	
Austria-Hungary	.	4·25	Norway . . . free	
Roumania	. .	2·43	Sweden . . . free	
Serbia .	. .	2·02	Greece . . . free	
Bulgaria	. .	2·02	Great Britain . . free	
Denmark	. .	1·17	United States of America 2·78	
Germany	. .	1·0	Japan . . .	2·09
Belgium	. .	0·81		

TABLE VI

DUTY ON SHEET IRON of a thickness of 1 millimetre

Russia	13·85	Denmark	1·17
France	10·93	Belgium	0·81
Italy	9·72	Switzerland	0·49
Austria-Hungary	8·50	Turkey	11% (ad valorem)
Serbia	8·10	Netherlands	5% (ad valorem)
Portugal	6·80	Greece	free
Spain	6·48	Norway	free
Germany	4·50	Great Britain	free
Sweden	4·50	United States of America	5·56
Roumania	4·08	Japan	2·61
Bulgaria	3·24		

TABLE VII

DUTY ON SEWING NEEDLES, of a length less than 5 centimetres

Russia	641·20	Denmark	75·0
Spain	243·0	Italy	64·80
Portugal	226·75	Sweden	45·0
France	202·50	Switzerland	40·50
Roumania	162·0	Belgium	13% (ad valorem)
Austria-Hungary	144·50	Netherlands	5% (ad valorem)
Greece	126·52	Great Britain	free
Germany	100·0	United States of America	25% (ad valorem)
Serbia	97·20		
Bulgaria	89·10	Japan	175·89
Norway	84·38		

Export Duties. While in the case of import duties the protectionist influence has become completely dominant, in that of duties on exports the commercial policy interest falls far behind fiscal considerations. This follows from the circumstance that the opportunity less and less frequently presents itself of securing important raw materials for a particular national economy by restricting exportation. An increase in the revenues of the state can be anticipated only in case the country holds a monopoly in the goods upon which an export duty is levied, for only in such a case will the foreign producer be compelled to pay the price increased by the export duty. It is true that the monopoly need not be so absolute that the article is exclusively the product of a single country as, for example, saltpetre of Chile. The position of relative monopolization may suffice, as when one country alone is able to furnish an important quality of the product; such a position is occupied by Sweden in the case of high-grade iron ores. Or again, in consequence of a combination of varied factors as to situation and means of transportation (by rail or water), a country may occupy an exclusive position in regard to supplying particular markets. An example of this is to be found in the situation of Canada relative to the demand of the United States of America for rough timber. Such situations are much more likely to arise in the case of colonial products than with those of European industry, which will explain the fact that in oversea countries revenue duties on exports for the special products of the country are frequently met with. Examples are the export duties on coffee and caoutchouc in Central and South American countries, on ivory, rubber, and ostrich plumes in African districts, animal products in South America, hemp and other articles in the Philippines, tin in the Straits Settlements, &c. This source of income is rather insecure, however. The monopoly of a country may be broken down by the discovery of new sources, by the transplanting and acclimatization of animals and plants, or by the transfer of consumption to substitution products. Moreover, no monopoly is unrestrained in its price policy; each and every one must reckon with the possibility of reduction in consumption and the entailed increase in production costs. The history of the export duty on spices in Ceylon, of that on tea in China, and of that on coffee in Brazil and the Central American States, affords abundant proof of this thesis.

In European countries the mercantilistic school emphasized the importance for commercial policy purposes of export duties, which were to be so designed as to secure to domestic industry a cheap supply of production goods and hence an advantage over foreign competition. But in the course of time the most important raw materials became staples in the world market, and as a result export duties in a single country can no longer make it difficult for any industry to secure its supplies. After the displacement of mercantilistic ideas in the free-trade era, export duties also disappeared from European customs tariffs. This change occurred in England in 1845, in France in 1857, in Prussia in 1865 (with the exception of a duty on rags), and in Austria in 1865 (with the exception of the duties on rags, hides, and bones). Recent years have, however, brought with them a partial revival of the commercial policy interest in exportation.

The export duty on various waste products, which has survived in some degree to the present, is subject to special considerations. We are here dealing, not with products which can be increased in quantity at will, but with a given stock of goods which may be marketed at home or abroad, according to the policy pursued. The article of greatest significance in this connexion has been rags, which formerly constituted almost the sole raw material for the manufacture of paper. But with the development of the publication of books and periodicals this source soon became insufficient to meet the rapidly rising demand for paper. The industry has since, to be sure, got over the difficulty. After many experiments a new raw material was found in wood, which after conversion by mechanical means into wood-pulp, or by chemical processes into cellulose, was rendered admirably suitable for paper manufacture. None the less, the export duty on rags has been retained in many of the new tariffs, as rags continue to form an important raw material for some special articles at least. Germany discarded the duty in 1873, but it is still to be found in the tariffs of Austria-Hungary, Italy, Russia, Spain, Greece, &c. In addition, the Swiss tariff contains export duties on skins, hides, bones, and old iron, that of Russia on old rubber, the Roumanian on old leather, hides, and bones, and the Italian on old silk refuse, &c.

In recent years wood has become an object of concern for commercial policy. In consequence of the enormous require-ment for wood in manufacturing and in building, the countries which control large forest resources are solicitous lest wasteful exploitation and large-scale exportation may work to the disadvantage of their domestic wood-working industries. Frequently a foreign country may in this way be placed in a position to compete with such domestic industries; thus the German and Italian paper manufacture is maintained with Austrian wood, the Spanish bent-wood furniture industry with Austrian beech splints, the paper industry of the United States with Canadian wood, &c. On this account the following countries levy export duties on the products indicated: Norway on lumber and building timber, Sweden (since 1905) on timber and wood pulp, Roumania (since 1905) on oak timber in the rough, and the Canadian provinces of Ontario and Quebec on wood suitable for paper manufacture (pulp-wood). As Russia has a natural monopoly of aspen wood, which is indispensable in the match industry, the manufacturers demanded a duty on this variety of wood. Similarly, in the discussion preceding the enactment of the Tariff of 1906, certain Austrian industries, such as paper and bent-wood furniture, proposed export duties for the protection of their raw material supply.

Another important raw material to be considered in connexion with an export duty levied with a view to commercial policy is iron ore. Such a duty is levied in Spain, where are produced large quantities of ore free from phosphorus and with a high iron content, which has become indispensable to Germany and other industrial countries of Europe. The same question has been much discussed in Sweden, which, on account of the high quality of the ores rather than the amount of production, furnishes raw material for the entire European iron industry. In the year 1905 the government introduced a bill in which an export duty of one krone per ton was imposed. In the Swedish-German commercial treaty of May 8, 1906, however, as well as in that of May 2, 1911 (Art. 10), Sweden assumed the obligation of leaving the exportation of ore duty free.

In the tax commission of the German Reichstag the

proposal was made, on March 1, 1906, for introducing export duties on crude potassium salts and potassium products, coal, lignite, and coke.[1] The purpose of the export duty on potassium was to utilize the natural monopoly held by Germany in potassium mining to procure a new source of income for the state, and also to afford an advantage in price to German agriculture over American, and finally to protect valuable natural resources against too rapid exhaustion. But it was pointed out by the opponents of the proposition that at higher prices the German potassium can be replaced in America by potassium from other than mining sources, such as cotton seed meal; also, that domestic agriculture already possessed an advantage without the duty; that in the United States the principal demand for potassium comes not from the grain-producing northern states, but from the cotton- and tobacco-growing South; and finally, that exhaustion of this German natural resource is not to be feared since, according to official statements, the supply is sufficient for thousands of years. As to German coal, it was shown that it has in no case an uncontested market in which it could shift an export duty to the purchaser; it is everywhere in competition with the English, Belgian, and Austrian product. A reduction in the domestic price, moreover, was not to be anticipated, as the coal-mining industry, in consequence of its highly developed combinations, can diminish production to correspond to the lessened demand. As a result of the unfriendly attitude of the government, the proposal fell through at the second reading before the Tax Commission on April 27, 1906.

The export duty on coal and coke, amounting to one shilling per ton, which Great Britain imposed in April, 1901, was motived by fiscal considerations and resulted from the increased financial needs of the state arising from the Boer War. It was, however, no doubt intended to serve subsidiary commercial-policy ends as well. In the districts not subject to foreign competition—that is, in South America,

[1] Hermann Levy, *Ausfuhrzölle und die deutsche Handelspolitik*, Berlin, 1907.

West Africa, and the Mediterranean region—a rise in the price of English coal was in fact effected; but the result in other markets was so much the more unfavourable, and the extent of the competitive field of course grows *pari passu* with the loss by England of her dominant position in the world's coal market. The export duty was for this reason quickly laid aside.

2. FREIGHT-RATE PROTECTION

Genesis of Protection by Freight Rates. The extent of the market for any product, and the competitive relations dependent thereupon, are not determined by geographical distances, but by the means of transportation and the cost of freight. When a productive industry is secured against foreign competition through the fact that the foreign product, on account of the lack of transportation media or because of the high transportation-costs, is unable to overcome the disadvantage of distance, the industry is said to enjoy freight protection. If, on the other hand, the freight rates are designedly set at different levels by the carrier, for the purpose of favouring some branches of production to the disadvantage of others, the case is one of freight-rate protection. Protective duties have repeatedly been made necessary by the very fact that with the development of new means of transportation, or through reduction in the previously obtaining rates, a need arose for equalizing the increased competitive power of foreign producers. As duties were thus used to offset freights, freights soon came to be used as a weapon against duties.

The sudden requirement for protection on the part of European agriculture, for example, was the result of a revolutionary change in transportation facilities. In the first place, the American railways, by their growth and competition in rates, reduced freights to such a point that the difference in the price of wheat in New York and in the interior of the United States fell in the period from 1860 to 1890 with astonishing rapidity. According to the official statistics of the Department of Agriculture in Washington, the average price of wheat in the years 1862–66 was in New

York 135.1 cents per bushel (208.6 marks per ton), and in the interior of the country 90.7 cents per bushel (142.0 marks per ton); in the years 1887–90, on the other hand, the New York price was 80 cents per bushel (124.7 marks per ton), and the interior price 76.4 cents per bushel (116.4 marks per ton); that is, at the earlier period the difference in price was 44.4 cents (66.6 marks per ton), while at the later period it was only 3.6 cents (7.3 marks per ton). The railway freight charge between Chicago and New York was reduced from an average of 13s. 11d. per quarter in the years 1866–70 to 3s. 7d. in the years 1901–4; the ocean freight from New York to Liverpool, moreover, actually fell from an average of 2s. 11d. in the years 1871–5 to 4d. in the years 1901–4.

The starting-point for freight-rate protection was very different from that for protective duties. A duty is a tax collected at the frontier of a country, and the determining factors in fixing its amount have always been found in considerations relating to the economic interests of the community. They have been levied for the purpose either of increasing the income of the state or of protecting domestic productive establishments. Freight rates, however, are adjusted according to the yield of the transportation service, and hence are determined by considerations of a purely private-economic character. The general economic interest first made itself felt with regard merely to the height and application of the railway rates as a whole. The railway enterprises were forced by charter provisions or by a settled policy of rate regulation to keep the transportation charges at a moderate height; and the principle also gained general recognition that each rate in the schedule must be general in its application, excluding all special favours to individuals. But the interest of the community may be injured by too low as well as by too high rates, and by especially favourable conditions with regard to goods as well as by those of a personal character. The railways sought to make their freight earnings as large as possible, and so attempted to attract foreign shipments by low rates on importations and through traffic. This brought them into conflict with the economic policy of the state, which, in the contrary direction, seeks to facilitate exportation relatively to importation. The railway schedules operated, in the words of Bismarck,[1] as a ' compensatory duty ' against the customs tariff. Recognition of this fact was all that was necessary to insure the transformation of the schedules into an instrument of governmental economic policy.

Schedules affecting Imports. An injury to domestic production relatively to foreign competition could be brought about by the railway freight tariffs, even in case of uniform rates, as these might in fact be susceptible to better utilization from abroad than at home. The simplest case which may occur is that in which a foreign producer operating at lower costs than domestic industries is enabled by a low transportation rate to deliver his goods at a domestic consumption point at a price to meet the domestic competition. This is illustrated by the following diagram :

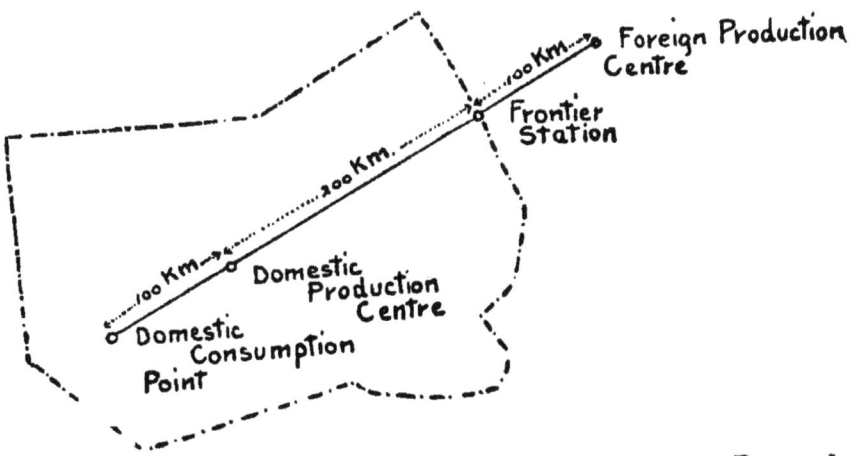

		Per 100 *kg.*
Domestic production costs	. . . .	60 *M.*
Foreign production costs	. . . . . .	54
Inland freight, normal, 2 pfennigs per km., for 300 km.	.	6
Inland freight, reduced, 1 pfennig per km. for 400 km.	.	3
Foreign freight, 2 pfennigs per km. for 100 km.	. . .	2

[1] Communication to the Bundesrat, December 15, 1878.

It will be seen that the example illustrated gives the following competitive data :

PRICES IN INTERIOR OF COUNTRY WITH NORMAL FREIGHT RATES

Domestic Commodity—   *M.*
   Production costs 60
   Freight   2
                                           —
                                           62

Foreign Product
   Production costs 54
   Freight (Inland) 6
   Freight (Foreign) 2
                                           —
                                         62

PRICES IN INTERIOR OF COUNTRY WITH REDUCED FREIGHT RATES

Domestic Goods—   *M.*
   Production costs 60
   Freight   1
                                           —
                                         61

Foreign Product—
   Production costs 54
   Domestic freight 3
   Foreign freight   2
                                           —
                                         59

Thus the foreign product would bear the same price as the domestic goods under the normal rates, and two marks cheaper after the rates were reduced.

It is possible that the foreign producer may be favoured even under equal production costs, in case of inequalities in the rates of different railways, which may be combined to give him an advantage at the domestic consumption point. Let us assume that the railway A in the sketch below represents the means of communication with a foreign production centre, a coal-mining district for example, and the railway B that with a domestic centre equally distant from the consumption point. The railway A will naturally strive to secure coal freights, and will grant rate concessions which the railway B may not feel called upon to meet for the reason that the domestic coal-field has access to no other market than the domestic consumption point in question. The situation will then be as follows :

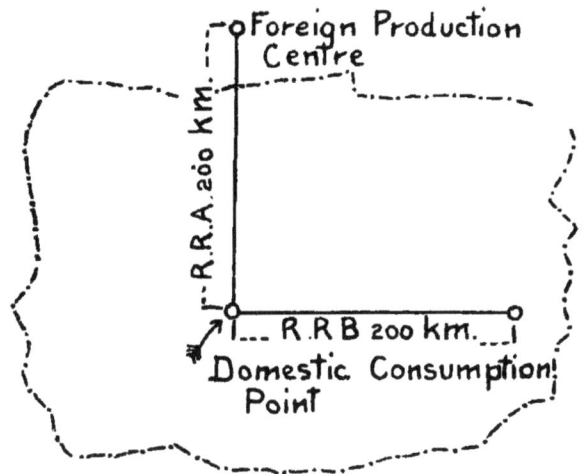

	Per 100 kg. M.
Domestic production costs	60
Foreign production costs	54
Freight (normal) 2 pfennigs per km. for 200 km. . . .	4
Freight (reduced but only on R. R. " A ") 1 pfennig per km. for 200 km.	2

The competitive conditions are these:

PRICE AT CONSUMPTION POINT FOR DOMESTIC PRODUCT

	M.
Production costs	60
Freight	4
	64

PRICE AT CONSUMPTION POINT FOR FOREIGN COAL

	M.
Production costs	60
Freight	2
	62

Thus the foreign product will sell two marks cheaper than the domestic at the consumption point, even though the freight rates of both railroads apply uniformly to all goods without distinction as to their foreign or domestic origin.

In the previous cases the rate policies of railroads operating according to private-economy principles lead undesignedly to a preference for imported goods over home products. But there are many instances in which the discrimination in favour of foreign industry is deliberate, and in which private-economic and national-economic interests come into open conflict. Such rate concessions may operate to modify or completely offset the effects of import duties. All these cases may be reduced to a competition between routes, either between two domestic transportation enterprises (railways, canals, &c.) or between one domestic route and a foreign route. The operation of competition between domestic routes may be seen from the following diagram :

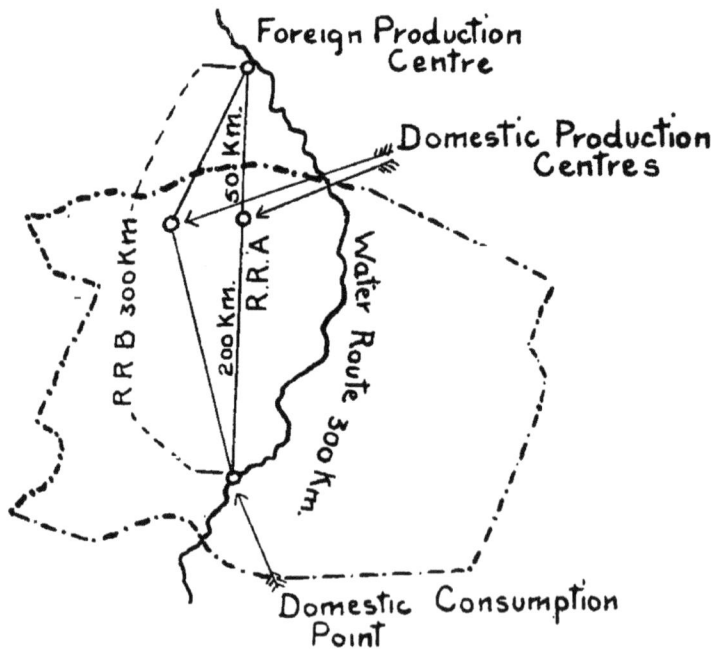

It will be seen from the sketch that the longer but cheaper water route (river or canal) will fix the freight charges from the foreign production centre to the domestic consumption point, and hence that the railways A and B must lower their rates at least on certain articles and for certain seasons. In the case of shipments from domestic production centres this necessity does not apply, since they lie on the railroads only and not on the water-way. It is therefore possible that the freight on foreign goods will be not merely relatively but also absolutely lower than that on the home product.

The following diagram illustrates the case of competition with foreign transportation enterprises :

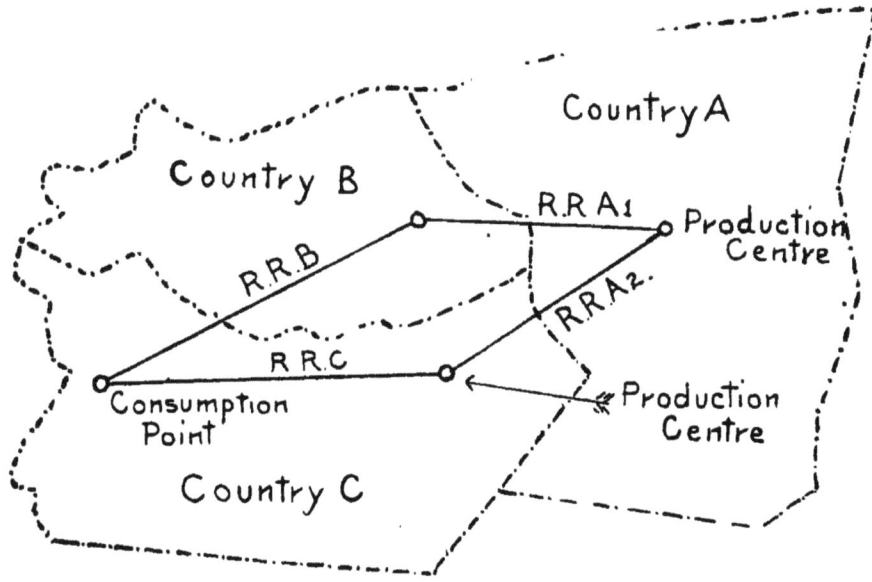

The railways B and C stand in a competitive relation with regard to the freights from the production centre of country A to the consumption point in country C. The line C may be forced by this competition to grant exceptionally low rates to freight from the country A, while no such compulsion exists in motives of private profit for the granting of similar rates to the domestic centre of production of the same goods, since to the latter no other road to market is available. The foreign product will in fact be given more favourable terms than the domestic. A particularly apt illustration of this procedure was afforded by the competitive struggle, especially keen in the decade of the 'nineties, between the German and Austrian railways for the transportation of Russian grain to southern Germany.

Such occurrences drew public attention to the economic significance of railway tariffs; the economic interest of the community received continually greater emphasis, and finally the freight rates on imports were transformed from an obstacle into an instrument of the protective policy, from a compensating into a supplementary impost. In this process, however, a difficulty had to be overcome which lay in the generally recognized commercial-policy principle of inland parity or uniformity of treatment within the home country. It is to be borne in mind that three principles come into play in the mutual economic relations of sovereign states. These are the principles of (1) reciprocity, (2) most-favoured-nation, and (3) inland parity (*Inlandsparität*).

Reciprocity carries over into the relations of economic states the private-economy viewpoint that to every concession must correspond a definite compensating concession of equal value. A foreign country will therefore be granted participation in a new concession only when it purchases the right to such participation by itself granting a new privilege. But the development toward world economy was impeded by the fact that the more frequently commercial agreements were concluded the greater became the danger that a privilege once purchased would become valueless through the subsequent grant to a competing country of still greater concessions. It was recognized, moreover, that in the competitive struggle it is not specific advantages which are so significant, but rather general uniformity in the competitive conditions. As a result, reciprocity ceased to be a factor in European tariff policy, and retained its position in that of America only because of the peculiar economic situation of the countries in that part of the world. At best it was only applied in special cases in which the issue was not merely a negative toleration but positive action on the part of the political power in favour of private enterprises. Such cases are found in the admission of business corporations or travelling agents, which may be conditioned on some special concession or privilege, or in connexion with the protection of working-men and working-men's insurance, where political institutions are made accessible to foreigners, or the like.

Protection against future injuries through the granting of further advantages to other countries was offered by the most-favoured-nation principle. Under this system all later concessions granted to any state whatever were guaranteed to the power concluding the treaty, without compensation and without further negotiations or a new agreement. This means, however, that one foreign nation is placed on an equality with other foreign nations, i. e. only ' foreign parity ' (*Auslandsparität*) ; in the nature of the case, therefore, it affects only such measures of economic policy as relate exclusively to foreign goods and foreign persons, such as regulations regarding duties and customs administration, the admission of consuls, &c. On the other hand, for those measures of economic policy which affect in the same way foreign and native persons and goods, and which involve no positive action, but only a negative sufferance, recourse was had at the same time to the principle of inland parity, which places the foreign country on an equality, not with other foreign nations, but with the home country, and so as a general rule goes farther than the most-favoured-nation principle. Examples of this practice are found in the treaty stipulations with regard to freedom of domicile and engagement in trade, granting to citizens of foreign powers the opportunity of taking up residence and carrying on business, acquiring real estate or practising trade in a country under conditions the same as those which apply to its own citizens ; also in the provisions relating to the whole field of commerce on roads, rivers, canals, railways, and sea-going ships.

It will be seen that railway tariffs are governed by the principle of inland parity, which, for example, is formulated as follows in the commercial treaty of December 6, 1891 (at present in force), between Austria-Hungary and Germany (Art. 15):

> With regard to railway transportation, no distinction shall be made between the inhabitants of the territories of the parties to this treaty, either as to rate charged or as to time and manner of performance of the service. In particular, parcels consigned from the territory of one of the parties into the territory of the other, or passing through the latter, shall not receive unfavourable treatment, either as to handling or any circumstance of the transportation, as compared with parcels either leaving the latter territory or remaining within it.

This application of the principle of inland parity was no ' remarkable phenomenon ',[1] but rather a logical consequence. In the first place there was already at hand in the customs duties a protective instrument so adaptable to every requirement that there was no occasion to sacrifice freedom of transportation also to this end, while railway freights constitute primarily a compensation for transportation service, and hence do not admit of such elastic manipulation. In the second place, railroads had formerly been managed after the manner of private enterprise, even when they were in the hands of the state, and hence had been allowed to negotiate with every patron for a special freight rate if they so desired ; but since the state had come to protect its own inhabitants against economic injustice by prohibiting all special favours to individuals (rebates), the treaty stipulation quoted involved only a carrying over of this principle of justice into the international sphere.

Not until the beginning of the 'nineties did Germany adopt a policy of restricting inland parity in her commercial

[1] Ernst Seidler and Alexander Freud, *Die Eisenbahntarife in ihren Beziehungen zur Handelspolitik* (Leipsic, 1904), p. 10.

treaties, which was finally done under pressure of the existing tariff policy. The application of the principle was restricted to the same route and direction of haul, and hence the policy of differentiating between the rates on imports and exports was openly adopted. Article 19 of the commercial treaty with Russia of February 10 (January 29), 1894, accordingly contained the following phraseology :

Both parties to this treaty reserve the right to adjust the transportation rates over their own railroads as they may see fit. However, no distinction shall be made between the inhabitants of the territories of the parties to this treaty with regard to either the rate of transportation or the time or manner of its performance. In particular, no higher rate shall be charged on German railroads for freight shipments consigned from Russia to a German station or forwarded through Germany than is applicable to similar German or foreign products passing over the same route and in the same direction. The same shall apply on Russian railroads to shipments from Germany consigned to a Russian station or carried through Russia. Exceptions to the foregoing provisions shall be permissible only in the case of transportation at reduced rates for public or benevolent purposes.

Although as a rule inland parity is more extensively applied than foreign parity or the most-favoured-nation principle, yet this does not exclude cases in which a country may grant to a foreign country, in case of a product whose importation does not work a disadvantage to domestic production since it cannot be produced in the home country, a freight-rate even lower than that applicable to domestic goods. To be sure, this higher domestic rate is in such a case merely nominal, and in fact is generally made merely for the purpose of evading the principle of inland parity. Since in economic measures affecting only foreign persons the principle of foreign parity is the only safeguard against disadvantageous treatment, it follows that under certain circumstances the most-favoured-nation principle must be applied in the field of railway tariffs also. The question whether an economic measure applies only to foreign countries or to the home country as well, is of course to be decided according to the actual, and not according to a supposititious, condition of affairs. For example, the commercial agreement between Austria-Hungary and Bulgaria of the date of December 9/21, 1896, contains in Article XII the most-favoured-nation principle side by side with that of inland parity :

With regard to the conditions of forwarding freight shipments, the rates, accommodations and other advantages connected therewith, the Bulgarian Government obligates itself to treat the goods and products either of the soil or of the industries of the Austro-Hungarian monarchy which may be carried by rail in Bulgaria, on a basis of complete equality with the goods of the most-favoured-nation or with domestic products.

The cause of the phenomenon that railway tariffs were brought into use as an auxiliary to customs duties in the furtherance of the protective policy is mainly to be sought in the fact that in the last quarter of the nineteenth century the need for protection on the part of production in general, and especially that of agriculture, increased so rapidly that import duties were unable to keep pace with the growing requirements. A change in duties could be effected only by means of a law, and the parliamentary procedure connected with legislation is, in view of the importance of the interests involved, uniformly time-consuming and by no means free from political danger. Furthermore, important duty rates were bound up in long-time commercial agreements with other nations, so that a change by one party alone was altogether out of the question. Railway tariffs, on the other hand, could be changed at will and in any particular, and were the more readily susceptible to employment as a correction of the duties since the purpose of economic protection could easily be concealed in a procedure connected with private enterprise such as is afforded in the adjustment of a freight schedule. Since in an international treaty it is not the text of the agreement, but the community of interest underlying it, that has binding power, the principle of inland parity formed no insuperable obstacle. It was simply evaded for the time being, and in due course subjected to formal limitations. The method adopted for introducing such protective transportation rates on imports was that of establishing special rate provisions, the wording of which was such that they could in fact be taken advantage of only by domestic production and could not be claimed by the competing foreign producer. The invention of such provisions afforded a rich field of activity to the administrative organs concerned. For example, this special rate might be granted from a specified station exclusively (station-rate), or occasionally only in case of consignment beyond a specifically named station (direction-rate). But as even in this case a utilization of the special rate by the foreign shipper was possible through intermediate unloading of the goods, the further condition was attached that the parcel must be delivered at the shipping-point by wagon transfer or by private industrial track. Eventually it became the custom to require the delivery at the shipping point of a specified quantity of goods such as only a productive establishment in the immediate vicinity could supply. The same result was achieved by limiting the special rate to goods bearing a particular mark or produced in a particular locality. Occasionally even, the special rate was expressly limited to goods of domestic production in open contradiction to the principle of inland parity established by treaty.

A general view of measures of this character taken by the various countries of continental Europe is hardly possible, as they are frequently so concealed under general provisions that they are apparent only to the parties directly concerned, while in addition they are subject to many and rapid alterations.

Transit Tariffs. It was again the private economic motive of increasing freight-earnings which led to the establishment of reduced rates on transit shipments. The incentive was generally the competition, already discussed, of foreign transportation enterprises, which may be illustrated by the following diagram :

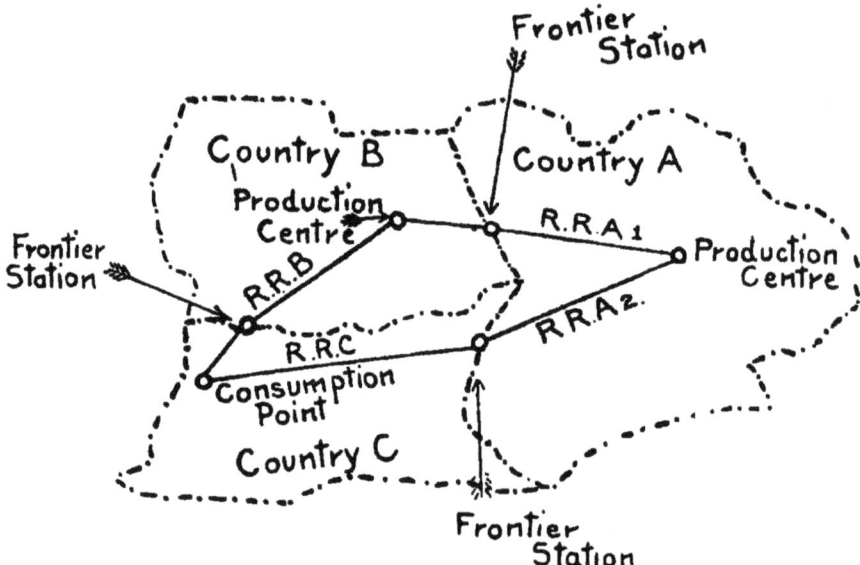

The railroad B will find itself obliged by the pressure of competition on the part of railways A2 and C to place its rates on through-traffic below the level of those applicable to domestic products, which, however, may seriously reduce the competitive efficiency of domestic production with regard to exportation to the consumption point in country C.

Such a case of competition may arise not merely through connexion with the same market region, but also through connexion with competing ports, as will be made clear by the sketch below :

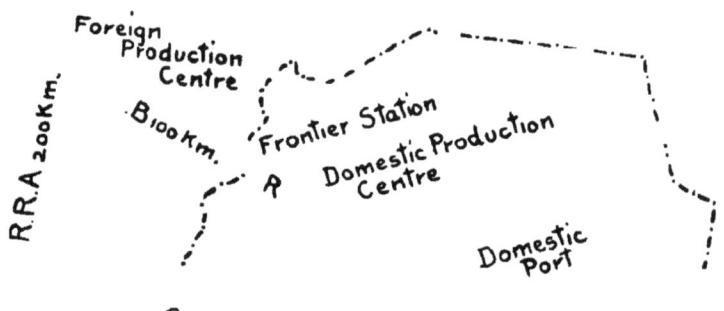

If the railway C wishes to secure the freight shipments of the foreign production centre for itself and for the domestic port, the combined rate on the lines B and C, together with a combined length of 300 kilometres, must not be greater than that of the railway A with a length of 200 kilometres. The transit rate of the railway C from the frontier station to the domestic port will therefore quite possibly be lower than the domestic rate from the production centre within the country.

Even without the competition of foreign transportation enterprises, the endeavour to increase freight earnings may lead to similar results, in case the ability of the foreign goods to compete in the market in question is completely dependent upon a reduction in the transit tariff. Let us assume the case represented in the following diagram :

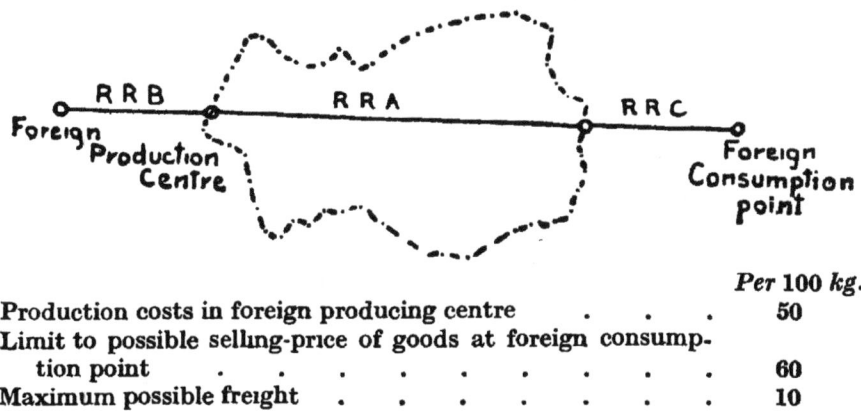

	Per 100 kg.
Production costs in foreign producing centre . . .	50
Limit to possible selling-price of goods at foreign consumption point	60
Maximum possible freight	10

The railway of the transit country will be forced to attempt a reduction in the rates on its transit traffic to such a point that when added to those on the connecting road in the foreign country they will not exceed the difference between the production cost in the foreign production centre (fifty marks per 100 kg.) and the sale price obtainable at the consumption point (sixty marks).

This reduction of the railway tariff on private economic

grounds will not in itself constitute an evil, for the increase in the traffic brought about by the addition of the foreign freight will increase the efficiency of the road, and hence will work to the benefit of domestic production. It is true that it will operate as a burden on exportation in case a similar domestic product competes with the foreign goods in the market of the consumption point. Private economic motives alone will not always impel the road to grant to the domestic product the concession made to the foreign, and it may even be inclined to recoup itself at home for any sacrifice involved in securing the foreign traffic. From the standpoint of the economic interests of the community, however, the principle which has come to be recognized in modern railway policy is quite justifiable, viz. : that transit rates must not be lower than the rates on goods exported from the home country.

In commercial treaties the principle of inland parity which is applied to the rates on imports is usually extended to the transit tariff as well. A more extensive unification was temporarily in force in the relations between Austria and Hungary. This was a mutual application of their respective transit tariffs to the foreign traffic. The Compromise (*Ausgleich*) of the year 1899 contains an agreement which was put into effect in Austria by a decree of the minister of railways on September 22, 1899. The obligation was twofold. On the one hand, the reduced rates established for transit traffic in the other country up to the year 1899 were fixed as a maximum, and on the other hand the state railways bound themselves to grant to shipments from the other country all further reductions made to foreign traffic consigned to the same terminal station. This stipulation involved a greater sacrifice on the part of Austria, since much larger quantities of Hungarian freight are carried through Austria by the state roads than conversely ; furthermore, foreign transit traffic is carried over much longer stretches of road than those affected by the common rate in Hungary. This agreement was dropped in the following *Ausgleich*, and in fact gave place to a tariff war.

3. ADMINISTRATIVE PROTECTION

The Genesis of Administrative Protection. Difficulties have multiplied with time in the way of both customs-duty and freight-tariff protection. The introduction or increase of duties calls forth even within the country attempting it numerous conflicts of interest between the extractive and the elaborative branches of production, and in addition a legislative act so deeply affecting material conditions is bound to offer to the political parties of the opposition many points of attack ; finally, foreign countries will find means of taking retaliative measures, or, in their negotiations for commercial agreements, will demand compensation. Freight-tariff protection avoids some of these difficulties, since in its manipulation legislative action does not need to be resorted to, but its effect is lost in the case of those very manufactures which most need protection—those of high value—and it may also involve considerable fiscal sacrifices. For these reasons, means have been sought for by which to place in the hands of the administrative authority such control over the application of laws regulating economic activity that an actual, though of course not a formal, protection might be afforded to domestic production against foreign competition. Possibilities of this character have been discovered in the most varied fields, in connexion with the agrarian policy, industrial policy, and domestic commercial policy.

A characteristic fact regarding the genesis of administrative protection is the circumstance, somewhat strange at first sight, that the measures comprehended under this term have reached their greatest development in Hungary and in England. Quite different causes have in these cases led to the same result. Hungary was bound by its customs-union with Austria to grant free trade to its most formidable competitor, while none the less constituting an independent economic organization with its own legislation and administration. The productive conditions of the two countries have become increasingly differentiated. As a result, Hungary was early impelled to seek out some substitute for the tariff protection excluded by the agreement. In England, on the other hand, the free-trade doctrine had become so firmly established on account of its theoretical background and its tactical advantages, that in the course of time corrections which had become necessary could be carried out only in the application of the principle and not by modifying the principle itself.

Veterinary Police-power Exclusions. Among the measures adopted by governments for combating the recurrent devastating epidemics of live-stock diseases, are to be found not merely provisions for the killing of affected animals with a view to stamping out at the earliest possible moment any disease which may be prevalent within a country itself, but also protective measures designed to prevent as far as possible the introduction of such diseases from abroad. In accordance with the general principles of international commercial policy with respect to regulations to secure the public health and safety, this protection may be extended to prohibition of importation. Now there is no such thing as absolute freedom from live-stock diseases in any country, and each government is free in prescribing the conditions of exclusion in so far as it has not restricted itself to measures of a specified character through special live-stock epidemic agreements, and these have grown rather unusual. Hence the temptation to use this veterinary police exclusion for the quite different purposes of commercial policy was immediate and strong.

The immediate incentive to this course was afforded by the introduction of rinderpest in the early 'sixties from Russia into the countries of western Europe, where the live-stock industry suffered frightfully. The countries affected sought by stringent laws and veterinary control to protect themselves against the danger. Great Britain in particular issued temporary prohibitions on the importation of live ruminants. In this connexion the presence of a subsidiary purpose of a commercial policy character was not admitted. In Schleswig-Holstein, Oldenburg, and Holland, however, the remarkable coincidence was pointed out that these prohibitions on importation were put in force in the particular periods of low prices, and were directed rather against competing regions than against those infested with the plague.[1]

German agriculture found in the procedure adopted to check the importation of diseased live-stock a possible excuse for an increase in the protection on agricultural products. As a result of the pressure it brought to bear, Germany also closed its doors to the importation of cattle from Russia and Austria-Hungary, and later extended the prohibition to that of hogs and sheep also, on the ground of the threatened danger of introducing foot-and-mouth disease. In the treaty negotiations of 1877 and 1881, the question of moderating these harsh veterinary regulations formed one of the greatest difficulties.[2] In the year 1894, the German Reichstag adopted a resolution in favour of a stricter administration of veterinary regulation; this was directed especially against Russia, as a live-stock epidemic agreement had been concluded with Austria-Hungary in the commercial treaty of December 6, 1891. The situation came to an open conflict in 1896 in consequence of the fact that the importation of pork from Russia was obstructed and that of geese entirely forbidden. Not until the agreement of February 9, 1897, were some moderations in the provisions granted, and then the German Government retained in principle a free hand in regard to its veterinary policy. In this connexion it was admitted,

---

[1] *Die Handelspolitik des Deutschen Reiches vom Frankfurter Frieden bis zur Gegenwart* (Berlin, 1899), p. 199.

[2] Alexander von Matlekowits, *Die Zollpolitik der österreichisch-ungarischen Monarchie und des Deutschen Reiches seit 1868* (Leipsic, 1891), pp. 38, 78.

even officially, that the protection against competition was regarded as at least as important as protection against disease.   The Prussian Minister of Agriculture asserted in the Reichstag session of January 10, 1899, that such a veterinary policy is the most effective means ' for maintaining German agriculture in such a condition—and this is what circumstances demand of us—that the needful supply of meat can be produced in the country '.[1]   In the relations of the United States of America and other oversea countries, the meat-inspection law of June 3, 1900, has also been of considerable importance.   Its principal object was to secure an expert inspection of slaughtered animals in order to determine whether the meat was suitable for human food. A considerable hindrance to importation was also involved, inasmuch as fresh meat was required to be shipped in whole or half carcasses only, in connexion with which certain internal organs (lungs, heart, kidneys, &c.) had to be left in their natural position.   The importation of meat in hermetically sealed cases or similar receptacles, as well as of sausage and other mixtures of minced meat, was entirely forbidden, on the ground that an adequate inspection of such meat products is practically impossible.

The example of Germany again incited Austria-Hungary to imitation, the more so in view of the fact that Germany had repeatedly pointed out that Austria-Hungary is especially exposed to danger of infection by epidemic disease from the great infected herds of Russia and Roumania.   As a result, Austria-Hungary, in the law of February 29, 1880, prohibited the importation and transit through its territory of cattle from these countries, temporarily at first, and then, on January 1, 1882, until further notice.   The importation of sheep and hogs was also temporarily suspended.   Roumania was so deeply affected by this action that the govern-

---

[1] Walther Lotz, *Die Handelspolitik des Deutschen Reiches unter Caprivi und Fürst Hohenlohe (1840–1900)* ; *Schriften des Vereins für Sozialpolitik*, vol. xcii, 3, p. 151.

ment took measures of reprisal, and the situation degenerated, after the expiration of the commercial treaty then in force, into a tariff war, which lasted from 1886 until 1890. Nor did the new commercial treaty of December 21, 1893, improve conditions. In the commercial treaty of May 6, 1881, Serbia had secured a live-stock epidemic agreement which permitted the importation of Serbian cattle into Austria-Hungary by way of certain specified stations of entry, and subject to careful veterinary inspection, but also only on the condition that Serbia should itself prohibit importation from the other Balkan States and should enforce veterinary regulations identical with those of Austria-Hungary. The live-stock disease clause included in the next commercial treaty of August 9, 1892, even increased the stringency of the conditions, and on expiration it was not renewed. The live-stock epidemic agreement concluded with Switzerland, December 5, 1890, was similarly denounced soon after it came into effect. As the commercial relations between Austria-Hungary and the Balkan region had suffered considerably as a result of the exclusion of live-stock, the import prohibitions were modified by special provisions for importation of limited numbers of slaughtered animals. This action, as taken, involved public recognition of the commercial-policy motive back of the regulations, since it is inconceivable that the danger of infection could begin only when the imports passed a certain mark. In the commercial treaty of March 14, 1908, Serbia was granted a provision for the importation of 35,000 cattle and 70,000 hogs, slaughtered, but the agreement remained in force only provisionally and for but seven months. The Austro-Hungarian Government yielded to the representative chamber merely to the extent of consenting to a most-favoured-nation agreement, and this was rejected by Serbia for the reason that it no longer contained the most important provision, viz., that relating to the importation of live-stock. In the later commercial treaty of July 27, 1910, the numbers that might be imported were fixed at 15,000 cattle and 50,000 hogs. Roumania was granted a limited importation in the auxiliary treaty of April 23, 1909, fixed in the case of cattle at 10,000 head for the first year of the treaty period, and increased to 35,000 head for the last three years (1915–17), and in the case of hogs the number was fixed at 50,000 head, to be increased to 120,000. In the commercial treaty of April 22, 1912, Bulgaria was granted an importation of 12,000 cattle per year. The importation of meat from countries outside of Europe was, by the ministerial edict of July 9, 1906, conditioned upon a special permit, which again, according to the *Ausgleich* Treaty with Hungary in 1907, cannot be granted by the Austrian Government without the concurrence of Hungary. In consequence of the unusual rise in the price of meat, chilled meat from Argentina was admitted in the year 1911, but only for a short time and in a narrowly limited quantity.

In France similar difficulties arose in the conclusion of commercial treaties as a result of a temporary prohibition on the importations of cattle and sheep.

Exclusion through Measures for the Protection of Industrial Property. Modern jurisprudence extends protection to the products of mental labour as well as physical, and hence secures to an inventor the right to the utilizable value of his invention (patent-right), to the producer the right to the exclusive use of a certain external form for his product (design-patents), and to the seller of a commodity the right to the exclusive use of a specific designation (trade mark). But as the question here relates to intangible economic values, the value of this protection can be determined only under conditions which make possible the verification of this value. In this connexion opportunity was afforded for placing foreign competition at a disadvantage while granting formal equality of conditions.

In this field the English Merchandise-Marks Act of 1887 has become particularly famous ; it not merely regulates the protection of marks on imported articles, but also forbids the use of false commercial designations, and includes under this head misleading statements as to the country of origin. According to Section XVI, goods bearing false marks and commercial designations are subject to confiscation on importation from abroad. This provision was further construed to mean that all foreign goods imported into England must bear a true statement of the country of origin. The much discussed 'Made in Germany' was intended to discredit the foreign goods, but as a matter of fact it advertised them so effectually that already a Bill has been introduced into the English Parliament forbidding the specific designation of the country of origin and prescribing for imported goods the general designation 'Made abroad'.

The United States of America has adopted into its legislation a regulation of greatest practical importance in the Dingley Bill of 1907. According to the Underwood Bill of 1913 also, imported commodities which can without injury be provided with marks, stamps, tags, and the like, as well as the wrappers of such commodities, must indicate clearly in the English language the country of origin and the quantity; when this information is wanting, or the designation as to quantity is incorrect, importation of the goods is forbidden.

Hungary has issued industrial police regulations forbidding the use of Austrian marks on the ground of alleged deception as to the origin of the goods. Accordingly, in the latest *Ausgleich* Treaty of 1907 (Austrian Law of December 30, 1907, Hungarian Statute LIII, 1907), there were enumerated on the basis of previous experience, certain cases in which the protection may not be denied. A mark does not lose its protective power simply because it does not correspond to the regulations in force in the other country as to the nature and outward form of marks, in so far as it satisfies the legislation of the registering country. Official coats of arms are not regarded as free symbols, and the registry of marks containing them is therefore restricted to the party who has the right to use them. The use of a language current in the territory of both countries is not to be regarded as a deceptive indication of origin. On the other hand, such industrial marks are excluded from registration as in their total effect, by the use of the national colours in their heraldic order, or by the use of representations of national emblems, monuments and architectural works of either country, of the names or portraits of historic personalities or others famous in the field of statesmanship, art, or science, would necessarily operate as a clear indication to the consumer of the origin of the goods in the country in question, unless the true origin is also indicated with sufficient clearness. The use of the national colours for producing inscriptions, arabesques, &c., as well as of border designs, as constituent parts of a mark, is not to be regarded as in itself an indication of the origin of the goods. It need not be pointed out that such casuistry affords no certain protection against further injurious deceptions.

In France, the Minister of Commerce has indicated it as desirable that foreign goods should bear the mark *produit non français*, or *produit étranger*; an indication of the country of origin he thinks should be avoided, in view of the experience of England.

Another measure which worked as a protection in England was the compulsory utilization clause placed in patent rights by the Patent and Designs Act of 1907. It is true that most patent laws have recognized the principle that a patented invention must be brought into use within a reasonable period of time in the country granting the patent, or the protection will be withdrawn from the inventor. But as England applied this principle for the first time in 1907, when numerous patented articles of foreign countries had already come into general use, many German and American firms were forced to found new factories in England in case they did not wish to forfeit their patent rights.

Protective Provisions in Regulations affecting Food Products. The modern policy in regard to food products, subjecting trade in foodstuffs and refreshments to a public regulation for the purpose of combating adulteration injurious to health, leads to restrictions on trade which admit of placing obstruction in the way of foreigners in a most unobtrusive manner. Either especially stringent regulations are issued affecting those foodstuffs which are exclusively furnished by foreign countries, a procedure for which modern hygiene always affords sufficient justification, or the application of provisions affecting domestic goods as well as foreign are more strictly interpreted in the case of imports than in domestic trade. Hence evidences of this tendency in protective policy are to be sought not merely in tariff laws, but also in laws against adulterations of food products.

In Turkey, for example, the irade of February 6, 1900, subjected various pharmaceutical preparations and foodstuffs to a chemical analysis at the customs-house. The requirement was manipulated in a manner which prohibited importation to such an extent that foreign powers entered vehement protests, and succeeded in 1905 in securing a more equitable regulation.

Exclusion Measures connected with the Letting of Public Contracts. With the progressive extension of public administrative activity in various fields of private economy, the state and the other municipal corporations have achieved an ever-increasing importance as consumers and purchasers. The requirements of the army and navy in particular, and those of state railways, of the administration of justice, and of education, come into prominence on account of their extent and high degree of concentration. The textile and clothing industries, iron and machine industry, and the building trades, are the most intensely affected. The state and communal authorities and institutions dare not, like the private individual, be guided exclusively by their own advantage in supplying their needs, but because they expend public money they must have regard also to considerations affecting the public interests. Among the principles which have come to be recognized in this connexion is the rule that domestic production must be given preference over foreign. It is true that to-day this is not possible unless conditions are otherwise equal, hence also when the price is the same. In comparing the domestic price with foreign prices, however, any customs duty applicable to the latter must be added to the price even when the public authority or institution in question is entitled to duty-free importation of goods for its own use ; the protective duty is a right granted to domestic production. A further extension of the principle in the sense that domestic workmanship is to be preferred even in case of more favourable offers from abroad, or that such foreign offers are to be unconditionally excluded, conflicts, to be sure, with the principle of free trade laid down in commercial treaties ; yet it is in fact practised by manipulating the character and form of the public specifications for the delivery of goods.

In England the provision of public service requirements is made a means of giving preference not merely to domestic but also to colonial production. Press and Parliament take a most hostile attitude toward any office or institution which purchases anything whatever from abroad, even when the need is pressing, and cannot be so quickly supplied within the empire. Cheaper foreign bids have been repeatedly rejected without consideration. On the other hand, English goods are given a preference in regions under the political control of England. In Egypt complaint has been made that the time-limits prescribed for furnishing goods are made extremely short, and that the interested English firms have been informed in advance of the forthcoming contracts. It was asserted that in the case of cement, for example, a particular brand has actually been specified, which of course can be furnished only by the particular firm intended.[1]

[1] Josef Grunzel, *Bericht über die wirtschaftlichen Verhältnisse Ägyptens* (Vienna, 1905), p. 104.

The extent to which these discriminating methods have developed is further shown by the fact that in the agreement regulating conditions in Morocco, express reference to them was made. The Acts of the Algeciras Conference of April 7, 1905, stipulated that the Moroccan Government in awarding public contracts shall grant fully equal consideration to European industry. In the Franco-German Moroccan treaty of November 4, 1911, the French Government further binds itself (Art. 6) ' to guarantee that contracts for labour and supplies which may be required for any construction of roads, railways, harbour improvements, telegraph lines, &c., shall be let to the bidder offering the most advantageous terms '.

According to the regulations in force in Austria regarding the purchase of supplies and hiring of labour for public purposes, foreign bids may not be considered unless disproportionately higher prices are demanded within the country. According to an official statement of the Minister of Commerce, a difference in price of eight per cent in favour of domestic bidders is to be regarded as corresponding to the necessary protection to domestic industry. On the occasion of contracts let abroad in the year 1912, for certain naval supplies, the industrial and commercial bodies made the demand that the same principles should be made applicable also to the expenditures of the authorities of the Dual Monarchy, as for example, the officials of the military establishment. They asked that a definite difference in price, reckoned on a percentage basis in favour of home industry, should be fixed, within the limits of which the letting of contracts abroad should be prohibited. They maintained that such an increased price was only a fair equivalent for the less advantageous conditions of production within the country.

In Hungary, public contracts are granted in principle to domestic industry exclusively, in so far as the goods are produced in the country. In the *Ausgleich* negotiations with Austria in the year 1893, a unified mutual equalization of position between the citizens and products of the two countries in connexion with such contracts was discussed, but no understanding could be reached. Certain general provisions for dividing the army contracts were agreed upon in view of the fact that the military establishment is a common institution of the two countries.[1]

Italy also has changed the regulations affecting public contracts so that domestic industry is favoured in comparison with foreign competition. The official figures for the value of supplies furnished to the Government for the five years 1906–11 are as follows : from Italy, 1,714,000,000 lire ; from abroad 507,400,000 lire ; of this total amount, the portion belonging to the fiscal year 1910–11 was 364,200,000 lire from Italy and 68,800,000 from abroad. It will be seen that while the ratio of the value of the public supplies obtained in Italy to that obtained abroad was seventy-seven per cent to twenty-three per cent on the average for the five-year period, it was eighty-four to sixteen per cent for the last year, which indicates a rapid movement toward excluding the foreign contractor.

In Roumania, the law of 1912 for the promotion of industries brought about a modification of the strict prohibition previously enforced. While the earlier laws had established the principle that in awarding contracts for supplies, the districts and communes should give preference under all circumstances to domestic products of the same character over foreign competitors, the new law provides that discrimination in favour of domestic enterprises is to be made only in case their bids are not more than five per cent higher.

According to Art. 37 of the Bulgarian Law of March 7/20, 1911, for the promotion of industry, all state, district, and commune authorities are required to procure from domestic industrial enterprises any articles needed by them, in so far as the articles in question are to be had and are produced

---

[1] Josef Grunzel, *Handelspolitik und Ausgleich in Oesterreich-Ungarn* (Vienna, 1912), p. 134.

within the country, even in case the price is five per cent above that of foreign goods. Article 40 stipulates that the uniforms to be provided by the authorities named must be made within the country and from fabrics and materials of domestic manufacture. The Ministry of Commerce and Agriculture is required by Art. 41 to prepare with the assistance of the industrial council and to keep revised to date a catalogue of the articles produced in the country and which fulfil the official requirements.

The Turkish Government submitted to the Parliament in 1909 the draft of a law for the promotion of industry, but it failed of passage. By Article 9 of the Bill, the Government was required in making purchases to give the preference to domestic industry, even when its prices should be fifteen per cent higher than those of foreign competitors.

Other Protective Measures. That numerous other means of administrative protection are still to be sought out is abundantly proved by the struggle of Hungary against the duty-free competition of Austrian industry. Thus in 1911 a gauging ordinance was passed which makes it practically impossible for the pressed-glass factories of Austria to furnish gauged receptacles to the Hungarian market. Factories located in Hungary are exempted from the gauging fee, and they possess the further advantage that they can furnish vessels already gauged, while the patrons of the Austrian factories must themselves assume the trouble and expense of the gauging process. A new law affecting instalment payments has effectively combated the sale of sewing-machines in Hungary on the instalment plan, and given a tremendous impetus to a domestic factory. Pressure is exerted on the retail sales-managers of the state tobacco monopoly not to handle cigarette-paper and playing-cards of Austrian manufacture, &c.[1]

---

[1] *Bericht über die Industrie, den Handel und die Verkehrsverhältnisse in Niederösterreich während des Jahres 1911.* Handels- und Gewerbekammer in Vienna, 1912, pp. 32, 89, 294, 296.

4. Protection by Concerted Popular Action

The Genesis of Protection by Concerted Action. The recognized means of protection by duties and the means, not recognized it is true, but none the less practised, of special freight-rate and administrative protection, can be utilized only by the government and legislation of a country, which in consequence becomes morally responsible before other nations. Measures of too arbitrary a character will eventually be met by retaliatory steps on the part of the foreign state affected, and hence their value will in general be lessened or destroyed. In recent years, however, protective measures have been more and more brought into play, which do not involve government and legislation, and may even be formally condemned by the latter. These arise from the modern principle of concerted popular action.

From the very origin of the nation as an economic organism, its economic policy has oscillated between two extremes, the absolute dominance of the state, and the freedom of the individual. Mercantilism demanded on the part of the state a minute regulation of the whole economic life, while the classical school, on the contrary, advocated the crassest individualism; socialism again came forward on behalf of unlimited state power, which, however, was no longer to be controlled by the possessing classes, but by the non-propertied masses. An intermediate position is, it is true, assumed by the various organizations, as well the obligatory ones which the state organizes for its aims, as free combinations which are developed on the initiative of individuals. Both classes have, in addition to their special shortcomings, the common defect that they are permanent organizations with a fixed programme. But the complexity of economic relations calls for a struggle between various groups and on shifting fronts. The antagonist of yesterday may be the ally of to-morrow. The final result is, of course, always a compromise, but an advantageous compromise is not to be expected without a previous struggle. For such purposes only a temporary combination is suitable, and for its establishment an informal agreement, even the coining and dissemination of a slogan embodying a general popular sentiment, is fully adequate. Thus came into being concerted popular action, which first developed in the relations between employer and employees and between the sellers and buyers of certain goods, but which gradually spread into international affairs also. It produces economic effects even when its immediate motive is of a non-economic (political or religious) character. In the present connexion, two principal forms are to be distinguished: it appears either as a boycott of foreign goods or as an effort to arouse the national consciousness. It will be seen that in the first case it is more aggressive than in the second, though the object is the same in both.

The Boycott of Foreign Goods. The boycott of foreign goods aims at the injury of a foreign country by preventing the marketing of its products. The concept of the boycott originated in the agrarian struggles in Ireland, and later found its most frequent application in European history in the conflicts between employers and employees. At present, it has become a weapon even in the field of foreign politics.

Turkey, for example, has in recent years repeatedly made use of the boycott on goods as a political weapon in her conflicts with European countries. After the annexation of Bosnia and Herzegovina, on October 8, 1908, this weapon was directed against Austria-Hungary. In the most important ports boycott committees were formed which agitated against Austrian merchants and goods. The stevedores (*Hammals*), who were organized in the form of guilds, refused to unload Austrian goods, and even threw them into the sea. In response to complaints on the part of the diplomatic representatives of Austria-Hungary in Constantinople, the Turkish Government promised indeed to take all possible means to suppress the boycott, but it did not in fact possess the power, and perhaps also not the inclination to fulfil the obligation. It was not ended until the formal agreement between the two governments was concluded on **February 26, 1909,** by the terms of which Turkey received a money indemnity and various considerations. In the year **1910–11** a boycott was instituted against Greek goods and ships on account of the Cretan question. Its effect was especially injurious to the commerce of Salonika. An immediate result was that shipping companies took advantage of the opportunity to increase freight charges, the pressure of Greek competition being removed. The exportation of Greek products was blocked or effected only at higher costs by way of Constantinople, where the boycott was less stringently enforced. Finally, during the **Tripolitan** War of **1911–12** Italian goods were boycotted, but the effect of the action was negligible.

In the course of the Balkan War, the Serbian Chamber of Commerce in Belgrade passed a resolution on April **10, 1913,** in which the intention was declared of placing Austrian and Hungarian goods under a boycott, in case Austria-Hungary did not modify her political policy of hostility to Serbia and Montenegro. An executive committee was appointed which was to elaborate the plan and take the necessary measures for its execution, but the occasion for carrying out the project did not materialize.

The harsh attitude of the United States of America against Chinese immigrants became the occasion of a boycott of American goods to China. On May **10, 1905,** such a resolution was adopted with great enthusiasm in Shanghai, and was communicated to all the ports. Firms which handled American goods were placed on the index. Orders in America were cancelled. All the stevedores refused to handle cargoes containing American goods. Newspapers refused American advertising, and even the theatres placed themselves in the service of the propaganda. In the summer the boycott became general, and its effects were even unpleasantly felt by the visiting American Secretary of State, Mr. Taft, in person. The financial damage to the United States was estimated at 100,000,000 francs; the moral effect consisted in a moderation of the discriminations against the Chinese.

Japan likewise responded to the measures taken by California in the year 1906 with a boycott on California fruits, hygienic grounds being alleged as a basis for the action. An understanding reached by the two governments, however, removed the occasion before the boycott became severe. In Russia, the denunciation of the American-Russian commercial treaty in the year 1912 was answered with a boycott. The agricultural congress of Kasan and other zemstvos decided to stop purchasing agricultural machinery of American manufacture.

In Hongkong in 1912, Chinese merchants boycotted English goods because the English street-railway company refused to accept as cash certain repudiated Chinese small coins, but the legislative council took its stand against the people. In Manila in 1912, Chinese traders boycotted Japanese goods to express their disapproval of the Japanese political aggressions in southern Manchuria.

In the recent political crisis the question of a French boycott of German goods was raised.[1]

The idea of the international boycott has also been proposed in connexion with the peace movement itself. In the World Peace Congress held at Ghent, September 22–28, 1912, the French delegate, Léon Bollack, pointed out that international treaties and arbitration treaties and arbitration awards require some guarantee, since at present there is no security that a state affected by such an action will conform to the terms of the award. To this end he proposed that the nations should bind themselves to punish any state for breach of international law in failing to comply with an arbitration treaty or arbitration award by a general economic boycott directed against the products of that country. At least the duty on the goods of such a country should be increased.

[1] Artur Dix, *Französischer Boycott, deutsche Abwehr.* Krefeld, 1913.

In the succeeding debates, however, attention was called to the impropriety of organizing an increase in protective duties in connexion with a development toward free trade as well as to the further injustice of penalizing private individuals for the guilt of a government, and finally to the fact that the neutral countries would also suffer. The result was that the measure failed of adoption. Again, a popular petition was addressed by certain pacifists to the nations represented in the third Hague Conference for the conclusion of treaties by which international conflicts should be avoided. In connexion with such treaties, according to the views of the petitioners, the nations should mutually obligate themselves

against any states or group of states which shall be guilty of breach of faith with regard to the world treaty, to erect protective duties which shall prevent the exportation of its mining, agricultural, and industrial products, to withhold credit from such nation or nations, &c., &c., in short to concertedly threaten them with a universal boycott.

It was thought that this supreme international political power created by the common action voluntarily taken by all free states would prove itself a reliable and effective preventive means, and especially that it would be one whose organization would cost nothing.

Protection by Appeal to the National Consciousness. The exclusion of foreign goods is more effective and permanent when it takes the form of a national movement directed toward increasing the economic efficiency of the home country and people. It is in this form that the concerted popular-action idea has most frequently been operative in international commerce.

For example, British India, where public sentiment is designated as ' overwhelmingly protectionist ',[1] in view of the impossibility of introducing protective duties, instituted in the year 1905 the swadeshi movement. (*Swa-deshi* means

[1] Pramathanath Banerjee, *A Study of Indian Economics* (London, 1911), p. 213.

' produced at home '.) The object of the movement was to develop in the purchasing public a preference for domestic manufactures, and in this way to build up the industries of the country. The weakness of the organization, however, which did not command any considerable financial resources, as well as various pacificatory precautionary measures of the government, prevented it from achieving any notable success.

In England, in recent years, numerous organizations have been formed varying widely in strength and significance, which carry on a propaganda for protectionistic ends, and which have become known under the general name of the ' All British ' movement. In March 1911, an ' All British ' shopping week was set apart by several societies, especially by the ' Union-Jack Industries League '. In the same year the ' All British Industries Association ' was founded, which by its motto, ' Buy British Empire manufactures and produce,' publicly announces its purpose of accomplishing in England results similar to those achieved by organizations of the same type in Canada and in the United States. Again, the ' British Empire League ' proposed the idea of a British Empire trade-mark which should designate and commend to the public all products of the British dominions. On April 20, 1910, the first steps were taken toward registration in accordance with Section 62 of the Trade Mark Act of 1905 ; but as the formation of a regular corporation was found necessary for this purpose, such an organization was effected after two great mass meetings (October 26, 1910, and March15, 1911) and chartered under the name of the ' British Empire Trade Mark Association '. The official representatives of the colonies (High Commissioners and Agents-General), about 130 chambers of commerce and several hundred business firms have joined the association. Its members receive in return for a yearly payment the right to affix the national trade mark to their goods, provided of course that the latter have in fact been produced in some part of the British Empire. For the determination of this question local committees were

appointed, though an appeal from their decisions to the
central committee in London is permitted. The mark is not
obligatory, and indicates the origin only, not the quality of
the goods. It includes a blank space for the addition of a
more specific designation of the part of the empire in which
the goods were produced, as ' Scotland ', ' Canada ', &c. In
addition, the usual trade-mark of the firm itself may be
affixed. The promoters of the movement proceed on the
assumption that large quantities of foreign goods are purchased in England merely from ignorance of the facts. Not
merely are the marks of British firms imitated by foreign
competitors, but a great number of foreign articles are given
a British designation after importation into England. This
deceives the purchaser as to their origin without involving
fraudulent procedure, as it is not illegal for a British firm
to place its name or mark on foreign goods. It is assumed
again that, under otherwise similar conditions as to quality
and price, British goods would be preferred to foreign. The
High Commissioner of Canada, Lord Strathcona, declared in
his memorandum : ' It is generally recognized that the
British public would on their merits give a common-sense
preference to British goods over similar competing foreign
goods, all things being equal, and it is absolutely necessary
to afford such buyers definite information by means of the
proposed mark to give this preference the full effect.' Opposition has not, to be sure, been wanting. The Chamber of
Commerce and many firms in Manchester declared that they
did not consider the adoption of the mark desirable in the
case of textile products. In some cases, too, misgivings as to
the results of placing English manufacturers on an equality
with those of the colonies seemed to have formed an obstacle.

The original inspiration for the whole idea came somewhat
strangely from a movement which was directed against
England. The Irish were endeavouring to establish a preference among their compatriots for Irish goods. The movement was set on foot by an exposition in Cork in the year

1902, on the basis of which the ' Cork Industrial Development Association ' was founded. At the ' All Ireland Industrial Conference ' held by the association in 1905, it was
decided to have registered a national trade-mark, which
should bear in Gaelic script the words ' made in Ireland ',
and should designate all goods of Irish production. The right
to use the mark is secured by payment of annual dues into
the treasury of the ' Irish Industrial Development Association ', a corporation organized for registering the mark. At
present about 550 business houses make use of the mark.
Independently of this movement, an analogous action was
undertaken in South Africa, by the ' South African International Union '.

III

PROTECTION AFFECTING COMMODITIES, BY POSITIVE MEASURES

1. BOUNTIES ON EXPORTS

Governmental Export Bounties. Direct expenditures of money on the part of a state to secure exportation of goods have never played a large rôle. They correspond, it is true, to the general ideas of mercantilism, which sought to improve the balance of trade and to favour the flow of money into a country by promoting exports as much as possible. The disordered condition of public finance was, however, an obstacle in the way of such action, so that even the greatest of mercantilistic statesmen, Colbert, could command only very moderate means for export bounties. The form of encouragement at that time was related in general to persons rather than to goods; bounties were attached, not to the value embodied in the products, but to the person of the enterpriser or to a trading company. As a result they consisted less in cash payments than in various privileges and exemptions, which, to be sure, under some circumstances possessed a high money value. The direct object, also, was not so much promotion of exportation as promotion of production, which in itself was expected to bring about an increase in exportation. Export bounties, therefore, represented mainly mere offshoots of production bounties.

The direct premium on exportation has become best known in the case of the grain bounties of England, which formed the subject of animated controversy in the classical literature of political economy.[1] In the year 1689, a bounty of five

---

[1] Adam Smith, *Wealth of Nations*, vol. iii, chaps. iv and v; David Ricardo, *Principles of Political Economy*, chap. xxii; Robert Malthus, *Principles of Population*, vol. iii, chap. ix.

shillings was placed on the exportation of wheat at a price not exceeding forty-eight shillings per (Winchester) quarter, while similar bounties were placed on the exportation of rye, barley, and malt within specified price limits. This system underwent successive alterations, and in fact became practically of no effect subsequent to the year 1766, as after that date the importation of grain became necessary. It was not finally repealed, however, until 1814. The bounties granted at the same period to the herring and whale fisheries partook more of the nature of production bounties. France, under Colbert, paid bounties on the silk culture as well as on various industrial enterprises ; these applications of the principle were again primarily bounties on production, but in some cases their amount was proportioned to exportation.[1] In Austria, Maria Theresa and Joseph II endeavoured to promote exportation by bounties.[2] In Germany, in spite of the mercantilistic aspirations of Frederick the Great, this point was never reached. A remnant of these ancient direct bounties on exports is found in the bounties still granted in France for the exportation of cured fish ; these, however, are combined with bounties on fisheries, and stand in an intimate relation to the navigation policy of the country. A reversion to the practice is occasionally found in oversea countries, predominantly in connexion with the products of tropical agriculture, and hence forming a counterpart to export duties. In 1910, e. g. Venezuela temporarily placed bounties on the exportation of sugar-cane products, various textile fibres, fruits, oil, and starch-containing substances, and also animal products. By the terms of the Australian Bounties Act of the year 1907, several production bounties are paid, and among them also one on combed wool and on silver when they are destined for exportation.

[1] A. des Tilleuls, *Histoire et régime de la grande industrie en France aux XVIIe et XVIIIe siècles*, Paris, 1898 ; W. Lexis, *Die französischen Ausfuhrprämien*, Bonn, 1870.

[2] Adolf Beer, *Die österreichische Handelspolitik unter Maria Theresia und Josef II* (Vienna, 1898), p. 29.

More recent governmental export bounties have originated unintentionally and unconsciously through the refund by the state, on occasion of the exportation of certain articles, of an amount for consumption tax or import duty greater than was in fact paid on the goods. The consumption taxes on food-stuffs (meat, bread, salt, sugar), beverages (beer, brandy, and wine), and various articles of use and enjoyment (petroleum, tobacco, matches, &c.), are finally borne by the consumer, but on account of the minute subdivision of their consumption they are collected not from the consumer but from the producer or dealer. In order to facilitate control and to reduce the cost of administration the raw material before transformation, or some more easily taxable intermediate product, or even a typical device used in the manufacture, has frequently been chosen as the basis of taxation. On exportation, however, the tax paid for the raw material or partly manufactured product had to be repaid on the basis of the finished goods. In consequence it became the difficult task of legislation to establish an equitable equivalence between the basis of taxation and that of restitution. But even in case this was successfully done, the natural endeavour on the part of the spirit of technical invention would be to increase the proportion of the finished product by improving the manufacturing plant, by the installation of more efficient machinery and apparatus, the utilization of by-products, &c. With every increase in the actual ratio of quantity of product to the taxation basis over that presumed in the law, a larger amount would be refunded on exportation than had been paid in taxes.

In an entirely analogous way, a difference may arise between the amount of import duty paid and the amount refunded as a drawback on exportation when the imported goods have in the meantime undergone elaboration within the country. In this case, however, there lurked a second possibility for concealed export bounties in view of the difficulty of proving identity, since in the finished manufacture on exportation the quantity and character of the raw material subject to duty which had been utilized in its production could no longer be determined with certainty. As a means of avoiding this difficulty, drawbacks on exportation independent of any proof of importation were adopted as a substitute for the refunding of duties paid. In the law of April 29, 1816, France introduced such specified exportation drawbacks applicable to refined sugar and to cotton goods; the law of June 7, 1820, applied the same principle to woollen goods, and it was later extended to other less important articles. Such drawbacks became true export bounties when importation at a reduced rate of duty was permitted, or when raw material produced in the home country, e.g. raw sugar from the colonies, was subjected to a more moderate duty than that from foreign countries. Furthermore, a domestic beet-sugar industry arose, the products of which received a drawback without ever having paid any duty. The attempt was now made to restore the original character of the export drawback by requiring the presentation of a receipt for duties previously paid. At first the receipt was made out in the name of the importer, and the refund was payable only to him; it was often provided in addition that exportation should take place by way of the same custom-house which had passed the raw material on importation. The exporting manufacturer, however, often finds it advantageous to procure his raw material from a domestic dealer and not direct from abroad, and, moreover, the most convenient custom-house for the importation of the material is not always the most advantageous for exporting the finished product. In consequence, these formal requirements were later abandoned. The customs receipts were made out in blank, and soon became pure negotiable instruments which could be freely dealt in. The importer sold his receipts on the exchange, receiving for them a lower or higher price according to the conditions of export trade, and the goods purchased of him were in fact relieved in large part of the burden of the duty.

The exporter, however, could work up domestic raw material also, and on exportation receive as a virtual export bounty the difference between the customs drawback paid to him and the price which he paid for the customs receipt. The producers of the region exposed to competition from imports now entered complaints on the evasion of the duty, while the consumers of the exporting district similarly complained of the increase in the price of the goods by the amount of the duty and the export bounty. These export drawbacks were first applied in France in the year 1822 to sugar, and later to soap, leather, copper, brass, lead, straw hats, &c. ; they fell away in the free trade period of the 'sixties as a result of the dropping of protective duties, or were replaced by the method of manufacture in bond. In England similar export reimbursements were applicable to wine, currants, and silk.

In modern commercial policy there are two methods of relieving goods of import duties on re-exportation. The first is that of the 'drawback', in which the duty is regularly paid on importation and refunded on re-exportation. The other is that of manufacture in bond, where the duty is condition-ally credited on importation, and later written off on re-exportation of the goods. Either proof of identity of the imported and exported articles may be required, or a rate of equivalence established on the basis of an assumed utiliza-tion factor. If the proof of identity is waived in this manner, customs drawbacks and manufacture in bond may experience an extraordinary development through the use of so-called importation permits or certificates. These reverse the techni-cal order of procedure. The exportation of the goods is taken as the starting-point, the exporter receiving permission to import at will, and duty-free, the same quantity of the same commodity or a corresponding quantity of the raw material or part-manufactures worked up in the exported product. If these certificates are made freely negotiable, they may become the basis of an extensive speculative trade. The relations of the various methods of procedure may be represented by the following scheme :—

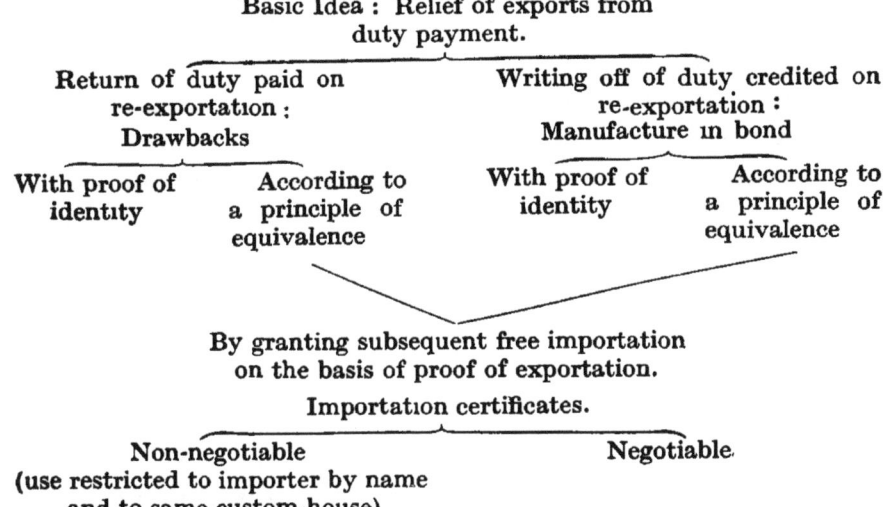

Basic Idea : Relief of exports from duty payment.

Return of duty paid on re-exportation : Drawbacks

Writing off of duty credited on re-exportation : Manufacture in bond

With proof of identity

According to a principle of equivalence

With proof of identity

According to a principle of equivalence

By granting subsequent free importation on the basis of proof of exportation.

Importation certificates.

Non-negotiable (use restricted to importer by name and to same custom-house).

Negotiable.

Manufacture in bond and drawbacks may in themselves lead to export bounties when strict proof of identity is not required. Thus the ratio of utilization may be fixed in such a way that the producer receives more as a drawback on the exportation of his manufactured product than he has in reality paid in duties on the foreign raw material. The provisions for proof of importation may be drawn so liberally that under certain conditions the drawback may also be secured on domestic material which has paid no duty. It is further possible that finer qualities of raw material may be imported for domestic consumption, while for exportation poorer qualities produced at home are worked up. For example, the United States of America refunds on exportation the duties, less one per cent, paid on any foreign raw material contained in the exported goods, but requires only a sworn affidavit of the exporter as proof of the fact in question. By the royal decree of February 27, 1896, Italy grants restitution of the duty on exportation of cotton yarns and fabrics ; but as the duty is but three lire per 100 kilograms while the amount of the drawback is four lire per 100 kilograms in the case of yarns, and four and a half in the case of fabrics, and in addition the tax provisions are very liberally administered, an export bounty is the result. A similar situation obtains in Russia, where, on the exportation of certain cotton and woollen manufactures, a drawback at fixed rates is paid for the duty on machinery and raw material used in their manufacture, the payment taking the form of an issue of receipts which are accepted in payment of duties on raw cotton and wool.

An export bounty appears most frequently in case of negotiable certificates of importation, and may in fact make its appearance in two different ways. In the first place, that part of domestic production which comes from the home district most favourably situated commercially and geographically with respect to a foreign market region can be more effectively exported because of the fact that on exportation the producer can sell his export certificate for the approximate amount of the import duty in another part of the country where an import demand for the goods exists; but this import demand will again be increased because the producing region best situated for exportation can now compete on the foreign market under conditions more favourable than it previously could in the more remote domestic markets. In this case the industry will at once be assured of a domestic price profiting by the full amount of the tariff protection, i.e. (neglecting freight-charges) a price equal to that in the world-market plus the duty, while the exporting district will receive the same price, viz. the price in the world-market on the sale of the goods, and an amount approximately equal to the duty from the disposal of the importation certificate. An export premium may also result when the quality of the imported raw material or part manufactures is better than the quality of the material put into the exported final product, since similarity in quality is still harder to verify than equality in amount. This import certificate system first reached an extensive development in France in the course of the nineteenth century in the case of cereals and iron; it was later taken over by Germany for grain, and in recent years has found ardent advocates in Austria-Hungary.

Sugar Bounties. The most important group of export bounties which have arisen out of duty refunds is formed by the sugar bounties. The growth of the European beet-sugar manufacture in the first half of the nineteenth century cheapened sugar into an object of popular consumption, and led the producing countries to introduce consumption taxes (France, 1837; Germany, 1841; Belgium, 1843, Austria-Hungary, 1849; &c.). But on account of the difficulty and expense of administration the tax was laid, not on the raw sugar, but on the beets or the sap on the basis of an assumed percentage of yield. But the percentage of yield assumed in the law could not always correspond with the actual ratio, as the sugar content of the beets varies from place to place and from time to time, and is subject to change by every technical improvement in the industry. In this way a factory using better beets or more efficient appliances would at once receive a concealed production bounty.[1] The French law of July 24, 1884, placed a tax of fifty francs on each quintal of refined sugar, assuming a yield of six per cent under the diffusion process. A factory which in fact secured only six quintals of sugar from 100 quintals of beets would therefore pay a tax of 300 francs, while a factory which obtained ten quintals of sugar would pay the same amount; in the first case, the burden of the tax would be the intended amount of fifty francs, while in the second case it would be equivalent only to a tax of thirty francs, so that in comparison with the first factory the second would even here receive a production bounty of twenty francs. But on exportation the tax paid had to be refunded in order not to reduce the power of the product to compete in the world-market, and since the tax was computed on the basis of the raw material or

[1] Grunzel, *System der Handelspolitik*, second edition (Leipsic, 1906), p. 509.

half-manufacture, and the reimbursement on the basis of the finished product, there arose in addition an export bounty to the amount of the difference between the actual yield ratio and that assumed in the law. All these bounties, moreover, were unequal for the different factories, and therefore unjust, although they furnished a powerful spur to technical improvement as their amount varied with the efficiency of the plant. These provisions resulted in a considerable loss of customs receipts to the state, but could not be repealed with impunity as they had become essential to the existence of an extensive industry, and one of great importance for agriculture. It was decided, however, in the interest of juster distribution, to introduce direct export-bounties in place of the indirect, and this was done by Austria-Hungary in 1888, by Germany in 1891, and, in part, by France in 1897. In Russia an indirect export-bounty arose in the same way and became more or less a fixed institution in the course of the later period in connexion with the growth of a Kartell system. The Russian government, by means of a Kartell system, controlled by the minister of finance, fixed specific amounts to be produced by the several concerns for domestic consumption under the ordinary rate of taxation of 1·75 roubles per pood. Any sugar produced beyond the amount thus specified must either pay an additional tax of 1·75 roubles per pood or be exported. By the aid of this organization of the production and the high import-duty (four roubles per pood), the ministry of finance has succeeded in raising the domestic price to a point—from 4·15 roubles per pood upward on January 1, 1912—that the industry is very profitable. A Russian sugar factory will therefore endeavour to secure the allotment of as large a percentage as possible of the production for the home market, and hence will increase its production by every available means, since the division of the production for the home market among the several factories is made on the basis of their average output. Production, however, can be increased only by exportation, which as a result may be carried on at a loss in view of the high domestic prices. These high domestic prices maintained by combination and by duty obviously represent an indirect export-bounty.

The sugar bounties have led to increased consumption in the countries where the product is marketed, but also to the destruction of the sugar industry in those countries. The idea originated in England of neutralizing the effect of export bounties by levying compensatory duties on sugar subject to them. A Parliamentary investigating commission appointed in the year 1879 proposed such ' countervailing duties ' in its report of August 1880, but the English Government took no corresponding action as it held fast to free-trade principles and did not wish to injure the interests of the consumers, and, moreover, regarded the collection of duties at different rates according to the country of origin of the goods as a breach of the most-favoured-nation provisions of existing commercial treaties. In the United States of America, however, the tariff law of August 27, 1894 (the Wilson Bill), in addition to a duty of forty per cent *ad valorem*, placed a uniform super-tax of one-tenth of a cent on each pound of imported sugar which had enjoyed in the producing country either a direct or an indirect bounty. The Dingley Bill of July 24, 1897, fixed the equalizing duty at the amount of the bounty granted by the producing country, which amount was to be determined for this purpose by the Secretary of the Treasury of the United States. India, under the law of March 20, 1899, went still farther in the collection of such equalizing duties.

Although duties of this character unquestionably produced the result that on importation into the consuming country the bounty paid on the sugar in the producing country was taken off, and hence that the producing country paid the bounties not to its own industries but to the foreign customs agents, yet they did not break up the practice of giving the bounties, but only changed the marketing points for the beet-sugar produced. The attempts to do away with

1569.14   P

the sugar bounties by means of international agreement likewise met with little immediate success. Negotiations and conferences repeatedly entered into from 1864 on, between the European nations concerned, were without result. The International Sugar Conference held in Brussels in December 1901 also failed to get beyond academic pronouncements, until suddenly England issued a declaration that equalizing duties would be introduced unless some agreement were reached for the removal of the bounties and moderation of the excessive import duties on sugar. Under this pressure from England, the most important sugar-market, the Brussels Sugar Convention was finally signed on March 5, 1902. The states party to the treaty assumed in it three essential obligations, as follows : First, to remove all direct and indirect production and export bounties on sugar ; second, to reduce the import duty exclusive of the consumption tax (the so-called super-tax) to the moderate level of six francs per hundred kilograms of refined sugar, and 5·50 francs for other grades ; third, to levy upon sugar coming from a country not a party to the Convention an equalizing duty equal to any bounty granted in that country. The enforcement of the Convention was placed in the hands of a standing commission in Brussels, and it was to remain in force in the first instance for five years from September 1, 1903. England, which had aimed by its action to quiet the complaints of the colonies over the injury to their raw-sugar industries, was soon confronted with a violent opposition on the part of the sugar-using manufacturers (chocolate, marmalade, and cake industries) who, by the aid of the extraordinarily cheap sugar, had captured the markets of the world, and the intention was soon formed of denouncing the treaty. It is true that England finally concurred in the extension of the period of the Convention for a further five years, signed August 28, 1907, but only on condition of being freed from the obligation to collect equalizing duties on sugar upon which bounties had been paid. Russia, which had not been a party to the original Convention, now joined in the agreement, but also received an exceptional position. It was permitted to retain its customs and tax legislation which produced an indirect bounty, but was allowed to export over the western frontier only one million tons in the six years from September 1, 1907, to August 31, 1913. Exportation to Finland, to Persia (both by way of the Caspian Sea and across the land frontier), as well as to other adjacent Asiatic countries with the exception of Asiatic Turkey, remained unrestricted. On March 17, 1912, the Sugar Convention was again extended for five years, or until August 31, 1918, but the demand of Russia for an increase in the amount that might be exported was granted, and further, England and Italy no longer joined in the agreement.

Although the fate of the Brussels Sugar Convention has thus become somewhat uncertain, there is little probability that the bounty system will ever be restored to the former extent ; it would be a financial burden to the state, and moreover such measures are not popular in modern representative legislative bodies. The following summary gives a general view of the present situation in this field :

Belgium, Germany, France, Holland, Austria-Hungary, and Switzerland are bound by the Brussels Sugar Convention concluded on March 5, 1902, and extended August 28, 1907, and March 17, 1912, to the removal of the direct and indirect bounties formerly subsisting.

Sweden has joined in the Brussels Sugar Convention, but may retain its tariff and tax system favouring the industry so long as it does not export.

Italy joined in the Brussels Convention under the same conditions as Sweden, but withdrew in the year 1912.

Great Britain subscribed to the Brussels Convention with certain reservations, but withdrew in the year 1912.

Russia joined in the Brussels Convention when it was renewed in 1907, but occupies a special position, as it is allowed to maintain the export duties arising from its tariff and Kartell system, but is limited as to sugar exportation toward the West.

Denmark does not subscribe to the Brussels Convention, but, according to the decision of the Brussels Commission in 1912, it is no longer to be regarded as a bounty-paying country.

Spain grants export bounties which, according to the determinations of the Brussels Commission, amount to 19·75 francs per 100 kilograms for raw, and 19·50 francs for refined, sugar.

Roumania pays export bounties which, according to the determination of the Brussels Commission, amount to 22·50 francs per 100 kilograms on refined, and 17·75 francs on raw, sugar.

Japan pays a bounty on crystallized sugar amounting, according to the Brussels Commission, to 2·61 francs per 100 kilograms.

The United States of America does not subscribe to the Brussels Convention, but collects special duties to the amount of the export bounty from sugar from the old bounty-paying countries.

Bounties on Distilled Liquors. Another group of government export bounties which have grown up in connexion with customs drawbacks are those on distilled liquors. These have not, to be sure, achieved by any means the significance of the sugar bounties, for the reason that the manufacture of spirits from the very beginning sought and found its equilibrium in the world-market. Of the spirits production of the world, amounting to between 3,500,000,000 and 4,080,000,000 litres, only from fifty to sixty million litres enter into international commerce. This limitation, again, is a consequence of the intimate relation between brandy distillation and agriculture. The raw material originally preferred was that in which alcohol already occurs, i. e. wine, and it was not until later that use was made of starch-containing substances, among which, again, first place was soon taken by potatoes—the most advantageous crop for the poorer and lighter soils hardly adapted to any other culture. The manufacture itself offers the advantage that on account of the favourable relation between bulk and value, the product may be transported to great distances, and hence its production makes possible an expansion of the productive activity of regions remote from the world-trade and carrying on an extensive agriculture. In addition, alcohol removes no fertility from the soil, so that all the valuable elements can be restored to the land in the by-product, the distillery slop forming an especially valuable stock-feed and an excellent fertilizer. Most countries have therefore excluded importation of spirits by enormously high duties, besides which, the three most important exporting countries have taken legislative measures to combat over-production. Germany, in the law of June 24, 1887, introduced an allotment system permitting only a limited quantity distributed among the different distilleries, to be produced at the minimum rate of the consumption tax, of formerly fifty, now 105 marks per hectolitre; any further amount was subject to a higher rate of seventy, now 125 marks. Another measure aiming at the same result is an auxiliary tax, the so-called ' establishment impost' (*Betriebsauflage*), which is graduated according to the size of the distillery and is subject to increase in case the average amount distilled according to a specified process is exceeded. These examples were followed by Austria-Hungary, where the consumption tax is likewise divided into two rates, one for an allotted amount (fixed by the law of June 8, 1901, at 90 kronen per hectolitre of pure alcohol), and another rate (110 kronen) for any further amount. In Russia, the law of June 6, 1894, which inaugurated the fiscal monopoly of the spirit trade, was unfavourable to exportation, which has almost ceased. France and England, on the other hand, are prevailingly exporters of distilled liquors (cognac and the like).

The necessity of collecting the intended consumption tax at the beginning or during the course of the process of production was more conspicuous in the case of the distillation of spirits than in the beet-sugar industry, as distilling, on account of its closer connexion with agriculture, was largely divided-up and scattered among small establishments. Not until the most recent legislation has the principle of levying the consumption tax on the finished product finally achieved exclusive application. Formerly the principal emphasis was laid on those methods of taxation which fixed upon the raw material or some intermediate product, especially the malt liquor, or upon the capacity of the productive establishment, i. e. the cubic contents of the vats (*Maischraumsteuer*) or the distilling apparatus (still tax) as a basis. In this way the possibility of indirect production-bounties would have been present, as in the case of the sugar industry. Such bounties arose, too, but not, as with sugar, in favour of the most efficient plants, but, on the contrary, to the advantage of the small establishments. Legislation designedly favoured in an extraordinary degree the small agricultural distilleries which work up potatoes or grain of home production and carry back to the land, either as stock feed or as fertilizer, the residues of the distillation process. In Germany the farm distilleries remained subject to the vat tax even after the introduction of the consumption tax; their payments were measured by the cubic contents of the mash-tub (1·31 marks per hectolitre and for each course of operations), and hence a premium was placed on the efficient utilization of the space and the use of materials with the largest possible starch content. Fruit distilleries paid also a material tax of 0·25 marks per hectolitre in the case of fruit skins, 0·35 for stone fruits, 0·45 for berries, 0·50 for brewery refuse, and 0·85 for stone fruits and wine; this also placed a premium on intensive utilization. The new Imperial law of July 15, 1909, has indeed discarded these special taxes, but it provides for reductions in the consumption tax for the smaller distilleries. In Austria-Hungary the smaller farm distilleries which use starchy material, and also those utilizing wine refuse, fruit, and the like, pay a production tax which is nominally equal to the lower rate required from other distilleries (90 kronen per hectolitre of alcohol), but which is adjusted according to a lump-sum provision based on the capacity of the distilling appliance, or is compounded according to an estimate of the probable amount of production. In addition, the agricultural distilleries are favoured in the distribution of the allotments subject to minimum tax and receive bonuses of six, eight, and ten kronen per hectolitre of pure alcohol within the allotment, and of 2·4 and six kronen when exceeding it.   In France, home distillers (*bouilleurs de cru*) who distil spirits in small quantities from raw materials produced by themselves have always enjoyed freedom from taxation.   In Russia, the brandy tax which was introduced in 1863 has since been increased from four to eleven kopecks per wedrograd (12·3 litres per cent), and which is still in force in that part of Russia not covered by the monopoly, is collected on the basis of the raw material, on the assumption of a specified normal production constant for each kind of material used—grain, potatoes, molasses, &c.   The excess distillate (*Überbrand*) remained tax-free down to the year 1890, as a compensation for which the agricultural distilleries were granted tax-exemption on from one-half to four per cent of their spirits production according to the amount produced.

On exportation of taxed spirits, the custom is to refund the amount of the tax.   When the tax was levied on a basis of the raw material, an intermediate product, or the productive establishment, an indirect export-bounty usually arose in connexion with the drawback, which of course can only be made according to the finished product.   This bounty never achieved the significance of the sugar bounty, for the reason that it hardly sufficed to offset the enormous import duties in the purchasing countries.   The duty amounts in Germany to 160 marks per hundred kilograms of cask brandy ; in Austria-Hungary, to 110 kronen ; in France, to 70 francs, to which, however, a high municipal impost must be added; in Great Britain, to 10s. 4d. per gallon of proof spirit; in Italy, to 180 lire per 100 kilograms, with various special imposts; in Sweden, to 100 kronen; in Norway, to from 265 to 280 kronen, &c. The indirect export-bounty which was paid in Germany in the days of the mash-vat tax was determined by the actual duty imposed of 9·95 to 13·63 marks per hectolitre of pure alcohol, and the drawback on exportation amounting to sixteen marks per hectolitre. Indirect export-bounties subsist also in Austria-Hungary and Italy. In the law of May 2, 1894, Russia changed to the system of direct bounties, reimbursing the tax, and in addition paying a bounty of three and one-half per cent of the spirits tax and five per cent in case of pure spirits of at least ninety-five degrees proof, and even then was unable to make good the loss of the valuable Spanish market. Germany pays a direct export bounty, the rate of which is annually determined by the Bundesrat, and which usually amounts to five or six marks per hectolitre of alcohol. Austria-Hungary pays a similar bounty of ten kronen per hectolitre. Great Britain refunds the tax on exportation, and in case of plain spirits, spirits in imitation of wine, and distilled liquors denatured with wood spirit, the amount paid is threepence per gallon normal strength, and in case of rectified spirits fivepence per gallon. The United States of America regarded this as an export bounty, and on January 21, 1911, placed a special extra duty on British distilled liquors, but these were later removed, as the American Secretary of the Treasury declared himself convinced that no bounty was contained in the payment. The determination of the facts as to whether an indirect export-bounty is paid, and its amount, is peculiarly difficult in the case of distilled liquors.

The 'Titres d'acquits à caution' in France. The importation certificates system first came into general use in France in connexion with grain. The business of manufacture in bond which had been carried on since 1828 was facilitated in the

edicts of January 14 and June 1, 1850, by the elimination
of the requirement of proof of identity and of the limitation
requiring exportation to take place through the same customs
office. The ratio of product to material was fixed according
to grade at 90, 80, and 70 kilograms of flour per 100 kilograms
of wheat. The period of manufacture was fixed for the time
being at twenty days, but was extended to three months by
the edict of August 25, 1861. The southern provinces dependent upon the importation of grain now secured their imports
duty-free through sale of the certificates in the flour-exporting
north. When the harvests were bad and the importations
large, the millers secured the lion's share of the bounty, while
under the reverse conditions, when the amount of importation was small, the grain traders in the south raised the price
on the certificates. The landlords in the south soon began
to complain that they were not sufficiently protected against
the growing oversea competition resulting from the lowered
duties on imports, while some foreign countries also, especially
the Belgian government, protested against this form of export
bounties. As a result, the edict of October 18, 1873, restored
the provision that the importation of grain should take place
through the same customs-office by which the corresponding
exportation of flour had gone. The new regulation did not
impede the phenomenal development of the Marseilles milling
industry, which immediately took advantage of the provision for manufacture in bond (*admission temporaire*), imported foreign grain and exported the flour manufactured
from it to the near eastern countries, Egypt and Turkey. In
the year 1909 the wheat importation of Marseilles amounted
to 4,400,000 quintals, of which 3,400,000 quintals were re-
exported in the form of flour, grits, pastry, crackers, and
starch. In recent years the trade in import certificates has
again been admitted. At present the millers in the north
export flour made from domestic grain and sell the import
certificates in Marseilles, where flour made from foreign grain
can be advantageously sold at home.

The *titres d'acquits à caution* have played an important rôle in the iron industry also since the requirement of proof of identity was dropped in the edict of September 8, 1851. The southern and western iron and steel works carry on a flourishing export trade in goods manufactured from domestic iron, while the northern works import the higher quality English pig-iron. This procedure led to complaint on the part of Germany, and the edicts of January 9, 1870, and January 24, 1888, introduced restrictions prescribing the transportation of the imported iron to the plant which desired to claim the drawback and which was to effect the manufacture (*obligation du convoyage à l'usine*); the new regulation brought to an end the commerce in iron certificates.

Import Certificates in the German Grain Trade. The above-described effects of the traffic in import certificates have been especially conspicuous in Germany also. Different districts within the country are interested in the commerce in grain in very different ways. The north-eastern Prussian provinces produce a surplus which, by the aid of cheap freights by water, they can market more advantageously in England than in the more remote consumption centres of Germany, while Russia and Austria-Hungary afford a more convenient source of supply for the industrial sections of middle and southern Germany. In the years 1887 and 1888, therefore, the landlords began agitating a demand for the issue of import certificates; in view of the fact that the question related to an extension of elaborative industry, they demanded abolition of the requirement for proof of identity. In the law of April 14, 1894, the desired change was introduced, and it has been retained in the latest tariff law of December 25, 1902. By the terms of the law, on the exportation of wheat, rye, spelt, oats, buckwheat, legumes, hops, rape, and beet-seed, and when the amount exported is at least 500 kilograms, certificates are issued which entitle the holder to import duty-free a corresponding quantity of the same commodity within an interval to be fixed by the Bundesrat, but in no case to exceed six months. As a further extension of this traffic, the proprietors of grinding and roller mills, to whom the privileges of manufacture in bond had already been granted in the tariff law of July 15, 1879, and also the proprietors of oil-mills, likewise received permission to use import certificates. They were given the certificates on exportation of manufactured goods produced by themselves within the customs domain, issued on the basis of the amount of raw material embodied in the products, and subject to the provision that this amount must be not less than 500 kilograms. The yield-ratio fixed in the exportation requirements is in the case of rye-flour seventy-five per cent, of barley-malt seventy-five per cent, and of wheat-malt seventy-eight per cent. The Bundesrat was further authorized to permit the acceptance of these import certificates in payment for duties on goods other than grains and legumes, and the permission was in fact granted in the case of a series of articles subject to purely revenue duties, including coffee, cocoa, tea, spices, tropical fruits, olives, rice, herring, petroleum, &c. The first limitation was imposed by a ruling of the Bundesrat on November 9, 1911, reducing the term of validity of the certificates from six to three months, and restricting their acceptability in place of cash in duty-payments to grains, legumes, rape, and rapeseed. These import-certificates were extensively employed in grain exportation, but in the case of flour the older provisions for manufacture in bond were found preferable. The immediate effect was that the prices of grain in those parts of the country which depend on exportation for their market and which formerly had to contend with depressed prices, rose to a point higher than the general world-market price by approximately the amount of the import duty. As a result, an equalization in grain prices within the German customs domain has come about, as in the exporting districts also the domestic price could now rise to the height of the world-market price plus the amount of the duty.

Private Export Bounties. While the governmental export bounties serve in the first instance for capturing foreign markets, in the case of private bounties exportation appears merely as an auxiliary regulating medium for the development of the domestic market. Those branches of production which have not from the beginning specialized for trade on the world-market will naturally prefer to dispose of their goods on the more accessible, better known, and heavily protected home market ; yet they will not be able to dispense with exportation if they expect to free themselves from danger of loss on account of the inevitable changes in the business situation without contracting production and dismissing employés. The larger the establishment, the more urgent is the requirement for continuous operation at full capacity. The foreign price, however, will usually be lower than the domestic price, as the most favourably situated producers meet on the world-market under conditions of free competition and sell their surplus product, even at a loss. It is true that in the discussions in regard to the German combinations (*Kartelle*) it has been brought out that at one time the prices obtained for coal in Belgium and Holland were higher than the syndicate prices at home, but such cases could not arise except under a very unusual and temporary concurrence of circumstances. If a producer wishes to sell unmarketable goods abroad in order to keep his plant fully occupied, he must bear the sacrifice of the difference in price. As an individual, he will usually be indisposed to this action unless the sacrifice amounts to less than his profit. But in case of an agreement or organization including the entire body of home competitors, he will take a much more deliberate and positive stand. Such agreements were already at hand in the earliest historic development of large-scale production. Thus, for example, as early as the beginning of the nineteenth century, the English cotton spinners sold at a loss on the Continent large quantities of yarn in order to cut off in its inception the competing industry there growing up. Adam Smith mentions the case [1] of an agreement among the manufacturers, who paid an export bounty out of their own pockets, and by getting rid of a part of their product, doubled the price of the remainder on the domestic market. The full development of the private export-bounty was, however, first achieved under the modern trade agreement and industrial combinations, which is to say, in connexion with organizations aiming at the substitution of a regulated for the normal free competition. Export bounties form one of the means of such regulation.

We distinguish two sorts of private export-bounties. The first variety immediately serves the purposes of the trust; the organization gives encouragement to the members themselves for the exportation of the commodity which the organization seeks to control, in order to relieve the domestic market of surplus goods and their price-depressing effects. The second variety serves the same ends indirectly; not the members of the combine, but domestic establishments using its products in their own elaborative processes, are given concessions for the purchase of the regulated commodity, with the object of increasing the competitive power of their product in the world-market. In both cases, the essential point is the unloading of the goods of the combine abroad, in the first instance in the crude state, through the agency of the members of the combine; in the second instance, in a further elaborated condition, through the agency of domestic purchasers. While it is true that from the national-economy standpoint it is certainly more advantageous to export completely manufactured than partly manufactured goods, since the important point in exportation is not the material value, but the labour value of the product, yet, from the private-economy point of view of

---

[1] *Wealth of Nations*, Book IV, chap. v.

the combine itself, the distinction between the two modes of procedure is purely formal, as the object in both cases is merely to unload its own surplus product. In consequence, the management of the combine itself commonly draws no distinction between the two varieties of export bounties. As a further result, the attempts made in the literature of the subject [1] to make a sharp division between export bounties and export drawbacks are not to be regarded as successful. The analogy with the similar favours granted by governments does not hold, since it is not that a previously levied impost (duty or tax) is refunded, but merely that a contribution is made for the equalization of a price-difference arising from a complicated set of circumstances. Nor is the character of the payment changed when the trust-controlled product is disposed of in a transformed and improved condition instead of in its original form.

The direct export-bounty represents for the member of the combine a cash payment computed on the basis of the quantity of the controlled goods exported, while for the manufacturer who buys the goods for further elaboration it represents a price concession in their purchase. The necessary means are collected by a contribution levied on the members of the combine on the basis of the extent of their operations. Exportation is facilitated and promoted in this way, since the sacrifice of profit or actual loss incurred by the exporting establishment is distributed throughout the group of competitors; yet, as a matter of fact, the amount of the bounty, as was repeatedly shown in connexion with the German Kartell investigation, always falls short of the actual difference between the domestic and the foreign price. Moreover, it is not a constant payment, as in the case of the governmental bounty, since their price-difference is not

---

[1] See Trescher, in *Kartellrundschau* for 1907, nos. 2 & 3 ; Fritz Diepenhorst, *Die handelspolitische Bedeutung der Ausfuhrunterstützungen der Kartelle* (Leipsic, 1908), p. 7.

uniform, but decreases with every improvement in the domestic market, and usually disappears entirely in periods of great prosperity. In the German iron industry, e. g., no export bounties were paid at the times of culmination of improvement in conditions in the years 1899 and 1906, but in the following periods of depression they were again introduced. The amount of the bounty also commonly changes in accordance with conditions: with the Rhenish-Westphalian Coal Syndicate the amount paid in 1896 was ten per cent, while at the high point of business conditions in 1900 it sank to three per cent, to rise again to six per cent in October 1901. A bounty will be paid to establishments using the trust products for further manufacture, i. e. to its domestic customers, only on condition that the resulting finished product is to be exported. In this connexion it may happen that such exportation again takes place, not immediately, but through the medium of still another elaborative industry, in which case the bounty received must be passed along, and may even be increased by a new bounty paid by an intermediate industry. Thus a chain of bounties following one another in regular succession has grown up in German industry. The coal and coke trusts paid an export bounty on each ton of pig-iron exported. The ore and pig-iron trusts paid bounties—partly in combination with the coal trust—on the exportation of half manufactures, and the combine controlling these products, with the aid of their predecessors in the production process, encouraged the exportation of wire-rods. The wire-rod works passed along the support received to the wire-nail factories, &c.

An indirect export-bounty arises spontaneously from the mutual interaction of trade combines and protective duties. This case has become famous under the catch-word of the 'dumping system', and may be explained as follows: Let us assume that the normal production of a certain commodity, sufficient fully to supply the home demand, amounts to

100,000,000 quintals, and let us further place the production costs at forty and the normal domestic selling-price at fifty marks per quintal. Under normal market conditions the account will stand as follows :

	M.
Selling-price of 1,000,000 quintals at 50 M. . . .	50,000,000
Production costs of 1,000,000 quintals at 40 M. . . .	40,000,000
Resulting profit	10,000,000

Now let us suppose an over-production of ten per cent. which depresses the domestic price to the cost of production. We shall then have :

	M.
Selling-price of 1,100,000 quintals at 40 M. . . .	44,000,000
Production cost of 1,100,000 quintals at 40 M. . . .	44,000,000
Resulting profit—Nothing.	

If, now, by concerted action the surplus product of 100,000 quintals can be sold abroad at a loss at a price of thirty marks (ten marks under the cost of production), only 1,000,000 quintals will be placed on the domestic market, and as a result the normal selling price will be obtained. The balance-sheet will now appear as follows :

	M.
Selling-price of 1,000,000 quintals in the home country at 50 M.	50,000,000
Selling-price of 100,000 quintals abroad at 30 M. . .	3,000,000
Total yield	53,000,000
Production cost of 1,100,000 quintals at 40 M. . .	44,000,000
Profit	9,000,000

In connexion with the German Kartell investigation it was brought out that the pig-iron syndicate had for years maintained the German prices for pig-iron higher than the English prices by the amount of the duty (ten marks) plus the freight from England to the Rhine district (from ten to twelve marks), or about twenty marks per ton on the whole.

Some foreign and domestic selling prices of coal and coke are shown in the following table :

GERMAN AND FOREIGN SELLING PRICES OF GERMAN COAL AND COKE

Year.	Coal.			Coke.		
	Marks per Ton.		Difference in %.	Marks per Ton.		Difference in %.
	Inland.	Abroad.		Inland.	Abroad.	
1900	10·70	9·82	—8·2	17·00	16·12	— 5·5
1901	11·01	11·22	+1·9	17·00	16·86	— 0·2
1902	10·45	9·84	—5·8	15·00	13·11	—12·6

The American trusts ordinarily sell their products at from five to ten per cent cheaper in foreign countries than at home. A particularly crass instance was that of the Steel Trust, which at one time sold sheet steel in England at $22.00 per ton, while it charged American ship-builders $32.00 for the same product.[1] An American soap manufacturer stated before the free trade congress in Antwerp in the year 1910, that borax was produced in the neighbourhood of his plant, but that in consequence of the high duty of two cents per pound it was so costly in the home country that he had bought borax in Paris and had it shipped to America via Liverpool. On the arrival of the shipment it was discovered that the stuff had been produced in the near-by American works, and so had only traversed an enormously roundabout course to bring up again at the place from which it set out.

Direct export bounties have reached their greatest development in the German iron industry.[2] The Siegerländer Pig-Iron Syndicate and the Rhenish-Westphalian Coal Syndicate granted bounties as early as the year 1882 to the members of the combines, and also to domestic purchasers, though only occasionally and for short periods ; not until the decade

[1] Hermann Levy, *Die Stahlindustrie der Vereinigten Staaten von Amerika* (Berlin, 1906), p. 276.

[2] W. Morgenroth, *Die Exportpolitik der Kartelle*, Leipsic, 1907 ; Fritz Diepenhorst, *Die handelspolitische Bedeutung der Ausfuhrunterstützungen der Kartelle*, Leipsic, 1908.

Q

of the 'nineties was a systematic exportation policy introduced. Since the year 1893, the Rhenish Westphalian Coal
Syndicate has set aside a variable percentage of the turnover to meet the costs of both sorts of bounties. From the
year 1892 until it was merged with the coal syndicate in
1897, the Westphalian Coke Syndicate paid a rebate of one
and one-half marks to the rolling mills for each ton of pig-iron
exported. The pig-iron syndicate also joined with the
Siegerländer Iron-Stone Syndicate in the payment of bounties
on the exportation of the manufactured pig-iron. Among
the establishments affected were the wire-rod mills, which
were especially interested in exportation and which in turn
granted price reductions to manufacturers using their products in case of re-exportation. In order to avoid friction
in the relations of so many organizations and enterprises,
a ' Clearing House for Exportation ' was established in
Düsseldorf in 1902 by the Rhenish-Westphalian Coal Syndicate, the Düsseldorfer and Siegerländer Pig-iron Syndicates, together with the half-manufactures' combine and the
organization of final producers. It was the business of this
institution to account for and distribute the export bounties
according to a uniform plan. The form of bounty represented by price concession was dropped. Every quarter,
maximum rates were fixed, within which the clearing house
might determine the bounties. At the end of 1902 these
maximum rates were as follows : 1·50 marks per ton for
coal, 2·50 marks per ton for pig-iron, exclusive of the bounty
on coal, and 10 marks per ton for half-manufactures and
final products, including the bounties on coal and pig-iron.
These rates were gradually increased to 4 86 marks for half-
manufactures and 20 marks for formed iron, but were
lowered at the beginning of 1906 in consequence of the
improvement of business conditions, and finally reduced to
zero. In the year 1908, under the pressure of declining
business conditions, the earlier practice was resumed, but
it did not achieve great significance on account of the rapid

return of prosperity. In May 1913, however, the steel works association raised its bounty to fifteen marks per ton, and the pig-iron combine took under advisement the question of re-introducing such measures, while the coal syndicate held aloof.

The German Kartell investigation showed also that the central organization for the application of industrial alcohol grants rebates on orders for distilled spirits to be used in the production of articles for exportation, but according to the statement of the association itself, only in years ˙ when it seems advisable to relieve pressure on the domestic spirits market by exportation '.

Interesting examples of bounty payment are also afforded by the textile industry. In the Austrian cotton-spinning industry in the year 1897, the owners of 2,100,000 spindles, or three-fourths of the total number of spindles in Austria, bound themselves, in view of the glut of the domestic yarn market brought about by large importations, to con-tribute for a period of six months, two kronen per spindle per month toward an exportation fund, out of which bounties were to be paid for the exportation of yarn. The consequence was a rapid growth in the Austrian exports of yarn to un-accustomed market districts—to Germany at first, and later to Russia. In the year 1913 a similar course of action was again entered upon in order to unload a surplus of production on the German market. The plan included concerted action with the cotton weavers, but this came to naught. The idea was that the spinners should supply domestic weavers with yarn at world-market prices, in consideration for which the weavers were to pay export bounties on fabrics out of a fund; for the maintenance of this fund an assessment of ten kronen per loom per year was proposed.

In the Italian cotton industry the ' Instituto cotoniero italiano ' was founded in the spring of 1913, mainly for the purpose of limiting production and increasing exportation. The spinning department was first organized, and later three other departments relating to weaving, printing, dyeing, and finishing are to be added. Of the 4,580,000 spindles in Italy, 3,800,000 are represented in the organization. An assessment of 0·50 lire per spindle is to be paid toward the expense of limiting production, and an equal amount as an export bounty fund. Accordingly, a sum of about 2,000,000 lire annually should be available for distribution, but in comparison with the total Italian exportation of cotton goods, which amounts to 200,000,000 lire per year, this is not of great importance.

Following this example the French cotton spinners in Rouen have set on foot negotiations looking toward organization. It was hoped to take in at first the establishments of Normandy and later those of the entire country.

The Russian cotton spinners in Lodz formed an export association in 1905, to which each member contributed one kopeck per spindle per week. By the aid of this fund 800,000 pounds of yarn were exported to Germany and the Orient during the first year of operation.

The Austro-Hungarian petroleum Kartell has also formed an export organization of its own. The ' Petrolea ', established in 1903, and including practically all the crude oil producers, has supplied the refineries with crude oil at reduced prices on condition that the exportation of a corresponding quantity of refined petroleum should be guaranteed. In the year 1907, however, the Kartell was dissolved. On the other hand, the organization of refineries (Petroleum-Produkte-Vertriebs-Gesellschaft, Ltd.) founded July 25, 1911, has taken up the question of placing bounties on exportation. The Central Committee is authorized under prescribed conditions to effect the formation in any year of the period of the agreement of an ' export subvention fund ',[1] into which is to be paid an assessment varying with the domestic price (half the amount of the price above twenty-seven kronen, but not more than four kronen per metric hundredweight of the

---

[1] *Verhandlungen der vom k. k. Handelsministerium veranstalteten Kartell-enquete. III. Mineralölindustrie* (Vienna, 1912), pp. 246, 247.

domestic allotment). On the other hand, the exporting refineries must pay into a reimbursement fund half of any export price received above a specified amount, and this fund is again distributed according to the domestic contingent.

In the case of the American trusts, export bounties to individual members do not come into consideration as the trusts themselves are consolidated enterprises, but price concessions are granted to manufacturers who further elaborate the products for exportation. In the tin-plate industry the employees have actually paid assessments from their wages into an export subvention fund.[1]

2. FREIGHT-RATE CONCESSIONS.

Special Rates on Exports. As in the case of railways the general economic interest steadily pushed the question of private gain into the background, the railway rates became not merely an auxiliary to protective duties, but in a still higher degree a means of encouraging exportation. Special tariffs applicable to exports have in fact achieved a higher development and a more extended application than those relating to import tariffs, though, like the former, they exert their influence in connexion with protective duties, special rates on imports being a means of increasing the tariff protection of a country itself, while special rates on exports on the other hand are a means of overcoming the effects of foreign tariff protection. In commercial treaties governments invariably guarantee only the treatment to be accorded to foreign goods, i. e. finally, their own tariff protection procedure, and not the treatment accorded their own goods in relation to other goods in foreign territory. Hence a special freight tariff on exports does not appear as an evasion of treaty stipulations inasmuch as it is not directed against a particular country ; it therefore offers less occasion for damaging retaliatory measures on the part of foreign countries.

[1] Hermann Levy, *Die Stahlindustrie der Vereinigten Staaten von Amerika.* Berlin, 1906.

On this account special freight tariffs on exports have from the very beginning been manipulated much more openly and publicly. Thus, in the decade of the 'nineties, the ' export classification ', so-called, was introduced in Austria-Hungary, Germany, and Switzerland. This means that the goods in question are placed in a lower freight class in case they are destined for exportation. In this way many commodities belong to two freight classes, a general and a special, or export, class. Special or exceptional rate-tariffs are, however, much more frequently met with in nearly all Continental European countries. In this practice either a special rate lower than the regular rate is introduced into the direct tariff applicable to traffic consigned to a foreign station, or else the rate to the frontier station is reduced on condition that the goods go on into the foreign country on a single way-bill. Direct tariffs or direct way-bills are thus the two means of determining the fact of exportation. Under certain conditions, however, it is possible for the foreign country to reap a share of the benefit of the reduced tariff on exports ; and this may make itself unpleasantly felt in case the foreign competitor is able, on account of more favourable productive conditions, to overcome the disadvantage of a location more remote from the market centre, or in case the special export tariff by virtue of its extremely low charges represents an actual loss to the nation which has established it to encourage its own exportation. The possibility of this participation in the reduced rate by foreign producers is clearly illustrated by the following diagram :

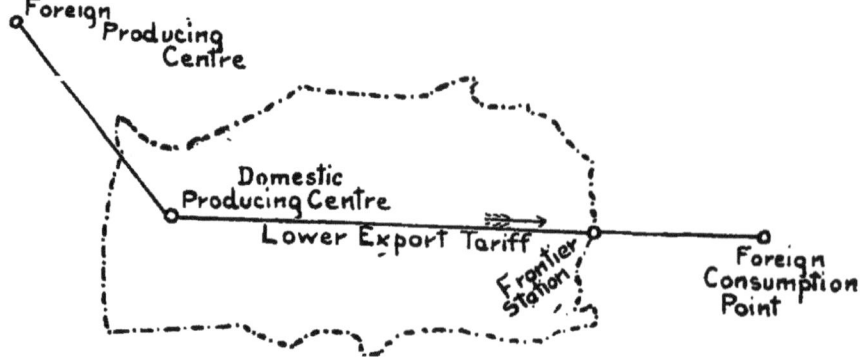

In the quest for means of obviating such participation, the device was hit upon of making purely formal requirements, such as have already been discussed in connexion with concealed special import tariffs. The applicability of the special rate has frequently been limited to a specified domestic shipping point, and often at the same time to a certain destination or transit station. Cases have been known in which the exporting manufacturing establishment was forced to prove that its raw material had been produced in the country.[1]

3. Measures for the Encouragement of Shipping

The Genesis of Artificial Support of the Merchant Marine. A favourable field for the promotion of national economy interests in the sphere of world-economy is afforded by ocean transportation, since the highway of the seas is international and every ship represents to some country an extension of the sphere of its economic power beyond its natural borders. Two objects have been pursued by the political authority in this connexion. The first is that of securing the largest possible share of ocean commerce for its own merchant fleet. The shipping of a nation brings freight earnings into the country from without, affords regular postal connexions with colonies and oversea countries, and also has great military significance since it secures a seafaring population, and in the case of war affords auxiliary ships for the transportation of troops and supplies, for carrying intelligence, &c. The second is the aim of making the ocean traffic subservient to the interests of the production and commerce of the country. Ships will visit home ports more regularly than foreign, and as a result foreign goods may be subjected by the lack of direct shipping connexions to costly and time-consuming transhipments, while also domestic goods,

---

[1] Ernst Seidler and Alexander Freud, *Die Eisenbahntarife in ihren Beziehungen zur Handelspolitik* (Leipsic, 1904), p. 58

even for selfish motives, will naturally be given lower freight rates and more favourable conditions of delivery.

The economic protective policy directed its attention first to means of transportation in order incidentally to stimulate the production of commodities also. The original secondary aim, however, became gradually the principal one, while at the same time a fundamental change took place in navigation policies. In earlier times negative measures alone were employed, the protectionistic navigation policy endeavoured to exclude foreign flags as much as possible from ocean traffic. The most aggravated form of exclusion is direct prohibition, in which the famous English Navigation Act of October 9, 1651, furnished an example to French and Spanish legislation also. At the beginning of the nineteenth century, however, such Draconian exclusion methods were found incompatible with satisfactory relations with foreign powers. Recourse was now had to the fixing of higher shipping taxes for foreign vessels, and the French legislation of 1816 set the example of increased customs duties on goods in ships under foreign flags (*surtaxes de pavillon*). Such additional duties on the ground of the flag were indeed revived in the recent tariff legislation of the United States of America (the Dingley Bill of 1897, the Paine Bill of 1909, and the Underwood Bill of 1913), and also in the French tariff law of 1910, but thus far only as a reserve measure for retaliatory use. In the course of time the practice of discriminating between flags was bound to operate to the greatest disadvantage of that very nation which had the largest merchant marine. As a result England, as long ago as the Law of June 25, 1849, laid down the principle of placing foreign flags on an equality with the home flag. Since that time the principle has secured universal recognition in modern commercial and navigation treaties.

In place of negative measures positive ones were now tried ; the protectionistic navigation policy was replaced by the granting of subventions. The latter employs two methods:

(1) ship subsidies, and (2) bounties.[1] Examples of both may be found in the earlier history of commerce; Venice and Spain at the end of the fifteenth century, and France under Colbert, paid bounties on shipbuilding and for maintaining service on specified routes. The policy, however, achieved its full development only in the course of the nineteenth century.

Ship Subsidies. A ship subsidy represents an absolutely definite material outlay, usually fixed for a term of years, granted by the state to an individually specified shipping company in consideration for the maintenance of regular lines. The basis of it is the idea of a mutual *quid pro quo* relation between the political power and private enterprise. The genesis of subsidies is intimately connected with the development of steam navigation. In former times the oversea postal service, especially that between mother country and colonies, was carried on by ships owned by the state— in England by the so-called ships of the Admiralty. When the use of steam became practicable, the state desired to secure for this service the more rapid and more certain transportation medium, but was repelled by the great financial risk from undertaking the service itself; or, in case it did take it over, as in France, its experiments produced the most unsatisfactory results, as the Government was not in position to meet the much higher operating costs by extending the freight service. As a result, agreements were concluded with private companies in which the latter undertook, in consideration for fixed payments, the free transportation of mail matter, and in consideration for tariff concessions or other privileges, the free carriage of officials and of Government property to and from outlying possessions, &c. A further inducement was added to this first motive for encouraging the growth of the nation's shipping. The difference between war ships and merchant ships was in the beginning so small that the idea readily suggested itself of securing a very respectable cruiser fleet in time of war by arming

[1] Josef Grunzel, *System der Verkehrspolitik* (Leipsic, 1908), p. 28.

private merchant vessels. In return for a corresponding subsidy the shipping companies now obligated themselves in case of war to undertake any transportation of troops or munitions of war assigned to them, to permit the transformation of the steamer into a cruiser, and in time of peace also to keep a certain number of ships at the disposal of the military authorities. Even in the drawing of the plans of the vessels they were to conform to the requirements of the military administration, and to fulfil certain minimal demands as to speed, and they were not to sell or rent the vessels to any foreign country. Gradually, however, these bounties came to serve commercial ends also. This is shown in the fact that in regard to freight charges minimum rates were laid down while the consent of the Government was made necessary before the rates could be changed; also that the owners were forbidden to enter into trade agreements, &c. A classification of subsidies according to their purpose is, however, found only in English legislation. This form of encouragement for the merchant marine has spread from France and England into all countries with large shipping interests.

The first postal agreement was concluded in 1839 between the British Government and the newly organized Royal West India Mail Steam Packet Company for carrying the mail to the Antilles and Central America. The later contracts with the Cunard Line and the Peninsular and Oriental Companies contained clauses in regard to the event of war. Since, however, commercial vessels are adapted to purposes of naval warfare in only a limited degree, and not all in the same way, the subsidies were divided in the year 1861 into three classes: postal subsidies or payments for carrying mails, military subsidies or Admiralty payments, and purely commercial subsidies. They are at present distributed among numerous companies with which special agreements have been concluded. In recent years many English colonies, as, e.g., Australia and Canada, have granted their own independent mail subsidies.

France has paid subsidies for carriage of mail since as early as 1827, and has also performed the service by direct governmental agencies in the Mediterranean. But as Government enterprise was productive of very bad results financially, the policy was changed in 1851 to long-time agreements with private companies, in particular with the ' Compagnie des Messageries maritimes ' and the ' Compagnie générale transatlantique'. The annual expense formed an item of 27,600,000 francs in the budget of 1912.

Italy likewise grants subsidies, principally to the ' Navigazione generale italiana ' for several lines in the Mediterranean and to Indo-China. The effort to renew the agreement, which expired on June 30, 1910, failed on account of the increased demands of the company referred to, with the result that bids were publicly opened, in which the Loyd Sabando and Pierce Parodi Companies came out victorious in October, 1909. But in consequence of a change in the Government, when the Giolitti Cabinet gave way to that of Sonnino on December 2, 1909, the project fell through. The idea of the new Government was to replace the subvention by general navigation bounties. But Parliament again failed to concur in this view, and the succeeding Cabinet of Luzzatti nationalized the intra-Italian lines, and effected the transfer of the others by means of a three years' agreement (1910–13) to the ' Società nazionale pei servizi marittimi ', which was organized for this purpose. Eleven Bills were introduced into the Parliament for a final settlement of the question after 1913, but most of these were rejected by the Giolitti Cabinet in 1911, and the rest were combined into a single measure which finally secured acceptance in 1912. The new law divided the thirty-two lines receiving subsidies into four groups, and again opened the contracts to public bidding. The first group, Alto Tirreno, embraces lines outward from Genoa ; the second group, Basso Tirreno, includes those from Naples and Palermo, among which are all the new direct connexions with Cyrenaica and the Tripolitaine; the third group, Adriatico, includes the lines from Venice and Ancona, and the fourth group, the fast service from Brindisi to Egypt. The thirty-two routes were to be plied by seventy-four ships, and were to be given an annual subsidy of 16,000,000 lire. The immediate result of the classification was, however, unsatisfactory from the start.

In Germany, after two unsuccessful attempts to secure the passage by the Parliament of the necessary Bills, the Government finally concluded an agreement in the year 1885 with the North German Lloyd; this was renewed in 1898 for a term of fifteen years, and carries with it an annual subsidy of 5,590,000 marks. In the year 1890 the German East African Line was added, which by the terms of the new agreement of 1900 receives 1,350,000 marks yearly. In addition, various companies are paid smaller sums for carrying mail.

In Austria, the Austrian Lloyd at first possessed a practical monopoly, and is now a subsidized corporation. According to the Law of February 23, 1907, this company receives mileage payments for twelve lines in the Mediterranean and to Eastern Asia, amounting to a maximum of 7,234,412 kronen, and in addition reimbursement for the Suez Canal tolls. Hungary subsidizes the 'Adria' for regular service to European ports and to Brazil, the 'Hungarian-Croatian Ocean Steam Navigation Company' for service in the Adriatic Sea, and the 'Hungarian Levant Shipping Corporation' for service from Galatz to points on the Black Sea and the Eastern Mediterranean.

Spain subsidizes the 'Compañía Transatlantica' and Portugal similarly encourages ocean connexions with her African colonies and with America. Russia grants fixed annual sums, mileage payments, and restitution of the Suez Canal tolls to several companies, and Holland, Belgium, Sweden, and Norway also pursue a subvention policy. Of countries outside of Europe, Japan and the United States of America have paid very large amounts to various companies.

Shipping Bounties. Shipping bounties are general payments open to any one in return for certain legally specified
performances in the interest of the national shipping. They
are distinguished from subsidies by the fundamental idea
underlying them, as in the former the relation between the
state and the commercial fleet is not conceived of as obtaining
between two private contracting parties, but as one between
the public authority and a number of enterprises upon which
an important public economic interest depends. As a result
bounties are based, not on agreements, but on laws, and are
applicable, not to a specified ship-owner, but to all alike.
For this reason, too, they take the form, not of subsidies
for regular lines, but of payments for encouraging general
navigation. While subsidies owe their origin to the change
from sailing to steam vessels, bounties arose out of the
economic change which followed from the introduction of
the principle of placing all flags on an equal footing. The
overwhelmingly dominant industry of England could only
welcome the throwing open of the world to free competition,
but other countries—especially France, which was most
directly exposed to English competition—found themselves
forced into a relatively disadvantageous position. A ship
is an industrial product, which by its very nature always
lies outside of all customs lines, and so can be reached by
no protective duties, and, furthermore, in its transportation
to another country it does not incur costs, but on the contrary earns freight. Shipbuilding, however, is not carried on
in the open sea but on the land. In jurisdictions affected by
tariff protection, the shipbuilding company must bear the
increase in prices on its iron and other materials resulting
from import duties, while with its finished product, the ship,
it must compete against the similar finished product of
English industry, which can be set down before its doors
freight and duty free. Duty exemption on shipbuilding
material, which has actually been introduced into the tariff
legislation of some countries, only partly equalizes even the

differences arising from the customs tariff. It is impossible to determine with absolute certainty the identity between raw material and manufactured product, and, moreover, in the refunding of duties on the basis of the quantity of material in the finished product, no account can be taken of the unavoidable waste in the material upon which also a duty had of course to be paid. The first bounty laws in France and Italy, whatever may have been their immediate instigation, are to be traced back to these very difficulties, and aimed at nothing else than the restitution to the national shipbuilding industry, in the form of a bounty, of the duty directly or indirectly paid on construction material. Shipping bounties arose from customs drawbacks just as sugar bounties arose from tax restitution, and as little as the former did they remain confined within the narrow compass of their original purpose, but steadily grew and spread. At the same time ship-owners had lost the protection which they had previously enjoyed through the more unfavourable treatment accorded to foreign flags, and this at a time when they were about to be confronted with the necessity of replacing their old construction material, now no longer available, with a new medium. It is to these considerations that service bounties owe their origin.

We accordingly distinguish two different sorts of bounties, building bounties and service bounties. The tonnage capacity forms the basis of computing building bounties, though in many laws a minimum size is prescribed. Separate bounties are often provided on the machinery, in which case either their weight, as in France and Austria, the horse-power as in Japan, or both, as in Italy, form the basis of the payments. Gradations in bounty rates are met with according as the ship is built of wood or iron, and fitted out with steam or sails. Occasionally a distinction is made as to whether the registry is to be under the home or under a foreign flag, and when this is done the duty is less in the latter case.

The adjustment of service bounties offers much greater

difficulties. The first Bill for this purpose in France (Report of the Parliamentary Commission, 1873) attempted to fix the bounty on a *per capita* basis for the crew of the vessel ; but as in modern shipping the size of the ship's company decreases relatively with an increase in the size and capacity of the vessel, the less advanced types would be favoured by such an arrangement. For this reason the generally recognized basis of the bounty came to be the product of the number of tons into the number of miles traversed. This, however, did not eliminate all the difficulties. The usual measurement in gross tons has the disadvantage that the actual commercial efficiency is not indicated with sufficient accuracy as ships could earn bounties even by sailing under ballast. In consequence, the practice later came to be that bounties were paid only on such ships as maintained a regular service between the home country and some foreign land, or else only upon the useful service rendered, determined by multiplying the number of tons in the cargo by the number of knots in the route to the port of unloading. The Sonnino Bill in Italy involved a close approximation to export bounties in case of a number of specified commodities the exportation of which was regarded as especially desirable, as it provided for an addition to the freight payments (*contributo di nolo*). The fear of retaliatory measures on the part of foreign countries led to the introduction of a change by which the lines were subjected to classification in case bounties were to be paid on the service, and the country of exportation was taken into account in the classification. Similarly in the agreement, not yet ratified, between the Austrian Government and the ' Austro-Americana ' a freight bounty is contemplated which is to be fixed at a higher rate on the exportation of domestic products, and at a lower rate in the importation of raw materials purchased abroad.

Cargo bounties are also graduated for ships built of wood and those of iron, and for steam and sailing vessels, and are also decreased with the length of time the ship remains in service, ceasing entirely after a certain age has been reached. They are usually applied to long journeys only, though in exceptional cases at lower rates for coastwise traffic also. A minimum tonnage is usually required in order to exclude the smallest vessels, and in addition, a minimum speed is prescribed, though there is nothing to be gained by favouring the higher speed service since in the freight traffic speed is not an important consideration.

The question was much debated as to whether service bounties should also be paid on foreign-built ships. If they are granted, the foreign shipbuilding industry is encouraged, and the benefit of the construction bounties may even be lost to the domestic industry. If they are not granted, the domestic shipbuilding industry receives a monopoly which forms an obstacle to the growth of national shipping, as it must not only pay higher prices for the ships, but must submit to less favourable conditions of delivery as well, which would impede the prompt replacement of vessels lost by accident, and also the speedy utilization of favourable opportunities. The French Law of 1881 adopted the expedient of granting half of the bounty to foreign-built ships, but this did not afford a satisfactory solution of the problem, and as a result in the Law of 1893 the service bounty was restricted to vessels built in France. The consequence was that a parliamentary investigation which was carried out established the fact that in the year 1893, the French shipbuilding industry received from twenty-five to thirty per cent higher prices, while in the year 1898 sailing vessels cost forty-four and a half per cent, and steamships from sixty to eighty-three per cent more than in England. In general the question of the distribution of bounties between shipbuilding and navigation is the most delicate and difficult question in the whole field of bounty legislation. The state is certainly deeply interested in the development of a domestic shipbuilding industry, since it thereby becomes independent of foreign countries, provides new employment for labour, &c.

Ability to compete with England in this field is, however, not easily attainable, as in that country the shipyards are concentrated as to location, and technically specialized, and they have immediately at hand coal and iron in unlimited quantities and at low cost. Further, they build ships of the commoner types not merely on special order but of standard sizes according to the same plans, and hence may operate more systematically than can yards whose market is so limited that special plans must be drawn for each single vessel. Finally, ships are not merely an industrial product, but also an article of commerce, and an immoderate increase in their cost sympathetically affects not only navigation but commerce also, and indirectly manufactures and agriculture as well. Bounty legislation has striven to promote both shipbuilding and navigation, but as a matter of fact it has oscillated between the two conflicting interests. As a rule, in view of the fact that the function of the service bounty has not been correctly conceived, navigation has borne the chief burden of shipbuilding. In order to attain a fairer distribution of favour, recent legislation has in many cases introduced, in the place of construction or service bounties, payments based on equipment, first cost, or cost of operation (*primes* or *compensations d'armement*), which can be drawn once for all at the time of the purchase of the vessel, or annually, according to the tonnage capacity and the proportion of the time in service, and which are equally applicable to foreign-built ships. This practice, however, is not free from objeetions, as it promotes only the numerical growth of the merchant marine, which is not always identical with an increase in its efficiency in serving the interests of the national commerce.

The proposal to introduce government bounties originated in France soon after the elimination of discrimination between flags in the year 1869, but it was first put into effect in the law of January 29, 1881. Duty exemption on shipbuilding material was dropped, and construction bounties were substituted as follows: sixty francs per ton for ships of iron or steel, twenty francs for wooden ships of 200 tons and over, ten francs for wooden ships under 200 tons, and forty francs for ships of wood and iron, that is, when the ribs and beams are entirely of iron or steel; in addition to these sums a bounty of twelve francs per 100 kilograms was paid for the machinery on board, and finally service premiums were also paid. The latter amounted to 1·50 francs per ton per thousand knots traversed, but were subject to an annual decrease of 0·75 francs for wooden ships and those of wood and iron, and 0·50 francs for ships of iron or steel; they applied exclusively to long voyages, and only half the amount specified was paid on foreign-built ships. The bounty was increased fifteen per cent on ships the plans of which had been previously accepted by the navy department. As the bounties were to be paid for only ten years from the date of publication of the law, the ship-yards were overwhelmed with orders for the first three years, and foreign builders also profited by the situation; then followed a notable slump. The half-bounties on foreign-built ships were set aside in the law of July 30, 1890, while the remaining provisions of the law of 1881 were continued in force until the new law of January 30, 1893, came into effect. By this law construction premiums were increased, and now amounted to sixty-five francs per ton for iron ships, forty francs for wooden ships of 150 tons or over, and thirty francs for wooden ships of under 150 tons, plus fifteen francs per 100 kilograms on engines. Service bounties, now restricted exclusively to ships built in France, were calculated on the gross tonnage and the number of thousands of miles sailed, instead of the net tonnage as formerly, and were fixed at the following amounts: For steamships of more than 100 tons, 1·10 francs with an annual reduction of 0 06 francs for wooden ships and 0·04 for those built of iron; for sailing-vessels of more than eighty tons, 1·70 francs, with an annual reduction of 0·08 francs for wooden ships and 0·06 francs for those of iron.

Ships engaged in the international carrying trade received two-thirds of the above bounties. Ships built according to plans of the Ministry of Marine might claim an increase of twenty-five per cent. In view of the unpleasant previous experience, the duration of the bounties was fixed at ten years from the date of registry (*moment de francisation*) of the vessel, and not as before from the date of the law. The error in this policy was soon manifest, as the smaller types, and especially sailing-vessels, had been disproportionately favoured. Foreign competition being entirely excluded, the industry of sailing-vessel building consumed the service bounty, and the share of the French merchant marine in the shipping of the country sank at a fearful rate. The succeeding law of April 7, 1902, was scarcely more fortunate. It retained the construction bounties at the old rates, but limited them to a total tonnage of 300,000 for steamers and 100,000 for sailing-vessels, and to a total amount of 50,000,000 francs ; in addition, steamship navigation bounties could not be paid on more than 50,000 tons annually, and sailing-vessel bounties on not more than 15,000. The law further introduced bounties on the fittings of ships, though only in the case of steam vessels, so that steamers and sailing-vessels were accorded quite different treatment. The service bounty was granted to every ship built in France of above 100 tons burden. The amount was fixed in the case of steamships at 1·70 francs per gross ton per 1,000 marine miles traversed, subject to an annual reduction of 0 04 francs for the first four years, 0·08 for the second, and 0 16 francs for the third four years of the twelve-year period for which bounties were granted, with a further deduction of 0 01 franc per 100 tons for steamships of over 3,000 tons, while all above 7,000 were rated for bounty purposes at 7,000 tons. For sailing-vessels the amount of the bounty was to be 1 70 francs per ton per 1,000 miles, reduced annually by 0·02 francs for the first, 0·04 francs for the second, and 0·08 francs for the third four years of the bounty period, and with a further reduction of

0·10 francs per 100 tons for ships of above 600 tons, and the rating at 1,000 tons of all sailing-vessels beyond that size. The bounty on fittings (*compensation d'armement*) was provided for ships of foreign construction of more than 100 tons burden, and amounted to 0·05 francs per gross ton per day of service (300 days of service per year being fixed as a maximum) for steamers up to 2,000 tons, to 0 04 francs for those from 2,000 to 3,000 tons, to 0·03 francs for tonnage from 3,000 to 4,000, and 0·02 for all above 4,000 tons, but increase in the bounty ceased at 7,000 tons. As a matter of fact, the service bounties, accessible only to ships built in France, were from two-thirds to three-fourths higher than the fittings bounty, so that the domestic shipbuilding industry continued to receive protection. The differential advantage accorded to the smaller types, and especially to the smaller sailing-vessels, was still greater than before, and as a result of the limitation of the sum to be paid out by the government in bounties, there followed such a boom in shipbuilding that all the funds appropriated by the law were exhausted in a single year. In consequence, a new law was passed on April 19, 1906, which set aside the service bounties and retained only those on construction and fittings. The construction bounties are now fixed for iron steam-vessels at 145 francs per gross ton, with an annual decrease of 4·50 francs during the first ten years in which the law is to run, and for iron sailing-ships at ninety-five francs, with an annual reduction of three francs. For wooden ships of 150 tons and over, the bounty is forty francs ; for those under 150 tons it is thirty francs, to which is added twenty-seven and a half francs per 100 kilograms for engines and boilers, subject to an annual reduction of 0·75 francs during the first ten years. For foreign-built ships specified classes were granted seven-tenths of these amounts. The fittings bounty is granted to all French vessels, wherever built, of at least 100 tons burden, and the amount per ton per day of service is 0·04 francs for steamers up to 3,000 tons, 0·03 francs for the same class of vessels of from 3,001 to 6,000 tons, and 0·02 francs for those of more than 6,000 tons; for sailing-vessels it is 0·03 francs up to 500 tons, 0·02 from 501 to 1,000 tons, and 0·01 above 1,000 tons. Proof is required that certain conditions have been fulfilled as to voyages made and transportation service performed; in particular, a claim to a bounty becomes valid only when vessels carry cargoes of at least one-third their capacity for at least half of the distance sailed. A minimum speed of ten knots is further prescribed, while an increase to fourteen knots entitles the owner to a ten-per-cent addition to the bounty, a speed of fifteen knots carries a twenty-per-cent increase in bounty, and of sixteen knots one of thirty per cent. A limit is fixed to the total amount of the bounty, but it is formulated differently than in the preceding law; steam vessels up to 50,000 tons and sailing-vessels up to 15,000 may be annually admitted to participation in the bounty. Certain defects have been overcome in this law, but criticism of its provisions was very animated even at the time it was passed. The budget for the year 1912 included 1,100,000 francs for construction bounties, and 21,900,000 francs for fittings bounties.

After the establishment of the principle placing the flags of different nations on an equality, Italy at first resorted to the expedient of granting duty exemption on shipbuilding material, but replaced this device in the law of December 6, 1885, with bounty provisions. The construction bounty was fixed at sixty lire per gross ton for iron ships and fifteen lire for wooden vessels, plus ten lire per horse-power for engines and six lire per 100 kilograms for boilers; steam vessels built according to plans approved by the Ministry of Marine were entitled to an increase of from ten to twenty per cent. A service bounty of 0·65 lire per ton per 1,000 nautical miles traversed was provided for ships built in Italy which plied routes to distant points; foreign-built ships were admitted to bounty participation only in exceptional cases. The bounties were further increased before the expiration of the ten-year term of the law. The new law of July 23, 1896, contained the following provisions: construction bounties of 77 lire per gross ton for iron and 17·5 lire for wooden ships, 12·50 lire per horse-power and 9·50 lire per 100 kilograms of boilers; a service bounty of 0·80 lire per gross ton per 1,000 miles for the first three years, with a reduction in each succeeding three-year period of 0·10 lire in the case of steamers and 0·15 lire for sailing-vessels. Entitled to the service bounty are only steamers of at least 500 tons burden and of iron, iron sailing-vessels of at least 250 tons, and wooden sailing-vessels of at least 100 tons. Ships built abroad receive half the bounty given to Italian-built ships. This law was again modified before its expiration. By the royal decree of November 16, 1900, the construction bounty was graduated according to speed; it was fixed at 45 lire for steamers of less than twelve knots and for iron sailing-vessels, 50 lire for steamers of from twelve to fifteen knots, 55 lire for steamers of over fifteen knots, and at 13 lire for wooden ships—per gross ton in each case. The law of May 16, 1901, reduced the construction bounty to 35 lire for iron ships and 13 lire for wooden ones, and in addition set aside the service bounties and introduced fittings bounties. The latter were made applicable to iron steamers of over 400 and iron sailing-ships of over 100 tons burden, and the rates were fixed at 60 lire for vessels launched before June 30, 1903, 50 lire for those launched before June 30, 1905, and 40 lire for those launched before June 30, 1907. Wooden sailing-ships were granted bounties of 50, 20, and 10 lire under the same conditions. The total bounty was limited to 40,000 tons, and to an amount of 8,000,000 lire per year. By terms of a bill introduced in 1913 the government would grant to every freight steamer a fittings bounty (*compenso di navigazione*) of two and a half per cent of the value of the ship for a period of ten years. The ship must, however, have a displacement of at least 100 tons, must be not more than twenty years old, and must pass at least 200 days in the year in actual travel; for less time in service, correspondingly reduced bounties would be paid.   An expenditure of 2,300,000 lire in this way was proposed.

Austria passed a law on December 27, 1893, for the encouragement of free navigation, so-called, introducing unit bounties and service bounties.   The unit bounty (*Betriebs-zuschuss*) was fixed at 6 gulden per ton per year for iron steamships, 4·50 gulden for iron sailing-ships, and three gulden for sailing-vessels built of wood.   These amounts were subject to a five-per-cent annual decrease, and ceased entirely after fifteen years, but were increased by ten per cent in case the ship was built in a domestic shipyard, and by twenty-five per cent if at least half the material was of domestic production.   The service bounty (*Reisezuschuss*), granted under certain prescribed conditions, was fixed at five kreuzer per ton per 1,000 miles traversed.   Under the influence of this law the merchant marine has in fact grown, though by no means at the rate hoped for, especially when the prosperous business conditions of recent years are taken into account. As a result, a new law was passed on February 23, 1907. By the terms of this measure, ocean-going commercial vessels devoted exclusively to free navigation, and at least two-thirds of which are Austrian interest, and which satisfy certain minimum requirements as to efficiency, receive, in addition to exemption from the industrial tax, both a unit bonus and a service bonus.   The unit bonus is granted to ships of at least 400 gross tons, and its amount is fixed as follows : for such ships built of iron and steel in domestic shipyards, 10 kronen per ton ; if built abroad, 7 kronen per ton, in case they are registered before the close of 1910, and 6 kronen if registered after that date ; for ships of wood or mixed construction, built in domestic shipyards, 6 kronen per ton.   This unit bonus is paid for fifteen years, but is decreased five per cent at the beginning of the fourth year and ten per cent at the beginning of the tenth.   Ships of over 7,000 tons are treated as 7,000 ton vessels.   The service bounty is granted only on

condition that the cargo amounts to at least a third of the
net spatial capacity, or corresponds to a spatial capacity of
at least 1,700 tons, and that it goes to an Austrian port; the
amount is ten heller per ton per 100 marine miles. Steamers
of over 5,000 tons are rated at 5,000. On condition of using
fifty per cent domestic material, shipyards receive a construction bonus, amounting in the case of steamers built of
iron and steel to 40 kronen per ton on the ship's hull, and
eight kronen per ton for machinery of domestic manufacture ;
in the case of sailing-vessels of iron or steel, the amount
received is 14 kronen per ton for the ship's hull; for sailing-
vessels of wood or of mixed construction, 10 kronen per ton
are allowed. The total amount of the bounty is limited, the
unit bonus to 18,000 tons per year, of which not over 3,000
tons may represent sailing-ships; the service bonus is limited
by the restriction of the total amount to be expended for
both forms of bounties to an annual sum beginning at
4,200,000 kronen, and increasing each year up to 5,600,000
kronen for the year 1912.

An analogous arrangement is to be found in Hungary.
By the terms of Article XXII of the Statutes of 1893, free
navigation enjoyed purchase bounties and service bounties
in case at least two-thirds of the ship in question was the
property of Hungarian citizens. The purchase bounty
amounted to 6 kronen per net ton for sailing-ships plying in
the long routes of the coasting trade, 9 kronen for sailing-
ships on distant routes, 9 kronen for steamers in long route
coasting trade, and 12 kronen for steamers in distant service
—all subject to an annual decrease of seven per cent, and
limited to a period of fifteen years from the date of launching
of the ship. The service bounty amounted to five heller
per registry-ton per 100 miles. By Statutes Article XXXIV
of the year 1895, construction bounties were also introduced,
as follows: For iron ships, 30 to 60 kronen; for wooden
ships, from 10 to 25 kronen ; for the engines, 10 to 15 kronen,
and for the boilers, 6 to 10 kronen per ton, the total

sum being limited to 200,000 kronen. After years of preliminary work a new system of regulations was undertaken
in Statutes Article VI of the year 1907. The first provision
grants for a period of fifteen years to iron ships with a minimum
speed of ten knots a purchase bounty amounting in the
first year to 8 kronen per gross ton, and sinking gradually
to 4 kronen. The bounty is increased by forty per cent in
case the vessel is built in a domestic shipyard and entirely
of domestic material, by thirty per cent if two-thirds of the
material is of domestic production, and by twenty per cent
when at least one-third is such. If the engines are also of
domestic material the bounty is increased by twenty per
cent. A further increase in the bounty takes place when the
average speed is twelve knots or more. A service bounty is
paid on vessels in the free-navigation service, and having
a gross tonnage of at least 1,500; the amount is 5 heller per
net ton per 100 knots for the long-route coasting trade,
and 10 heller for the distant service. Shipyards which are
equipped to build vessels of at least 1,000 gross tons receive
as a construction bounty 30 kronen per ton for ships of iron
and steel, when at least two-thirds of the material used in
them is of domestic production, and 15 kronen per ton if
at least one-third of the material is domestic. A bounty of
12 kronen per indicated horse-power is paid on marine engines,
one of 8 kronen per 100 kilograms on boilers and steam-
piping, and one of 10 kronen per 100 kilograms on various
auxiliary machinery. The total bounty is limited to 1,500,000
kronen per year.

In Spain, shipping bounties were introduced by the law
of June 14, 1909, and either service bounties or unit bounties
are paid on proof of a specified minimum performance. This
minimum amounts in the irregular service to fifty per cent
of the passenger and freight tonnage, with the condition that
thirty per cent of the goods carried must be Spanish products;
in the regular service the annual average must reach forty
per cent of capacity in case of exportation, and thirty per

cent in case of importation. In addition, the ships of the South American lines must have a speed of ten knots, those in the Mediterranean service must make 11·5 knots, and those of the lines to New York thirteen knots. The total amount of the bounties is limited to 4,900,000 pesetas.

In Russia, a bounty law was passed on May 21, 1912. By its terms Russian shipbuilding establishments receive for the original construction or the refitting of iron merchant ships a lump-sum bounty based on the tonnage capacity of the vessel and the horse-power of its engines. After the year 1922, an annual reduction of six per cent in the bounty rates is to come into effect.

Japan passed a bounty law on March 23, 1896, providing for construction and service bounties. A later law of March 24, 1909, made certain changes.

4. Other Positive Measures for Commodity Protection

Subsidies for the Promotion of Exportation. As long as the governmental encouragement of exportation does not go beyond the publication of commercial reports, the furnishing of information, and paying of salaries to young merchants, and other measures for directing and stimulating private initiative, an economic protective policy operating through commodities cannot properly be spoken of. Later in the history of the movement, however, the development abroad of a merchant class of the nationality in question has taken shape as the most important task. When now the state proceeded still further and granted financial support to the merchant engaged in the export trade, such government subsidy at once manifested the same evolutionary tendencies as merchant-marine subventions. The artificial encouragement is transferred more and more in the one case from the transportation medium, and in the other case from the commercial dealer, to the commodity, and is imperceptibly transformed into an export bounty, in spite of all steps which may be taken on the grounds of general principles to prevent such a change.

The transformation which has taken place in the Austrian policy of encouraging exportation is characteristic in this respect.   In the year 1897, at a time when a possibility of a customs separation between Austria and Hungary had to be reckoned with, four broad investigations undertaken by the corporations concerned brought out the necessity of developing exportation.   Beginning with the year 1898, a sum for the promotion of exportation, fixed at first at 80,000 kronen, was included in the national budget, and in the year 1907 the amount was precipitately increased to 1,000,000 kronen. These amounts were used to defray the expenses of ' commercial emissaries ' (Sendlinge), whose duty it was to travel in specified oversea countries with samples of Austrian products and to solicit orders.   In the period from 1898 to 1906, thirty-six such agents were subsidized to a total amount of 462,500 kronen, and in the period from 1907 to 1909 eight additional emissaries received 169,000 kronen ; according to the official figures these agents secured business to the amount of 18,700,000 and 2,800,000 kronen respectively,[1] but in these sums were included many Austrian special manufactures which ' sell themselves ', so to speak, and require no canvassing.   The policy ended in complete failure.   On the one hand, the commercial agents did not in general receive the necessary backing in the home country, as the branch export-syndicates desired by the government did not come into being.   On the other hand, the agents were unable to establish themselves in the oversea points, as would have been necessary in order to maintain the business connexions once created.   Only a few agents employed as representatives by a certain exporter in Vienna were able to maintain themselves, and in this case complaint was at once made that the state was paying the employees of a particular firm which

---

[1] *Verhandlungen und Beschlüsse des Industrierates*, Heft 28, *Fragen der Exportförderung*, Vienna, 1911.

would otherwise have had to pay them on its own account. In the year 1907 a new attempt was made, this time at subsidizing oversea branches of domestic business houses, but with no better success. As there is no longer any important foreign point in which Austria is entirely unrepresented, the subsidy represented a decided intermeddling in established competitive conditions. The subsidized branch houses were of course in a position to sell their goods cheaper than their competitors, and in fact underbid on exactly those goods to which the measures of encouragement had not been intended to apply. As a result, the Industrial Council decided in 1911 that such subsidies were to be granted only exceptionally, and on political and commercial policy grounds, in which case the merely business interest would be overshadowed by the special aims of the state; the recommendation of the employment by the government of foreign commercial emissaries was also couched in very sceptical terms. The idea was now repeatedly proposed of basing the subsidies on the quantity and value of particular articles sold, but this would have been an undisguised export bounty. The bill prepared by a member of the Industrial Council, and endorsed by that body, but which failed of passage, would also have been merely a roundabout road to the same result. It provided that a certain percentage of the tax on the turnover of each industrial enterprise corresponding to the ratio of its export to its total business should be reimbursed. The procedure of granting tax rebates, which has become familiar in the field of indirect taxes, was thus to be carried over into that of direct taxes, where it would, however, without doubt have led still more readily to abuses. In order to enlarge the market for national products, Italy, by the terms of the royal decree of December 25, 1909, grants to persons engaged in commerce who maintain on their own account commercial agencies in foreign centres a subsidy limited to three years, and to a maximum amount of 4,000 lire for European points, and 5,000 lire for points outside of

Europe. In addition, newly established agencies may receive for the first year a bonus toward the cost of the establishment up to 2,000 lire.

Encouragement of Exportation by Political and Capitalistic Influence. In a period in which political issues relate more and more exclusively to economic policy it is but natural that external political connexions should be utilized to open up new markets to a country's production. In the year 1906, for example, Austria threw its political influence into the balance in order to secure certain ordnance contracts in Serbia. Again, the Austrian paper exportation to Egypt has been falling off since 1903, because England brings strong pressure to bear on Egyptian officials in connexion with public contracts. In Morocco, also, the influence of France is decisive in business relations, in Persia that of Russia and England, &c.

Large loans to foreign states or foreign enterprises are usually granted under the condition, expressed or understood, that the debtor is to buy in the country making the loan the materials for the purchase of which it is made. Thus in the year 1910 Serbia obtained a loan of 150,000,000 francs in France, only on the implicit condition that a contract for arms for the Serbian army should be granted to the French firm of Schneider & Co., at Creusot. In the same way, orders were repeatedly obtained from Russia. In the year 1910 Germany held up a Bulgarian loan until assurance was forthcoming that consideration would be given to German industry. In the treaty with Germany of March 6, 1898, China was forced to obligate itself to purchase in that country the machinery necessary for the industrialization of the Shantung province, which was further connected with various economic concessions in the region.

IV

PROTECTION AFFECTING CAPITAL, BY NEGATIVE MEASURES

1. Obstacles placed in the way of Foreign Enterprisers

Employment of the Antipathy to Foreigners. It is only in the earlier stages of capitalistic production that foreign *entrepreneurs'* capital will be viewed by a country as desirable. As soon as the spirit of enterprise becomes active in the country itself, attempts will not be wanting to replace such capital by foreign loan capital, which leaves in the possession of the debtor country the excess of its earnings above interest, thus operating to enrich the latter more rapidly and at the same time eliminating the unavoidable personal influence of the foreign capitalist on the domestic economic policy. The most insistent opposition to the foreign *entrepreneur* will be found in the case of those enterprises to which is entrusted the safeguarding of any special economic interest of the community in the field of national defence, of trade, industry, or commercial policy.

The opposition to the foreign enterpriser may be indirect, through simply concentrating the attention of the national consciousness upon domestic industry. Not infrequently, however, a hatred of foreigners will at the same time be stirred up, either openly or under cover, by means of the press, public gatherings, political agitation, &c. In China, in the year 1908, a strong agitation was set on foot against the granting to foreigners of mining and railway concessions. The attempt was made to repurchase concessions already granted, the necessary capital being raised in part by national subscriptions. In a few years, however, these currents of hostility to foreigners subsided as the Chinese recognized that in view of the timidity of their own capitalists in making public investments, they were not for the time being in a position to dispense with foreign capital, and that, moreover, they required the technical and commercial leadership of the Europeans. The larger part of the enormous mineral wealth of the country lies still untouched for the reason that home enterprise is wanting for its utilization. Efforts are now being made in the direction of establishing mixed enterprises in which the home element will be assured an influence alongside of the foreign.

In Roumania the antipathy to foreign capital has received clearest expression in the different attitude of the population toward domestic and foreign banks. Deposits are given preferably to the domestic depositories and savings-banks, in spite of the fact that they are less solidly based, and many a small provincial bank shows deposits to many times the amount of ts capital stock. The market-price of the shares of the foreign banks is also relatively much lower in view of the amount of reserves and the dividend rates. Industrial enterprises suffer less, foreign capital being satisfied with a return as low as five per cent, while domestic capital earns eight per cent in safe mortgages.

In Greece also it is to be observed that domestic capital is given the preference. The Greek government officials themselves, when they must purchase supplies abroad, make use of the services of Greek merchants resident in the foreign country.

At the beginning of November 1912 it was announced in the *Times* in London that a nationalistic movement was in progress in Chile directed toward securing in the future for domestic capital a larger share in the saltpetre industry of the country. To this end the bidding of foreign capitalists for the saltpetre fields opened up by the government was to be restricted. Soon afterwards the *Times* received a communication from the Chilean representative in London in which it was explained that such unfriendliness to foreigners did not reflect the views of the Chilean government, which was well aware of the value and importance of larger movements of foreign capital into Chile.

A similar proposal for the utilization of the antipathy to foreigners was included in the form of a draft of a law by a nationalistic deputy in France in the year 1913. By the terms of this bill the use of the designation ' French ' would be forbidden in the following cases : 1. When the enterprise or company has one or more foreign administrative officers, when it is a branch establishment of a foreign enterprise or corporation, when more than ten per cent of its personnel consists of foreign employees, or when it is not carried on exclusively according to French laws ; 2. When the goods are not produced in France or in French colonies by exclusively French enterprises. Persons violating the law, in case they are foreigners, shall be expelled on repetition of the offence.

The Nationalization of Foreign Capital. The modern means of opposition consists in the nationalization of the foreign capital. The political allegiance does not inhere in capital itself, but follows in the first place from the citizenship of its owner. It can, therefore, be changed either without the transfer of the capital or after such transfer has been effected, and in either of two ways ; a new owner with a different citizenship may take the place of the former one, or the original owner may continue in possession but may change his allegiance. In this manner foreign capital may be nationalized and that of the country itself denationalized. A further distinction to be made in this connexion relates to the question whether the enterprise as such or only the capital invested in it undergoes the nationalizing process. The following examples may make clearer the procedure gone through in these cases. Let us suppose that a citizen of the German Empire founds a factory in Austria. He may either buy up a factory already in existence in

Austria, in which case a denationalization of Austrian capital takes place, or with the help of imported machinery, building material, and other capital goods, he may erect a new factory. If he maintains his residence in Germany, in Dresden, for example, while the factory is, let us say, in Aussig, the Austrian national economy will have to give up to the German the earnings of the factory, including the interest on the capital. A nationalization of the enterprise from the standpoint of Austria, and a denationalization from the standpoint of Germany can take place only if the German either sells his factory to an Austrian, or himself emigrates to Austria. The economically decisive factor in citizenship is, of course, the place of residence and not legal status. Again, the factory may be organized as a corporation, in which case the nationalization process may be effected easily and imperceptibly through the purchase of the shares by domestic capitalists. In this connexion the difference between enterprise and capital is often made manifest. The capitalist receives his returns in dividends or interest, while the enterpriser oversees the administration. The German corporation operating abroad may place its foreign establishments under the supervision of its own managers and employees, or by the employment of native labour power it may appear in Russia as a Russian, and in Italy as an Italian, enterprise. The nationalization struggle may also be fought out in countries which have themselves no interest in it; we need only refer to the conflicts of interest in connexion with the Anatolian and Bagdad railways. The capital of the latter is distributed by treaty, forty per cent being German and thirty per cent each Swiss and French. The capital and entrepreneur interests may also be separated; the Suez Canal Company continues in form a French enterprise, for the reason that statutory obstacles prevent the dominating English capital from securing administrative control.

The nationalization process is, to be sure, from the private-economic point of view, a capital transfer, inasmuch as the evidences of ownership, stock certificates, bonds, &c., pass from the hands of foreigners into those of citizens, but in the national economic sense no such change takes place. From the latter point of view, either no capital transfer at all is effected, as when an establishment already in existence in a foreign country is purchased by residents of the home country in question, or else the capital transfer is one which has previously taken place, without regard to the later nationalization, through the establishment of an enterprise within the country by foreign capitalists. In its national economic effects, however, nationalization is similar to an international transfer of capital, since it brings about a change in the direction taken by the income of the invested funds, which now remains in the home country instead of going abroad.

In still another way the nationalization of foreign capital invested within a country is of great value for the national economy. In connexion with those enterprises in particular which require the largest amount of capital and therefore exert the greatest amount of attraction on foreign capital, common economic and other public interests push themselves more and more into the foreground, a circumstance which makes it seem necessary, or at least desirable, that such enterprises should not be in the hands of foreigners. Thus, the railroads form an important implement of the national economic policy as well as the essential means in any mobilization of troops. A canal may be rendered useless for a considerable interval by the apparently accidental sinking of a vessel at a critical moment, as was shown in the case of the Suez Canal at the time of the Russo-Japanese War. The mining industry operates with natural-monopoly wealth of a country, and must, therefore, be subjected to regulations which should be carried out in the same spirit in which they were promulgated.

Mexico has effected the nationalization of its railways by the method of merging the different private companies into a large corporation (Lineas Nacionales de Mexico), in which the Federal Government secured for itself a sufficient number of shares to be able to dictate the railroad policy in the interest of the country.

In China, a strong nationalization movement set in in the year 1900, which, as already stated, aimed at the repurchase of the concessions granted to foreign nations and enterprisers.

On the high seas, no nationalization of enterprises important to the economic community is necessary, since in this case it is sufficient that a national enterprise be built up to offset those of other nations. Thus England finds it a considerable disadvantage from the military as well as the commercial standpoint, that the thirteen cable lines by which England is able to communicate with Canada are under American control, even though the employees are English. On this account the laying of the so-called ' all British ' cable is advocated for connecting England with the colonies. According to the plan proposed, one line should extend from the west coast of Ireland (Blacksod Bay) to Halifax, with a branch line up the St. Lawrence River to Montreal. A second line would be laid from Gibraltar to the Cape of Good Hope, and be connected with the West Indies through an intermediate station on the west coast of Africa (Bathurst or Sierra Leone).

2. DISCOURAGEMENT OF CAPITAL EXPORTATION

Discouragement by Influencing Public Opinion. The previously mentioned disadvantages to the country of the exportation of capital, the deadening effect on the spirit of enterprise, the injury to the domestic money market affecting loans in the home country, and the giving over of financial power into the hands of a political opponent—have attracted general attention to themselves in recent decades and led to the taking of preventive measures. It is impossible to check the exodus of the capital itself as international transfers of capital take place in the form of shipments of commodities. For this reason the prohibition decreed by Holland in 1720 was without effect.[1] The result can be achieved only indirectly by controlling to this end either the person of the capitalist or the technical media for the transmission of capital.

Influence may be exerted on the person of the possessor of capital by the attitude of public opinion, and in this connexion again, either his self-interest or his patriotism may be appealed to. Thus, on the occasion of the flotation of the Russian five per cent Government Loan in 1906, the internal political and financial condition of the Russian Empire was depicted in such gloomy colours in the German and Austrian daily press and technical literature that the price of the loan fell under eighty, while in November 1912, at a peculiarly critical time for Government paper, the same bonds did not fall below 102. Such an agitation can, however, be only temporarily successful, and loses its effect in proportion as the owners of capital become accustomed to forming their own judgements on the basis of current information, which constantly increases in abundance and accessibility. With especial frequency is the appeal to patriotism used to prevent an exportation of capital from strengthening a political opponent. Thus, at the end of the year 1911 an animated press campaign was carried on in France against the Austrian loan project which had become well known at that time, on the ground that the sums raised by the loan were to be used for strengthening the military establishment, and thus would be useful to the hostile Triple Alliance. Even earlier, in November 1910, the great French banks had been called upon not to support the loans of Hungary and Turkey (not admitted to quotation) by taking up treasury bills of those countries. The influence of public opinion has

---

[1] A. Sartorius, Freiherr von Waltershausen, *Das volkswirtschaftliche System der Kapitalsanlage im Auslande* (Berlin, 1907), p. 374.

also repeatedly asserted itself in America in connexion with the marriage of the daughters of millionaires with the impecunious heirs of European noble families and the consequent transfer of capital across the Atlantic Ocean.

Manipulation of the Technical Means of Transferring Capital. Of the technical mechanism for transferring capital, two forms especially—banks of issue and exchanges—are subject to political influence; in the regulations affecting the operation of these institutions, the taking up of the undesired capital loans of foreign countries in general or of a particular country may be rendered difficult.

An example of the utilization of the bank of issue to prevent capital exportation has been furnished by Germany. In earlier times many Russian Government loans and railway bonds were marketed in that country. On political and commercial policy grounds, Prince Bismarck, in November 1887, forbade the disposal of Russian securities through the Reichsbank. By this means not only was the flotation of new Russian loans impeded, but in addition a general unloading of securities already purchased was brought about. The capital assistance which Germany thus refused was granted the more willingly by France. Germany also affords an example of the obstruction of the utilization of exchange facilities by foreign securities. The admission of any issue to quotation is granted by a commission (*Zulassungsstelle*), whose primary purpose it is to guard against swindling schemes, but which serves as well to exclude foreign paper. Higher admission fees must also be paid as well as higher rates under the Imperial stamping law. None the less, complaint is still made on account of the exportation of capital. In the Prussian Lower House in February 1912, the Free Conservative deputy, Rahardt, moved the following interpellation:

A number of large banks have applied to the Minister of Commerce for permission to invest in an issue of 48,000,000 marks of four and a half per cent bonds of the Anatolian Railway Company. I ask the minister what he intends to do to prevent the exportation of German money at a time when the mortgage requirements are greater than ever before. Shall we assist a foreign people with German money at the expense of our own country ? This money would undoubtedly be taken from the middle classes to be used abroad.

The French quotation system is far more drastic. In an executive order of February 20, 1880, the French minister of finance expressly reserved the right to refuse to foreign securities admittance to official quotation, and hence the right to the utilization of exchange facilities. In the year 1912, it was even decided to make such decisions dependent upon the judgement of the ministerial council. According to the ruling practice, two conditions are required for admission, the political friendship of the borrowing country, and commercial policy advantages, especially the placing in France of orders connected with the services to which the foreign loan is destined to be put. Thus, in the year 1909, the quotation of an Argentine loan was refused for the reason that shortly before the Argentine Government had placed orders for artillery in Germany. In the year 1910, the French Government opposed the proposed Hungarian and Turkish loans, which, however, were floated in Germany as a result of this action. In 1912 the ' Chambre syndicale des agents ' in Paris decided to admit no more Italian securities to quotation until further notice ; this action was taken as a protest against the threatened injury to foreign capital through the establishment of the life insurance monopoly.

3. DISCOURAGEMENT OF THE DENATIONALIZATION OF CAPITAL

Self-Protection against Denationalization. The transfer of national enterprises into the hands of foreigners may be the result of economic aggression on the part of the foreign state which puts forward private enterprisers in order to gain influence in another economic domain. The history of both the Near and the Far East offers an abundance of examples of this sort. Or again, private-economic interests may lead to such expansion. Thus, the American trusts, which aim at a dominant position in the world-market, such as the Standard Oil Company, must obtain a firm footing in other producing countries also. An especially favourable field for denationalization is afforded by ' open door ' countries, where the lack of a national protective policy greatly intensifies international competition; similarly, the international ocean, which forms the field of activity of important national enterprises such as the ocean steamship corporations and submarine cable companies. Especial attention was attracted by the attempt at denationalization made in 1901 by the Morgan syndicate, which purchased through German and Austrian banks stock in the Hamburg-American Line and the North German Lloyd in order to bring these German shipping companies under American influence.

A means of protection occasionally effective, but inadequate in the long run, is the patriotism of the enterpriser. The activity of the Government, and still more the influence of public opinion, may bring it about that the enterprisers postpone the sale of their establishment, or accept less favourable offers, in order to prevent its passing into foreign hands. The accomplishment of this result is much more difficult when, as usually happens, the enterprise is organized in the form of a corporation or some other legal association of capital, since the stock or shares can generally be purchased on the open market, and hence the transfer may take place gradually and imperceptibly. If the danger is perceived in time it may perhaps be warded off for a while by an appeal to the large stockholders and the banks; but it can hardly be permanently prevented as the shares will not always be in the hands of financially independent persons, and, moreover, are not always purchased for the purpose of investment but for speculative ends as well, and hence must be sold at definite times depending on market conditions.

Corporations may secure a more reliable, if not absolutely safe, protection through their legal charters. A means of temporary defence is afforded if the right is granted to the company to increase its capitalization without a stockholders' meeting. That is, when the stock previously issued has largely passed into foreign possession, a sudden issue of new stock which is placed in the hands of reliable parties within the country, may restore majority ownership and control to the homeland. The obstacle to stock transfers afforded by the substitution of non-negotiable certificates for those made out to bearer, can seldom be realized in the case of large corporations such as those usually affected in this connexion, as it would render the issue unsaleable. Again, it may be provided by statute that the leading officers in the corporation (board of control, administrative officials, or directors) must be citizens of the country, and that regulations affecting the citizenship of the directing personalities, the business headquarters of the enterprise and its independence of foreign enterprises shall be under the protection of a qualified majority of the stockholders, or shall require the consent of a special stockholders' meeting. It was along this line that were reframed the statutory changes relating to the Hamburg-American Line in 1902. But even this device does not afford certain protection. When a majority of the shares are in the hands of foreigners, it will not be difficult to find citizens for all the important positions, who will obediently follow the dictates of those whom they serve.

Governmental Protection against Denationalization. Protection of private enterprises by the state against the aggression of foreign capital may be effective, but is applicable to only a limited degree. Especially must enterprises have some vital economic interest of the community bound up in them if they are to receive such protection, as a further extension of the principle would constitute violation of the international treaty principle of the freedom of industry, and hence would inevitably lead to retaliatory measures by other states. Furthermore, such protection would require considerable financial expenditures which naturally should not be made except in case correspondingly important common interests are to be safeguarded. The protection itself can be effected only by laying upon the enterprise certain obligations in the national interest, which foreign capital will either not assume at all, or not without special compensation in the shape of material advantages. The subsidizing of shipping companies affords special opportunity for the imposition of such conditions. Or again, the state may acquire a portion of the capital stock of the enterprise in order to secure some voice in the administration, and in combination with other reliable inland owners, may prevent a majority of the voting power from passing into foreign hands.

Nationalization as a Defence against Foreign Control. The most radical protective measure against foreign control of enterprises is the direct nationalization of the threatened productive industry, as in this way the property interest in the enterprise is entirely withdrawn from the commercial field. The word production is here intended in the general sense of the creation of any kind of economic values, and hence includes commerce, navigation, &c. But a pre-supposition of such action as here suggested must be the possibility of establishing a monopoly, as a governmental productive establishment is much impeded in its power to compete with other domestic or even foreign enterprises by its greater regard for the economic interests of the community, and the more formal and complicated methods of administration. For this reason, for example, the nationalizing tendency which in European countries has worked itself out triumphantly in the field of railway transportation, has not been successful in the domain of ocean navigation. The business of international water transportation, in view of the sudden changes in competitive relations, demands prompt and responsible decisions, and to these an organ of the political administrative machinery cannot be adopted because of its subordination to higher authority and to specific restrictions. The more clumsy character of state management will be less disadvantageous when as a result of more constant productive and consumptive relations, the field of business operations in question is more steady, and hence better suited to regulation by principles laid down in advance. In addition, the endeavour has always been to secure the advantages of commercial enterprise even in the field of public monopoly. In the beginning this was accomplished by leasing the monopoly to private concessionaries. This policy proved unsatisfactory, as only the financial interests could thus be safeguarded, and often these not adequately. In recent times new forms of organization have been developed by which the state may be relieved of the commercial administration, and yet be able to assert itself at any conjuncture on behalf of the interests entrusted to its care.

One of these forms is the compulsory combine (*Zwangs-kartell*). This is a legally regulated organization of the branch of production in question by means of which, especially in the case of commodities subject to a consumption tax, a control and distribution of the marketing at home and abroad can be carried out; over-production is warded off, exportation being subsidized to this end by the guarantee of higher domestic prices.[1] This plan may also be effective as a defence against foreign control, as the potassium combine in Germany has shown. Another form of organization is that of the private operating company for the Government monopoly, subject to constant oversight by the state; this is the plan which has been considered in connexion with the projected petroleum monopoly in Germany. A precedent for such procedure is, moreover, at hand in the development of banks of issue. The issue of banknotes has become a public monopoly in European states, but is entrusted to private banks which are commercially organized, yet forced in the broad outlines of their business policy, to give precedence

[1] Josef Grunzel, *Der Sieg des Industrialismus*, Leipsic, 1911, p. 93.

to the interests of the community at large over those of their stockholders.

The compulsory combination of producers of potassium salts in Germany was established by the Law of May 25, 1910, in order to forestall the threatened collapse of the private potassium Kartell, an event from which results inimical to the public interests were to be feared. The owners of the potassium works were compelled by law to market their products through the exclusive agency of the operating company formed for this purpose, the ' Potassium Syndicate ' (a limited liability corporation). A distribution committee fixes annually the quantities to be sold at home and abroad, and fixes at the same time the share of each member of the combine in these amounts. Such organizations for the control of marketing have usually been directed toward the end of making possible lower prices abroad by means of higher prices at home, that is, toward subsidizing exportation; in the reverse sense they aim also to utilize the lower foreign prices to secure higher prices at home by relieving the domestic market of the pressure of an excessive supply. In contrast to this procedure the policy of the German potassium combine will be to place the domestic purchaser at least on an equality with the foreign consumer; this action is justified by the fact that potassium salts are extremely important in agriculture, and that Germany has a natural monopoly in their production. In order that the operating company may not use the monopoly guaranteed to it by law to the injury of domestic agriculture, the domestic prices are fixed by the Bundesrat, while only a lower limit is set to foreign prices. These must not be lower than the domestic prices, but their adjustment above this minimum is left entirely at the discretion of the company. The preliminary report of the law clearly indicated that the fear lest the control of the industry should pass into foreign hands was a part of the incentive to this regulative action. The collapse of the private monopoly would have led to a fall in the value of the potassium works, which would have exerted a strong attraction on foreign capital. ' As a result of the marked fall in the value of the potassium plants,' says the report, ' foreign countries dependent upon this source of potassium would not have let pass the opportunity of acquiring numerous potassium works at low prices, and hence of securing an undesirable amount of influence in determining the policy of the German potassium industry.'

A Bill introduced into the German Reichstag in November 1912 is further designed to set a limit to the denationalizing commercial policy of the Standard Oil Company. As the deposits of petroleum in Germany are unimportant, the country must procure its supply from abroad, and in fact principally from the United States of America. In this field the American trust, the ' Standard Oil Company ', has secured a dominant position, inasmuch as it is not merely almost the only agency which furnishes American petroleum to the European market, but in addition controls the transportation media for carrying petroleum both on water (tank steamers) and on land (pipe lines). Even the European producing countries, Russia, Austria-Hungary, and Roumania, have not been able to keep themselves free from its influence. With the help of tributary companies it has erected its own refineries in these countries in order to use their own product in competing with their domestic enterprises, with the advantage of its enormous capital resources. In Germany it monopolized the entire trade through the agency of its own selling companies, the ' Amerikanische Petroleumgesellschaft ' in Hamburg, the ' Atlantische Aktiengesellschaft ' in Bremen, and the ' Mannheimer Petroleumgesellschaft '. The former petroleum dealers were forced out of the trade by the introduction of tank-wagons (*Kannensystem*). The English-French-Dutch competing organization, which, beginning with the year 1907, the ' Koninklijke Nederlandsche Maatschappij tot Exploitatie van Petroleumbronnen in Nederlandsch-Indië ' and the English ' Shell Transport and Trading Company ' have supported in community of interest, has been of no avail. It is now proposed to form a commercial monopoly for the wholesale trade in illuminating oil by utilizing the German ' Erdöl-Aktiengesellschaft '. This company controls practically the entire German supply of crude oil, owns refineries in Galicia, and has interests in Roumania, and quite recently, through the European ' Petroleumunion ', has also come into relation with the Russian naphtha production (the Nobel and Rothschild groups). The retail trade and that in petroleum not suited to illumination are to remain free. The private operating company to be established under state supervision will procure the petroleum through the free competition of the producers. The Standard Oil Company is not excluded, but it is expected that in case of necessity the commodity required may be obtained even without recourse to it.

V

THE PROTECTION AFFECTING CAPITAL BY POSITIVE MEASURES

1. THE ENCOURAGEMENT OF THE IMMIGRATION OF CAPITAL

Inducements Extended to Persons Living on an Income to take up their Residence in a Country. The immigration of capital may be of varied significance to a country. It depends in the first place on whether the owners of the capital also come to take up their residence in the country, or whether the capital alone is brought in; in the former case we have the further question as to whether the capitalists merely live on the income of their funds, or take an active part as enterprisers in the economic life of the country.

The accession of persons living on an income will always be welcome, as they are valuable consumers without at the same time being producers, and hence the productive capacity of the domestic population is increased. The state, however, can exert no direct influence in this direction, as the local conditions are decisive. Persons of this class seek an agreeable sojourn, and hence will avoid the industrial and commercial centres with their noisy business life and their prosaic pursuit of ' trade ', and will prefer places beautifully situated as to landscape, and where the prices of necessities are not raised by the proximity of industrial populations. Indirectly and unconsciously the immigration of such bondholders will be encouraged by a debasement of the currency in a country. The foreigners who draw in gold the income of their funds will be able to exchange the amounts for larger sums of domestic money, and hence the cost of living will be reduced. The depreciation of the currency in Spain, for example, has led to a strong movement of wealthy French people to Barcelona. Some cities, however, strive to attract persons of income, of their own nationality as well as foreigners, by increasing their attractiveness and by public advertising. As examples of such cities we may mention Wiesbaden and Munich in Germany, and Graz and Görz in Austria.

The Encouragement of the Immigration of Business Enterprisers. While a depreciated currency attracts foreigners of the classes living on the returns of investments, no better policy can be adopted by the state for bringing in foreign business enterprisers than that of assuring stability in its value standards. The India Currency Report for 1899 recommended the introduction of the gold standard into British India, asserting that only by this means could capital in large quantities be interested in the building of railways, canals, &c., in the country. Another essential in many cases is the introduction of protective measures relating to commodities. When, as the result of a new duty or patent law or the like, the foreign enterpriser either cannot market his goods in the protected region at all, or can do so only under very great disadvantages, he is likely, if the market is of sufficient importance, to decide to erect a branch factory in the territory. In such cases communes or local organizations often take the initiative and attempt to draw the attention of foreign enterprisers to themselves by communications addressed to the industrial corporations of the interested country, by advertisements in the daily and technical press, &c. Thus, after the enactment of the new Austrian Tariff Law of 1906, the central committee for the promotion of the industrial development of the Bohemian Erzgebirg district addressed a circular letter to all the German chambers of commerce setting forth that the region offered most favourable opportunities for the establishment of branch factories. The cities of Bodenbach and Linz also set on foot a similar agitation in their own behalf. After the passage of the new English Patent Law several English cities advertised in German and American journals offering cheap sites for the erection of branch plants. In Russia the textile industry of Lodz owes its flourishing conditions to Austrians and Germans, who were no longer able to market their goods on account of increased duties. Recently, it is asserted, the increased Russian duties on agricultural machinery and implements have induced the German capitalists to decide upon the erection of factories for these goods in Southern Russia and the Caucasus. In Brazil, also, many foreign producers have erected plants in order to retain their hard-won market in the face of prohibitive duties.

2. Encouragement of Capital Emigration

Encouragement of the Emigration of Business Enterprisers. The economic and political advantages of the expansion of a country through the sending out of enterprisers into foreign economic fields must form a strong inducement to the economic policy of the state to encourage such expansion. The opportunity for direct support of the movement will occur only in the case of colonies, countries under a protectorate, &c. Where the local government is in a position of external dependence, it may be induced to give the preference to citizens of a particular state in the way of public services, contracts, and orders. In countries with unrestricted sovereignty the road for the settlement of enterprisers can be smoothed only by commercial treaties. The freedom of domicile clause [1] in such agreements grants to the citizens of foreign states the right to move about at will in the territory of a country, to take up residence, acquire land, and carry on business. In modern civilized states this freedom is taken for granted, and is guaranteed even in the political constitutions. Only the acquisition of real estate is denied or restricted in some countries, as Roumania and Japan. The right to carry on trade and industry is usually regulated

[1] Josef Grunzel, *System der Handelspolitik* (second edition, Leipsic, 1906), p. 440.

in more detail. The foreigner is placed on an equality with the citizen, but certain exceptions are made with regard to druggists, commercial brokers, and itinerant merchants or pedlars.

Of all the enterprisers who go into foreign countries, merchants will naturally be looked upon with greatest favour by any state, as they carry with them relatively the least amount of capital, and provide a market for home products in the foreign land. In consequence, many European countries grant stipends to young merchants who take up their residence in oversea regions, a practice which in fact forms one of the essential means of promoting exportation.

The Encouragement of the Emigration of Capital. The mere emigration of capital will not be thought worthy of encouragement unless it can be brought into some relation with the exportation of commodities. In most instances it will suffice in connexion with actual exportation of capital, as especially in the case of the flotation of loans by the foreign governments, to secure this connexion by providing that the admission of the loan to quotation on the exchanges is conditioned on some consideration granted to domestic production. This procedure has already been explained.

On the other hand, we find in the case of oversea banks a direct provision for capital exportation for the purpose of encouraging the exportation of commodities. The purpose of such banks is not merely to finance the exportation of goods, but in addition to supply the need for capital in foreign economic fields. In this connexion are to be distinguished the commercial banks, which deal principally in the short-time credit of commerce and industry, and mortgage banks, which grant long-time loans to the farmers. England, Germany, France, Italy, and Holland have developed institutions of this character.

VI

THE PROTECTION AFFECTING LABOUR BY NEGATIVE MEASURES

1. The Discouragement of Emigration

The Principle of the Freedom of Emigration. A general prohibition of emigration could not be enforced under the present conditions as to the facility of international transportation, nor is it to be reconciled with the modern views of personal freedom of movement. Only as a retaliatory measure against a particular country is the emigration prohibition still met with in recent times.

As the principle of the freedom of emigration is generally established in constitutional law, it is usually not repeated in the statutes affecting emigration; only the Italian and Spanish laws state it explicitly. It is, however, universally subjected to various limitations. These may be divided into two groups, those directed toward safeguarding interests of the state which may be opposed to individual interests, and provisions for the protection of the emigrant himself. Following is a list of the laws relating to this subject to which reference will be made [1] :—

Hungary—Statutes, Article II, Year of 1909.

Italy—Law of January 31, 1901, with Supplementary Act of July 17, 1910, and emigration regulations of July 10, 1910.

Spain—Law of December 21, 1907, with enforcement provisions of April 30, 1908.

Germany—Law of June 9, 1897, with provisions for execution.

[1] A German translation of the more important laws has appeared under the following title : Franz Ritter von Srbik, *Die Auswanderungsgesetzgebung*, Vienna, 1911.

Switzerland—Law of March 22, 1888, with decree of July 10, 1888, for carrying into effect.

Belgium—Law of December 14, 1876, and January 7, 1890, with executive provisions of December 2, 1905.

France—Law of July 18, 1860, and Imperial decrees of March 9 and March 15, 1861.

Holland—Law of June 11, 1861 (July 15, 1869).

Austria—Bills of the years 1904 and 1908.

Restrictions for Safeguarding Public Interests. Under this head restrictions on the ground of obligation for military service take first place. The emigration of persons liable to such service between certain prescribed age limits may be entirely forbidden or granted only under prescribed conditions.[1] Occasionally lighter conditions for fulfilling the military service requirement are granted to citizens living abroad.

It follows from the juridical supremacy of the state that the emigration of those persons is to be forbidden who are convicted or accused of crimes or misdemeanours subject to punishment by deprivation of liberty.[2]

In the interest of persons needing protection the emigration of minors is made dependent on the consent of the parent or guardian, and in addition in certain cases, proper escort and respectable accommodation on the journey are provided for.[3] In Spain, a married woman must have the consent of her husband. Italy punishes the solicitation and removal of young persons to foreign countries for work, and of women for prostitution.[4] On the other hand, the emigration of parents may be forbidden if they design to leave behind them children unprovided for.[5] Or the same may apply to others leaving dependent persons unprovided for.[6]

A unique position is that of the Spanish Law relating to

[1] See German Law, sec. 23; Hungarian Law, sec. 2; Italian Law, Art. 1; Spanish Law, Art. 4.

[2] German Law, sec. 23, b; Hungarian Law, sec. 2, c; Spanish Law, Art. 3.

[3] Hungarian Law, sec. 2, a; Swiss Law, Art. 11; Spanish Law, Art. 5.

[4] Italian Law, Arts. 2–4.

[5] Swiss Law, Art. 11; Hungarian Law, sec. 2, d.

[6] Hungarian Law, sec. 2, c.

emigration in mass, a phenomenon which has been peculiarly conspicuous in Spain. The provision is as follows (Art. 6):

For any emigration in mass to any foreign country with the aim of settling a definite territory or with any other object in view, a special permit must be obtained from the Ministerial Council, to be issued on the basis of a report of the Superior Emigration Council, in addition to all other guarantees deemed necessary, even if not prescribed in this law. In the intent of this article, an emigration in mass is to be understood as any emigration leading to the depopulation of a particular region, a community, a village, or a parish.

If this limitation was designed merely to bring to the attention of the highest political authorities the menace of emigrations in mass, and to lead to a provision by economic and political measures for removing the underlying causes of the phenomenon, it would be justified. Otherwise, it represents a breach of the principle of the freedom of migration itself, and, moreover, it will probably not always be practicably enforceable unless at the same time freedom of movement within the country is to be denied.

Restrictions for the Protection of the Emigrant. It indicates a notable forward step when the state not merely safeguards its own interests but also protects the emigrant himself. It is true that the emigrant represents a loss to the state, but from the standpoint of emigration legislation it is an unavoidable one; hence it can only be the task of such legislation to mitigate the loss by proving to the departing citizen that the protecting hand of the home country does not abandon him even when he betakes himself into a foreign land for permanent productive activity. In this connexion four stages are to be distinguished, of which legislation may take account; these are the solicitation of the immigrant, his transportation, the sojourn abroad, and the return home.

The solicitation of emigrants by enterprisers engaged in their transportation, that is, by the steamship and railway companies, is forbidden in all laws. The extent of the activity permitted to them is the publication of the conditions of transportation, time-tables, descriptions of vessels, cost of passage, &c. To the same end the laws also forbid the so-called subsidized emigration, in which the transportation company receives any consideration of value from a foreign government or enterprise. The German Law forbids the transportation ' of citizens of the Empire for whose passage foreign governments, or colonization companies, or similar enterprises, have paid entirely or in part, or toward which they have made any advances '.[1] The Hungarian Law also [2] forbids the emigration of any ' to whom an entirely or partly free passage or the advancement of transportation charges have been offered in the furtherance of the designs of any colonization scheme planned by the government of a foreign state or by a colonization or similar company or by private persons '. The Italian Law [3] requires in such cases a special permission based on special guarantees, and the same is true of the Swiss executive decree.[4] The Swiss Federal Law itself prohibits emigration agencies and colonization companies from making contracts by which they ' obligate themselves to furnish a certain number of persons either to shipping companies, colonization or other enterprises, or governments '.[5] In order to guard against the possibility that the agents of transportation enterprises might be given some inducement to solicit emigrants, the Hungarian Law [6] prescribes that the managers and other employees of their offices must be paid fixed salaries, and that all forms of compensation varying with the amount of business transacted, as well as any sharing of profits, must be avoided. In many laws, however, solicitation is permitted on the condition of a special permit to be granted to enterprises which solicit the transportation of wage labourers to foreign countries, and those soliciting farmers for the settlement of oversea regions, such as colonization companies.[7]

[1] Sec. 23, c.   [2] Sec. 2, g.   [3] Art. 13.
[4] Art. 42.   [5] Art. 12.   [6] Sec. 13.
[7] Italian Law, Art. 18 ; Hungarian Statute, sec. 1; Swiss Law, Art. 12, relating only to colonization companies ; Austrian Bill of 1908, secs. 4–9.

By this method, however, solicitation within the country can alone be influenced. In case of solicitation from abroad, not the solicitation but only the solicited emigrant can be taken as the object of the influence to be exerted; hence, in this direction care is taken to provide for the establishment of a corresponding information service. For this purpose a governmental organization which distributes information gratis is always preferred; benevolent institutions are not usually employed as auxiliaries except in case of necessity, while commercial enterprises are in the nature of the case entirely excluded. The information service is purely governmental in the following countries, and is organized in the manner indicated: in Italy, it is under an Emigration Commission with local committees; in France information bureaus in specified cities are under the inspection of the Emigration Commissioner; Switzerland has an Emigration Bureau in the Department of Foreign Affairs; in Hungary the Bureau is in the Ministry of the Interior; Belgium has information offices under the supervision of the Minister of Foreign Affairs; Holland has supervisory commissions paid by the state in various communes; in Spain the service is in charge of the Higher Emigration Council, Third Section, with the assistance of local emigration commissions; England has the 'Emigrants Information Office' in the Colonial Office. In Germany the distribution of information is effected by the state-subsidized 'Central Information Office for Emigrants', and in Austria it is in the hands of several private associations.

All the laws at present in force require special official permission for the transportation of emigrants—a concession, patent, or the like. Among the conditions required, many laws include also the right of disposition over suitable ships.[1] The privilege may not be granted to foreign enterprises unless they have a responsible representative located in the country, and submit to its legislative and other requirements.

[1] Italian Law, Art. 13; German Law, sec. 5; Spanish Law, Art. 22; Austrian Bill of 1908, sec. 1, a.

This secures for the government an opportunity for working toward the bringing of the media for transporting emigrants under control of its nationals, as domestic shipping companies may be favoured, or the embarkation of emigrants at specified ports may be prescribed. In order to assure the fulfilment of obligations to the authorities and to the emigrants, the payment of a contingent deposit is prescribed. A special permit, and frequently also a special contingent fee, is required for emigration agents (called 'representatives' in the Italian Law), who are defined by the German Law (section 11) as persons who co-operate for a consideration with a licensed transportation enterprise by the preparation, transmission, or conclusion of transportation agreements. The Spanish Law prohibits them entirely (Art. 34), and permits the employment only of agents who assist the shipowners in the transportation of emigrants. For the protection of the emigrant the transportation contract is also legally regulated as to form and content. The formal requirements cover the drawing of an agreement in writing, and the provision for certain services; but as to content also, the freedom of contract is limited to the extent that the transportation company is legally compelled to assume certain obligations. Thus it must bind itself to carry the passenger to his port of landing, to provide for his needs, to furnish free medical attention, &c. Detailed requirements are laid down as to the character, construction, and equipment of the ships to be used in this service, and conformity to these specifications is made subject to the approval of special state officials. In the more recent laws the government also reserves the right of approval of the transportation rates for emigrants and their baggage.[1] In addition, the government has recently asserted the right of entirely prohibiting emigration to specified countries. For example, the Hungarian Law (Art. 4) says: 'The Minister of the Interior may for

[1] Italian Law, Art. 14; Hungarian Statute, sec. 10; Austrian Law of 1908, secs. 40-2.

a specified time prohibit either entirely or for persons of a specified occupation or age, emigration to any country or region where the life, health, morals, or property of emigrants is seriously endangered.' The Italian Law (Art. 1) empowers the Minister of Foreign Affairs to suspend emigration to specified regions on grounds of public policy or in case the life, freedom, or possessions of the emigrants may be endangered. The Spanish Law (Art. 15) is similarly worded. The Hungarian Law (Art. 5) also provides for the restriction of emigration to one or several specified routes, ' which from the standpoint of the public interest and with respect to the safeguarding of the interests of the emigrants may seem most advisable '; in this case, however, it is rather the nationalization of the emigrant transportation service which is aimed at.

The legislation for the protection of emigrants after reaching their destination is as yet little developed. Their interests are usually placed in the care of the diplomatic and consular service ; these officers are of course supposed to perform such functions for all their nationals, but watching over emigrants is often made a special duty. Only in the more recent laws are special emigrant commissioners or emigrant inspectors provided who are supposed to look after not merely the general problem of emigrant transportation, but in addition the interests of emigrants already living abroad.[1] In the royal decree of December 2, 1906, Italy has provided for certain special consular attachés to be temporarily connected with foreign consulates for the protection of Italian emigrants. The maintenance of some intimate connexion with the home country is still left exclusively to private initiative, which is especially inadequate in this field. The regulation of the important question of the conditions of money transmission is just beginning to be developed, after crass instances of exploitation of emigrants by swindling

---

[1] Spanish Law, sec. 47 ; German Law, sec. 41 ; Hungarian Statute, sec. 35 and sec. 36 ; Austrian Bill of 1908, sec. 56.

financial institutions have aroused the public interest. The Spanish Law contains (sec. 60) merely a general provision authorizing the government by the aid of consular officials to regulate the savings, accommodation, and money transmission of the emigrants. The Hungarian Law (sec. 31) assigns to the government the same task, to be performed with the aid of the postal savings system. The Italian government has probably best organized this money transmission service by the help of the postal savings banks and the ' Banco di Napoli '.

In view of the ever increasing· back flow, further provision must be made for the return of the emigrants. Up to the present only preliminary efforts on a small scale have been made in this direction. A possibility is offered in the inducement of transportation enterprises to grant return transportation to emigrants either free or at reduced rates. Thus the Italian Law (Art. 25) obligates the company to provide return transportation for a certain number of destitute Italians according to the size of the ship, at a price of two lire per day, including food and accommodation. The Spanish Law also requires that under specified conditions a given number of emigrants must be brought back at half price, the number being fixed at twenty per cent of those carried by the enterprise to the country in question during the preceding four months. In addition an emigration fund, composed of contributions, fees, and fines, is employed in repatriation besides its use for covering the costs of protecting emigrants.[1]

2. The Discouragement of Immigration

The Principle of the Freedom of Immigration. To the personal freedom of movement constitutionally secured corresponds the freedom of immigration. It is recognized in European countries also. In oversea countries, however,

---

[1] Hungarian Law, sec. 29 ; Spanish Law, Arts. 16 and 30 ; to some extent also, perhaps, the Italian Law, Art. 28.

a dual theory of immigration is maintained. Many governments encourage or even subsidize immigrants while many
exclude them, and occasionally even the same law contains
provisions both for encouragement and for exclusion, distinguishing between desirable and undesirable immigrants,
and between regions needing population and over-crowded
regions. We are here concerned merely with the exclusion
measures. These are to be reconciled with the principle of
personal freedom of movement only in so far as they are
dictated by the higher public interests of protecting the health,
safety, and morals of the people. Since, however, as already
explained, the equilibrium between wages, the products of
labour, and the standard of living subsisting in any economic
domain may be seriously disturbed by the accession of
immigrants, there arises a need of protection against cheaper
labour power on general principles. As such protection is
inconsistent with the principle of the freedom of movement
the end will be achieved indirectly, through the restriction
of the immigration of foreign labourers as much as possible
by sanitary and safety regulations and checks, as well as by
other requirements of various kinds.[1]

Such restrictions exist even in European states. Thus
England, in the Immigration Law of August 11, 1905, prohibits ' undesirable ' immigration absolutely. Subsequent
special provisions exclude prostitutes and their protectors,
destitute persons, or those who cannot prove the possession
of five pounds sterling and two pounds each for dependent
members of the family, persons of bad reputation, those
afflicted with incurable or repulsive diseases, the insane, and
criminals, in so far as according to the Law of 1870 they are
subject to deportation. This legislation was called forth by
the depressing effect on wages of immigrant Russians and
Italians. In Germany, the control of immigration is entrusted

---

[1] Cf. also Giuseppe Prato, *Il protezionismo operaio ; l'esclusione del
lavoro straniero*, Turin, Emmanuel Sella, 1910 ; *Der Wandel des Besitzes*,
German translation by J. Bluwstein, Munich and Leipsic, 1912.

to the individual states, and these have gone forward with the development of restrictive measures against foreign migratory labourers. In connexion with the public contracts of both states and communes, the contractors are required to give the preference to German labourers. The most stringent measures, however, are those introduced by Prussia in the Law of December 21, 1907. This requires immigrant labourers to provide themselves by payment of a fee of two marks, with identification cards in the German language, the cards being issued by officers on the frontiers, by the *Feldarbeiterzentral* in Berlin, or by officials in Essen or Berlin (*Zwangslegitimation*). In recent years proposals have frequently been made for the levying of an ' import duty ' on foreign migratory labourers.

Switzerland struggles simultaneously against labour competition and against anarchism. Foreigners must secure a residence permit card (*Permis de séjour*), the fee for which ranges from 0.50 franc in the canton of Appenzell up to twenty francs in the canton of Tessin. These permits are issued for a term of from one to twelve months, but may be revoked at any time on specified grounds.

In France a strong agitation has been carried on for decades against Italian labourers. The Law of August 8, 1893, established a number of police regulations, and required foreigners to be registered, for which a certain fee was charged. The demand for the introduction of a duty on foreign labour power has been frequently made. The enactment of August 10, 1899, limiting to ten per cent the employment of foreign labourers on public works, has been very effective.

Spain excludes foreigners entirely from public works. Roumania limits enterprises in the employment of foreigners to one-fourth the number of Roumanians employed.

The earliest and most stringent restrictive measures have, however, been taken by non-European countries, as the following summary will show. The laws to which reference will be made in connexion with the different countries are as follows [1] :—

United States of America—Law of February 20, 1907, with amendment of March 26, 1910, and regulations. Immigration Bill of 1913.

Canada—Law of May 4, 1910, amended April 4, 1911.

Mexico—Law of December 22, 1908, and the Colonization laws.

Argentina—Law of October 19, 1876, and Colonization Law of February 3, 1913.

Brazil—Edict of April 19, 1907, and Colonization provision of December 21, 1907.

Uruguay—Law of June 10, 1890.

Paraguay—Law of October 9, 1903.

Venezuela—Law of August 26, 1896.

Australia—Law relating to the Restriction of Immigration, 1901–10.

New Zealand—Law relating to the Restriction of Immigration, 1898, with amendment of 1910.

South African Union—Laws of the individual colonies.

Protection against Immigration by Sanitary and Public Safety Regulations. In this connexion, no objection whatever can be made to the prohibitions relating to diseases which threaten public health with the danger of contagion. The American Law (sec. 2) excludes 'persons who are affected with tuberculosis or any loathsome disease'. Canada (sec. 3) excludes persons who are affected with a loathsome or a contagious disease, or with any disease which might become a menace to public health. The Mexican Law (Art. 3) enumerates the contagious diseases; the following classes of foreigners have no right to admittance : '1. Persons affected with bubonic plague, cholera, yellow fever, cerebro-spinal meningitis, typhoid fever, pustular typhus, dysentery, measles,

[1] Some of the laws have appeared in German translation under the following title : Franz Ritter von Srbik, *Die Einwanderungsgesetzgebung*, Vienna, 1911.

scarlet fever, small-pox, or diphtheria, or with any other acute disease, which according to the decision of the government is to be regarded as contagious. 2. Persons suffering from tuberculosis, leprosy, beriberi, trachoma, Egyptian leprosy, or any other acute disease, which according to the decision of the government is to be regarded as contagious.' General regulations are also contained in the Argentinian Law (Arts. 31 and 32), as well as the Brazilian (Art. 2), the Australian (sec. 3, d), and New Zealand (sec. 14, c) legislation.

The second group of excluded immigrants consists of those who are apparently unable to earn a sufficient livelihood, and hence are likely to become a burden upon the community. These include, in the first place, persons having physical or mental defects. The American Law (sec. 2) names idiots, the insane, feebleminded, epileptic, persons of unsound mind, or those who have been mentally deranged within the preceding five years. Of a more general character are the provisions of the Mexican Law (Art. 3), and those of Argentina (Art. 32), Brazil (Art. 2), Australia (sec. 3), and New Zealand (sec. 14). But age may also constitute a cause of reduced earning capacity. The United States of America and Mexico exclude children under sixteen years of age, for whom adequate provision is not in evidence, while Argentina and Brazil refuse admission to persons above the age of sixty. The possession of a specified amount of money occasionally forms a further requirement. The United States of America enumerates among excluded immigrants those destitute of means (sec. 2), and demands a declaration as to the possession of fifty dollars (sec. 12) ; the Bill of 1913 contemplated an increase in this amount. Canada requires in the regulations of May 9, 1910, the possession of a ticket or the price of passage to the point of destination, and in addition a money sum of twenty-five dollars for each adult, and $12.50 for each member of the family between the ages of five and eighteen years. Paraguay grants certain encouragement to immigrants only on condition that the possession of fifty gold pesos by the father of the family and thirty pesos for each adult male member is proved. In the Transvaal and the Orange Free State the possession of twenty pounds sterling must be proved.[1]   Furthermore, it is not merely incapacity for work, but also a distaste for it which makes an immigrant undesirable ; hence many laws, as those of Canada, Argentina, and Brazil, expressly exclude beggars and vagabonds.   Finally, many countries protect themselves against immigration promoted by foreign societies or governments, as has been especially the case with Russia on religious grounds.   The United States of America (sec. 2) forbids the entrance of persons whose tickets or passage have been paid for with the money of another party, or who have been assisted by others in emigrating, unless it is clearly and satisfactorily shown that the persons concerned do not belong to one of the excluded classes, and that such tickets or passage were not directly or indirectly paid for by any association, organization, corporation, municipality, or foreign government.   The Canadian Law also names (sec. 3, h) ' immigrants to whom money has been given or loaned by any benevolent organization for the purpose of qualifying them to land in accordance with this law, or whose passage to Canada has been paid in whole or in part by any benevolent organization or out of public funds. . . .'

The third group of excluded immigrants consists of persons who constitute a menace to public morals.   All the laws exclude criminals, but the detailed specifications in this connexion are various.   The United States of America protects itself against 'persons convicted of a felony or misdemeanour or other offence involving moral turpitude, or who have confessed to the commission of such an offence ', but expressly declares that this provision does not apply to persons ' who have been convicted of a purely political offence '.   The Mexican Law (Art. 3, VI) names ' fugitives from justice, and

[1] It will be recalled that in the mother country, England, the possession of five pounds and an additional two pounds for each member of the family was required.

persons who have been convicted of an offence which, according to Mexican laws, would be punishable by confinement for more than two years, in both cases with the exception of political and military offences '. According to the Australian Law (sec. 3, e), admittance is denied to ' persons who have been convicted of crime and sentenced therefore to imprisonment for a term of one year or more, and who have not paid the penalty or secured its remission '. The New Zealand Law (sec. 14, d) designates as inadmissible :

any person who arrives in New Zealand within less than two years after the conclusion of a term of imprisonment to which he was sentenced on account of an offence which if committed in New Zealand would render him liable to death or to imprisonment for a term of two years or more, provided the offence is not of a purely political character and that no pardon for it has been granted.

The United States of America, Canada, and Australia combat prostitution in the same way. The most explicit is the American Law, which runs as follows :

Prostitutes or women and girls who come to the United States for the purpose of prostitution or for any other immoral purpose ; persons who are supported wholly or in part by the proceeds of prostitution or who receive an income from this source ; or persons who maintain prostitutes or women and girls for the purpose of prostitution or for any other immoral purpose or who attempt to bring such persons into the United States.

The American Law further adds polygamists or persons who confess adherence to the doctrine or practice of polygamy. Finally, legislation in some countries found itself called upon to take measures against anarchists. The American Law forbids the immigration of anarchists, and of persons who admit their belief in the overthrow by force or violence of the government of the United States or of all government or of all legal forms, or in the murder of public officials, or who defend such beliefs. The Mexican Law similarly excludes adherents of anarchist organizations, or persons who propagate, advocate, or profess the doctrine of the violent overthrow of governments, or the murder of public officials.

Protection against the Competition of Foreign Labour. The difficulty in enforcing protection against competition by foreign labour is twofold. On the one hand, the prohibition may formally conflict with the principle of personal freedom of movement, and hence must be brought under some higher interest of the state; on the other hand, it must not interfere with the immigration of foreigners in·general, and as such, but only of such foreign labourers as on account of their lower standard of living are liable to disturb the equilibrium established within the country between wages, the product of labour, and the standard of life.

One means to this end is afforded by the manipulation of the sanitary police regulations; if these are made very stringent they may become a potent obstacle to immigration, since in the determination of disease and crime considerable play is afforded for subjective estimation. In the United States of America this means of control is in fact so extra-ordinarily severe that the scenes on Ellis Island, where the immigrants are inspected, have acquired a certain notoriety and given the place the name of the ' Isle of Tears '.

Similar judgement must be passed on the head-tax provision, which is justified on the ground of the cost of immigration control, but which may degenerate into a protective duty on foreign labour power, just as registration fees often become a protective duty against foreign commodities. In the United States the head-tax, which must be paid by every foreigner who enters the country, has been raised from fifty cents to four dollars (sec. 1 of the Law of February 20, 1907). British Columbia introduced a head-tax on Chinese immigrants as early as the year 1878, and by the year 1903 it had been increased to 100 pounds sterling, while, in addition, the ships were forbidden to carry more than one Chinese to fifty tons of vessel capacity. In New Zealand, £100 must be paid to the customs office for each Chinese landed, and the landing is further limited according to the capacity of the vessels, one Chinese to 200 tons. Before the enactment of the federal legislation, the several colonies also levied high taxes.

A direct violation of the principle of the freedom of movement is offered by the exclusion of contract labourers, in which the United States of America has taken the lead. The law regards as contract labourers all who have been induced or persuaded to immigrate by the offer or promise of employment, or as a result of any oral, written, or printed agreement, expressed or understood, relating to skilled or unskilled labour of any kind (sec. 2). The prohibition is not to be applied to members of the higher professions such as artists or scholars, nor to personal or domestic servants. In addition, any person or organization is liable to punishment for supporting or encouraging the immigration of contract labourers in any manner whatever (sec. 4). That the United States of America was able with impunity to act in open contradiction to a universally recognized principle of international equity, is explicable in part from the strength of its economic position. It exports more raw material and imports more manufactured goods than other countries, and hence is less menaced by retaliatory measures on the part of foreign states. A further explanation is to be found in the fact that the foreign countries affected had no reason to encourage the solicitation of labourers for employment abroad.

The Canadian legislation assumes the character of a special solicitude for the immigrants, relating as it does to the adaptability of the race to the climate or to the special requirements of Canada. Section 38 of the Law of May 4, 1910, empowers the Governor-General to forbid, for a specified time or permanently, the landing in Canada, or at a specified Canadian port of entry, of immigrants belonging to a race known to be unsuited to the climate or conditions in Canada, and the provision applies to the landing of immigrants of any specified race, occupation, or description.

The Australian States have substituted for the earlier head-tax a remarkable means of selection in the form of the dictation test. By this means the higher interest of the state in the preservation of the cultural level of the population is protected, with the object of keeping out immigrants not belonging to the white race. The Federal Law designates as inadmissible immigrants, persons who cannot write at the dictation of an official at least fifty words in a specified language. A provision for designating the language to be used can be put in force only with the consent of both Houses of the Parliament, but none the less enormous difficulties have been met with in the execution of the provision. In the Law of 1905, agreements with foreign states are anticipated in consequence of which the nationals of the latter may be freed from the dictation test (Art. 4, A). In a similar manner, New Zealand (sec. 14 in the draft of the Law of October 25, 1910) has enacted that the following are not to be admitted :

any person of other than British or Irish birth or descent who on the demand of an official appointed by the governor in accordance with this law shall fail to fill out and sign with his own hand in the presence of such officer in any European speech whatever an application drawn up according to any one of the prescribed models which the officer in question may deem appropriate.

A Chinese, however, cannot land until he has copied in writing to the satisfaction of the customs officials, a printed selection of not less than one hundred words in the English language, selected at the pleasure of the customs officer. The Immigration Bill of 1913, which passed the United States Congress but failed to become law, excluded illiterates over sixteen years of age.

The most unscrupulous procedure in regard to the principle of freedom of movement has been followed in connexion with the protection of white labour (the ' white policy '), as the immigration of coloured labourers leads to political and social as well as economic dangers. The protective policy of Australia began as early as the year 1855 ; it was directed in the first place against the Chinese, and later against the inhabi-

tants of Polynesia, the Kanakas. The ' Pacific Island Labourers Act ' of the year 1901 unconditionally forbade the entrance
of Polynesian labourers after March 31, 1904, and further
provided that by December 31, 1906, all members of this race
must have left Australian soil. The struggle of the United
States of America against the ' yellow peril ' has had a
chequered history. California, where the movement originated, met at once with resistance on the part of the national
Congress. In the Law of September 13, 1888, the immigration
of all Chinese was forbidden, with the exception of officials,
teachers, merchants, and travellers for pleasure, in possession
of identification cards filled out by American consulates.
Repeated struggles with China followed, ending with the
Chinese boycott of American goods in the year 1905, which
led to a modification of the policy of hostility to the Chinese.
In the meantime, the immigration of the Japanese had
aroused concern ; in California especially a strong agitation
was set on foot. When, in the year 1906, the school board
in San Francisco denied admission to the schools of the
whites to Chinese, Japanese, and Korean children, there
followed a diplomatic correspondence with Japan ending with
the Japanese government taking action itself against the
immigration of Japanese coolies, so that the American states
would have no occasion to intervene. In the year 1913,
however, California undertook further repressive measures ;
a Bill was introduced into the legislature forbidding the acquisition of real estate by foreigners who had not declared
their intention of becoming American citizens.

International Regulation. While the protective measures
in the field of the exchange of commodities very early led
to international agreements, only the beginnings of such an
adjustment are yet to be traced in the field of population
movements. Their necessity, however, is gradually forcing
recognition. In the first place, the emigration countries are
recognizing that their enactments show a vital defect in that
they take no account of the provisions of the immigration

countries, for the steamship companies are equally bound to both. Some emigration laws, therefore, unconditionally prohibit the emigration of persons whose entry into the country of immigration is forbidden. The immigration countries in turn recognize that it would be more intelligent and humane to investigate immigrants who may encounter obstacles in landing at the port of embarkation, and in case of necessity to forbid their departure. It can be but a step from this point to the conclusion of international treaties in which these questions will be settled by joint action.

The Immigration Law of the United States of America (sec. 39) empowers the president to conclude agreements with other nations, to the end that emigrants may be inspected at the ports of embarkation by American Consuls and other officials, and that in this way the undesired immigration may be prevented with the assistance of the foreign government. The Australian Law also (sec. 4, A) authorized the government to conclude treaties with foreign states relative to the admission of their nationals which may free the latter from liability to the dictation test.

VII

PROTECTION AFFECTING LABOUR BY POSITIVE MEASURES

1. The Encouragement of Emigration

Colonization abroad on Non-Economic Grounds. The incitation of emigration will seldom occur on economic grounds, as it is usually regarded as involving a loss. Political and religious conditions, however, readily bring about encouraging activity on the part, if not of the state, at least of private associations, looking to the colonization under favourable conditions of members of a race, or adherents of a faith in which they are interested. As an example from our own times the German and Jewish agricultural colonies in Palestine may serve. In the year 1868, several colonies were established by a religious association founded in Württemberg, calling itself the ' German Temple '. One such colony is near Jaffa, another is three kilometres distant from the same city, in the plain of Sharon, one is situated a kilometre to the south of Jerusalem, and one on the narrow coastal plain between Mt. Carmel and the bay of Haifa. The ' Alliance Israélite ' has also settled in numerous colonies Jews driven from Russia.

Emigration for Relieving Pressure on the Home Labour Market. Just as the industrial corporations work for the maintenance of domestic prices through the marketing of goods abroad by means of private export bounties, so also the English labour unions have since as early as 1843 paid emigration bounties to their members. They were under the spell of the wages fund theory which fixed the level of the wages of labour in a purely mechanical way, according to the share of capital available in the country for the payment of wages and the number of labourers to be paid. The relief, however, proved of little value. In the first place, the financial means available were too small in proportion to the total labour market. Moreover, it was in particular the most industrious and enterprising people who volunteered to emigrate. Finally, the labour organizations in immigration regions of America and Australia assumed a hostile attitude to the practice.

The Repatriation of Immigrants. Other cases occur in which the re-emigration of persons is encouraged who have previously immigrated, and have subsequently shown themselves an undesirable addition to the population. Thus, in South Africa, where there was need of coloured labourers, as the use of white labourers in the mines would have threatened the position of the white population as the ruling class, —south of the Zambesi the ratio of blacks to whites is five to one—about 50,000 Chinese coolies were imported through a treaty with the government of China concluded in 1904. The measure met with violent opposition from the beginning in England itself, and in consequence of a change in the political system in the year 1911, all the labourers were repatriated. The mining companies have overcome the difficulty ; an offer of prizes which they made put them in possession of machine drills, which have made the human labour previously required largely superfluous. Australia also has taken special measures for the repatriation of the Kanakas or coloured plantation labourers to their native islands of Oceania, after the Federal Law of 1901 prohibited their remaining on Australian soil beyond the year 1906.

2. THE ENCOURAGEMENT OF IMMIGRATION

The Inducements contained in Immigration Laws. It has already been stated that many countries restrict immigration, while on the other hand many encourage it, and that occasionally even one country includes inducements and exclusion measures in the same law, distinguishing as to the character of the immigrants and their destination. Generally speaking, in regions with a predominantly agricultural production, the need of labour power is so far in excess of the supply that immigration will appear as desirable, while in regions of predominantly industrial production, the danger of underbidding the established wage-rate is so great that the working population will combat the admission of immigrants. The laws of the South American states are unreservedly friendly to the accession of new population from abroad. Canada employs stringent regulations against immigrants not wanted, but provides extensive measures of encouragement in favour of those admitted. The law of the United States of America contains a single paragraph designed to meet the wishes of the agricultural southern states for a larger accession of immigrants. The section in question provides for an information bureau to be established in the Immigration Office to secure the distribution of the immigrants admitted into the United States among the different states and territories of the Union by which immigrants are desired. Australia and New Zealand take a completely hostile attitude; their laws have already been described (under VI, 2).

The inducements offered may relate to five different phases of immigration—the solicitation of the immigrants, their transportation, arrival, sojourn in the country, and return to the old home. In connexion with the solicitation, we may mention the agreements which the governments of oversea countries have made with steamship companies, as do also the direct measures taken by these states themselves. Many governments maintain special agents in Europe, whose duty it is to carry on an active propaganda in favour of emigration to their respective countries. Thus Argentina, as early as the Law of October 19, 1876, empowered the government to appoint special agents in all countries of Europe or Asia regarded as suitable to the purpose; these agents were to use all the means at hand in carrying on the propaganda in the interest of immigration into the Argentine Republic, ' by advertising its natural, political, and social features, the principal branches of its industry, its colonial system, the advantages offered to industrious immigrants, the price of land and conditions of its acquisition, the rate of wages, the cost of food products and articles of consumption, and all information relating to the purpose of this law '. Canada has agents in Great Britain who set forth the merits of their country in pamphlets, public addresses, newspaper advertisements, &c., and in addition, two exhibition cars traverse the country. Brazil provides for the solicitation only through steamship companies who enter into formal contracts to furnish immigrants.

Inducements in connexion with transportation consist in the whole or part payment of the passage, and in requirements as to the character of the vessels used in the service. Argentina makes advances on the passage money to farmers under contract to settle in the colonies of the country. In Brazil the federal government grants to farmers of good repute, who arrive in company with their families, or are sent for by them, and who wish to settle as farm owners, third-class tickets from the port of embarkation to Rio Janeiro or any other port of landing, ' as long as the accession of voluntary immigrants into the country is not sufficiently numerous and shows no increase' (sec. 97). Contributions to the cost of passage are found also in Venezuela, Uruguay, and Paraguay. Especially explicit are the Canadian provisions for the protection of the immigrant on the journey (secs. 56–61). No ship may carry more passengers than one adult to each fifteen lighted square feet on each deck. The attitude of the captain and crew to the passengers is strictly regulated. Mexico prescribes in detail the arrangement of ships which bring in immigrant labourers (Art. 20 ff.). The law of the United States of America also (sec. 42) requires a specified relation between vessel capacity and the number of immigrants—one passenger to eighteen feet of lighted surface on the main deck and to twenty feet on the lower deck—

though the regulations probably aim rather at the restriction of immigration.

The most important chapter in the protection of immigrants relates to their arrival. Canada protects the newcomers against exploitation, of which they are usually the victims, by permitting persons engaged in bringing them into the country to recommend to them only those specified transportation enterprises, hotels, and boarding-houses which have taken out licences for this purpose (secs. 67–70). Landlords are compelled to post all prices conspicuously, and their lien on the effects of the immigrants is limited (secs. 71, 72). Argentina guarantees to every immigrant, ' who gives sufficient proof of good conduct and of capacity for any trade, art, or useful calling,' the following considerations : (1) Food and lodging at the cost of the state during the five days following his disembarkation ; (2) guidance in securing employment in the branch of work to which he wishes to devote himself ; (3) transportation at state expense to any place within the country where he may wish to take up his residence ; and (4) exemption from import duty on all effects of a personal or household character, or for use in plying his trade. In the most important immigration ports, Buenos Aires, Rosario, &c., immigrant homes have been erected, in which board and lodging are furnished directly by agents of the government. In the most important provincial cities and in the port towns, official immigration commissions are maintained, to whom are entrusted the securing of employment for immigrants and their further oversight and assistance. Any who move into the colonies enjoy in addition the benefits of the homestead law. In Brazil, every immigrant admitted who is a farmer of good repute, and desires to settle upon the soil, is entitled to free lodging and maintenance for the time necessary in reaching his final destination, and to free transportation by ship and railway to the station or port of destination. His baggage, agricultural implements, and all tools necessary for his calling are admitted duty free.

The expenses incurred are divided between the federal government and the different states in accordance with agreements for the purpose.

Special provision for maintenance is necessary only when the immigrants settle in closed colonies, as is the case in South America. Argentina, by the Land Law of February 3, 1903, has had public lands surveyed and investigation made as to their adaptability for different branches of production and for the founding of colonies. The lands are sold or leased on especially favourable terms, and even in part given free to first settlers ; agricultural holdings, however, must not exceed 100 hectares, and those destined to cattle raising are limited to 2,500 hectares, while a single person or company may not possess more than two agricultural allotments nor more than one grazing tract. The Brazilian immigration law provides for the formation of colonial groups by the federal government or by the various states, by private corporations, and by individuals. In the colonies of the federal government the allotments may not exceed twenty-five hectares in the vicinity of a railway or of a river steamship line, and elsewhere are limited to fifty. The town lots which form the future municipality are fixed at a maximum of 3,000 square metres. The immigrants who acquire such lots are encouraged in various ways, are furnished gratis with implements and seed, receive means of subsistence at reduced cost, free medical attention during one year, &c. The several states and private corporations and individuals founding colonies receive contributions and bounties from the federal government. In Canada, the railways have been the most zealous promoters of the agricultural settlement of the country. The Canadian Pacific Railway still has 7,000,000 acres for development. It advertised in December 1912 that bona fide prospective farmers (not land speculators) might in the future pay the purchase price in twenty years instead of ten as previously, with interest at six per cent. In addition, settlers are to receive $2,000 improvement credit on their new property, with twenty years' time for repayment, and are to be provided with livestock at cost price.

Under some circumstances return passage is also provided for immigrants. Thus Brazil pays the return passage of immigrants or members of their families engaged in agriculture who have been brought in on government account, and have maintained themselves at least two years in Brazil, if on account of special causes, such as death, incurable disease, accident, or the like, they are no longer able to earn a livelihood (Arts. 127–31). In addition, travel bonuses for visiting their homes are paid to immigrants who have been settled as farmers in Brazil for not less than three or more than six years, and whose conduct has given no cause for complaint during the time (Art. 132).

Propaganda of Private Enterprises. The encouragement of immigration is to the interest not only of certain oversea countries, but equally to that of the steamship companies, to which the transportation of emigrants has proved the most lucrative source of income, and also to the great railways which are under pressure to settle the regions traversed by their lines. These enterprises do not content themselves with soliciting persons who have decided to change their residence, but in addition employ a whole army of agents to stimulate emigration and give it the desired direction. These ' drummers ' work up an interest in the people, in their homes and on the railways, and employ the most despicable methods since they usually receive a specified sum ' per head ' for the emigrants they secure. Steamship companies have often entered into contracts to furnish to oversea countries a specified number of emigrants ; these contracts they can fulfil only by themselves granting bonuses. Since the countries of Western Europe have instituted strict surveillance over such commercialized proceedings, the operations of the private enterprises have been largely transferred to the Mediterranean region.

PART THREE

THE EFFECTS OF ECONOMIC PROTECTIONISM

I

THE EFFECTS OF COMMODITY PROTECTION ·

1. Effects of the Negative Measures

The Effect of Protective Duties on Prices. An estimation of the effect of protective duties on the prices of commodities is among the most difficult as well as the most important tasks of economic policy. The task is difficult for the reason that the problem of price determination, which is in itself one of the most disputed issues in economic science, is here to be considered under the influence of an artificial disturbing force, whose consequences make themselves felt in all the ramifications of national and world economy. The task is important as well, for the price changes òf the commodities form the most immediate and most obvious effect by which producers and consumers orient themselves in the attempt to determine the future of economic policy.

The first factor to be considered is the nature of this artificial disturbing force, which again involves, first the rôle of the protective duty, and further the character of the customs administration. A moderate duty will often exert no influence at all on prices, as the foreign producer may possibly offset it either by further reducing costs or by contenting himself with less profit, in order to retain his former market. The assertion that in this case the protective effect is lost,[1] is, however, incorrect, as the protection does not inhere in the price advance. The domestic producer receives protection if the cost is increased or the profit reduced for his foreign competitor. It may well happen, however, that the inevitable formalities of customs administration may notably heighten the protective effect. When in the year

---

[1] A. de Lavison, *La Protection par les primes* (Paris, 1900), p. 39.

1887 France levied duties of one or two francs on Italian silks, the silk producers of Eastern Asia preferred to send their silks to Milan instead of Lyons, in order to avoid the customs formalities, to which, in spite of exemption from the duty, their product would have been subjected. With an increase in the rate of the duty, the probability of a resulting change in domestic prices will increase, since the previous relation between supply and demand will be the more disturbed through the elimination of foreign competition. The higher the duty and the stricter the administration, the greater will be the premium on smuggling and the deception of officials. The price of smuggled goods will, to be sure, rise with an increase in the duty, as the trouble and danger connected with smuggling must be paid for, but the rise will not be equal to that in the price of goods on which duty has been regularly paid. The extent to which smuggling may be carried on even to-day is shown by an example from Greece. In the year 1909 the Greek Minister of Finance recommended a reduction in the sugar duty on the ground of the necessity of *increasing* the customs receipts, as it was estimated that up to that time about a third of the domestic demand had been satisfied with smuggled sugar.

Furthermore, in connexion with any measure, the adjusted condition of affairs must be distinguished from the permanent or normal. Supply and demand stand in a certain relation of equilibrium, which is suddenly disturbed by the artificial interference. The disturbance is especially violent when an extensive increase in duty is not promptly put into force by means of an embargo law or an embargo decree, but passes through the ordinary channels of introduction into the legislative assemblies. In this case all importers of the affected goods quickly bring in large stocks to be disposed of gradually after the increase takes effect. Thus a considerable interval must pass before supply and demand will again reach an equilibrium. The domestic price will perhaps finally be raised by the whole amount of the duty, but conditions in the period of transition depend largely upon the size of the accumulated stocks and the length of time they may be held by the individual importer in view of the general condition of business and his command of capital. But even in case the increase in duty is immediately put into force, the relations between the production costs at home and those abroad experience a disturbance to which the relations of supply and demand must adapt themselves.

The immediate effect on prices which is produced by a duty is exerted first on the supply, then through the supply upon the demand for the same goods ; in case the commodity is used for technical purposes and not for personal consumption, the effect is transferred to the supply of the product in whose manufacture it is used, through this again to the demand for the latter, &c. In the effect on the supply a question arises as to the relation between the amount of the domestic demand supplied at home and the part supplied from abroad. If the domestic supply of a commodity is drawn wholly or in large part from abroad for the reason that domestic production is impossible or is extensible only within narrow limits, the duty is really not protective, but is a fiscal measure, aiming at an increase in the revenues of the state. In this case the entire amount of the duty will generally appear in the price of the commodity, and hence will be borne by the domestic consumers. In particular will this be the case when the foreign country from which the supply is drawn possesses a natural monopoly in the commodity and when a reduction in its use is not to be feared. Only when the business is a very profitable one, and when the monopolistic production is threatened with a collapse in the existing demand, will it be inclined to assume part of the new burden of duty. The general case is that of competition between both producing and consuming countries. No disturbance in the competitive conditions will result from the imposition of a duty applicable alike to all foreign producing countries, even when the production costs of the various countries are different. The contrary assumption made by Fontana-Russo [1] is based on fallacious reasoning. If one country produces a unit of a given commodity at a cost of ten, and another country at a cost of twenty, a duty of five imposed in the market country will, according to his view, increase the total costs of the imported commodity to fifteen and twenty-five respectively, resulting in a change in the relative cost from one-half to two-fifths. But, as a matter of fact, the profit per unit of product is not changed by the fact that I compare it at one time with a higher and at another with a lower cost, as it is only the standard of measurement and not the object measured which changes. No interference in the competitive relations is produced until in the common market country one production country is favoured in comparison with another by a lower duty (preferential duty), or put at a disadvantage by a higher or discriminative duty. In this case the issue will hinge on whether the portion of the supply drawn from the country discriminated against is necessary to supply the domestic needs, or whether it may be dispensed with. If the latter is possible, the increased duty will hardly come out in the prices. In the case of a discrimination probably temporary, such as a tariff war, the producers of the unfavourably affected country will assume the burden of the higher duty in order to retain their customers. But purchasing countries also compete among themselves. Hence, if one of them undertakes to raise its duties, the producing countries will be thrown into sharper competition in the others, a circumstance which will tend to mitigate the effect of the increased duty on prices. The converse case is possible, but naturally of less frequent occurrence, in which one purchasing country, by lowering its duties, diverts foreign competition from the others; in these latter countries, in such a case, the effect of the duty on prices may be intensified. In this manner is to be explained the fact so often observed in recent decades,

---

[1] Luigi Fontana-Russo, *Grundzüge der Handelspolitik*, German translation (Leipsic, 1911), p. 381.

that the commercial policy measures of a state recoil upon regions apparently not concerned in it.

By far the most important as well as most frequent case, however, is that in which importation of the affected commodity from abroad may be dispensed with, or in which the country is to be rendered independent of such importation. Here the immediate effect of the duty is merely to secure the home market to inland production, and the price will now be adjusted by domestic competition. If the production is susceptible of extension, and if sufficient capital and labour for extending it are in fact at hand, the price may sink to the level of the world market price, so that the domestic consumer is not affected by the duty. If foreign competition, none the less, attempts to force an entrance, it must itself bear a part or all of the duty, as the consumer will not be inclined to pay higher prices for the foreign goods than for the domestic, other conditions being equal. To be sure, the spur to intensified competition through economies in production costs and price reduction will not be so great in the case of closed domestic markets as when the world at large also competes. In consequence, a price reduction to the level obtaining on the world market will be unusual, the duty will appear to a certain extent in the price, and on importation of the foreign commodity the burden of the duty will be divided between the foreign producer and the domestic consumer. A maintenance of the domestic price at the level of the world market plus the duty and plus freight will in the case of freely expansible production be possible in case the producers combine to secure a monopoly, and not otherwise; the industrial combination is thus a means for the complete utilization of tariff protection. A full exploitation of the duty will also take place when the domestic production is for any reason not expansible at will. In manufacturing, this may happen in case the commodity produced is protected by a patent, or in case the only factories in the country are branch establishments of some large foreign enterprise whose unlimited capital resources give it monopolistic power. In agriculture the natural limitation of the soil frequently results in restricting the expansibility of production.

But a duty may also affect the demand, through a change in the supply, and the producer must take account in adjusting the supply—which is to say from the very beginning—of the changeable character of the demand. The determining factor here is the elasticity of consumption, which usually falls off with a rise in the price, but does not inevitably or uniformly decrease. If the demand is fixed, or but slightly elastic, as a result of the fact that the commodity must be used without reference to the price, then the duty may more easily be shifted to the consumer, and so come out in the price. This is particularly true when a part of the domestic demand must be supplied from abroad. This category of inelastic demand includes not merely important food products such as wheat, meat, and the like, but also articles which are mere luxuries, whose consumption has become conventionally obligatory for certain classes of the population. Such are fashionable hats, new fabrics, champagne of famous brands, &c. In case a rise in the price will reduce consumption, the next question relates to the size of the consuming class which would fall away. Stratification in this connexion is very fluctuating, as it is based on the grouping of income relations. It is possible that a moderate increase in the price may leave consumption undiminished, while a somewhat greater one would result in a disproportionate falling off. For the individual enterprise, however, the decisive factor is not the profit attributable to a particular unit of the commodity, but the total profit, found by multiplying this gain per unit by the commodity turnover. Hence, a reduction of the profit per unit may under some circumstances be the lesser evil as compared with the reduction in the turnover, for 10,000 commodity units at a reduced profit of seven per unit still yield more (70,000) than 5,000 units at the full rate of ten (50,000). Especially great is the danger of a sudden and complete collapse in the demand, in case consumption can be diverted to some substitution product. Customs policy seeks with all the means at hand to prevent such diversion; cheaper goods, which might be substituted for higher priced articles, usually have the same duty imposed upon them. Thus the same duty is levied on oleo-margarine and cooking fat as on butter, on vegetable tallow as on animal tallow, &c. In all cases of this kind it will be more advantageous for the domestic producers to give up a part of the possible increase in price, and for foreign producers engaged in the import trade—unless they can secure other markets— to reduce their profits and assume a part of the burden of the duty. Thus the duty will be only in part transferred to the selling price of the goods.

The effect of the protective policy is not, however, limited to the prices of the dutiable goods alone. As a result of the increasing uniformity of income conditions, consumption goods stand in an intimate mutual relation; a change in the price of one commodity influences the consumption of others, as the distribution of the fixed income must be changed. Thus, for example, in the period of the recent culmination in business conditions a striking shift was to be observed in the consumptive relations. The shift was produced by the increase in the price of necessities which resulted from the intensified protection of agriculture; the employees of the state and of private enterprisers who draw a fixed income and who to-day form the most important element in the population of the larger cities, could not reduce the size of their dwellings, nor lessen their consumption of the means of life, and so were forced to limit their expenditures for clothing. In contrast with the prosperous conditions in other industries, the textile and leather manufactures suffered from a severe depression. Such a shifting of the effects further takes place in commodities for technical consumption, where the increase in price brought about by a protective duty must be transferred to the commodity. The attempt made by France in the year 1872 to introduce duties on raw materials was finally wrecked by the impossibility of carrying through the increases which became necessary in the duties on the corresponding manufactured goods. Since, in the case of exportation, consumption cannot be burdened in any way by inland protective measures, nothing is left but to neutralize by duty drawbacks or manufacture in bond the price-raising effect of the raw material duty on the manufactured product made therefrom. But this exemption from duty of foreign raw materials for the purpose of encouraging exportation, encounters so many difficulties in practical application that frequently either the relief from the burden is incomplete or else a bounty results.

A quantitative determination of the effect of protective duties on the prices of goods is bound to be extremely difficult, as the duty is only one of many factors in the determination of price. Hence an investigation must be made as to whether at the same time other influences have made themselves felt on the side of either demand or supply. Such probable influences would be improvements in the transportation situation, changes in the freight rates, speculation in securities, changes in income relations, shifts in consumption, and the like. Thus it comes to pass that in spite of the uniformity of protective relations within the customs domain, prices are very different on different markets, and develop along different lines. This is especially noticeable in the case of the bulky agricultural products. The price of wheat is higher in Berlin than in Mannheim, and has risen much more rapidly in recent years ; it is one thing in Vienna and another in Buda-Pest, is much lower in Odessa than in markets in the interior of Russia, &c.

Nevertheless, the general level of prices may be driven by a protective policy to extraordinary heights when the economic conditions permit of its working out its full effect. An example is offered by the rise in the cost of living in the Brazilian state of São Paulo. The Brazilian protective duties are extraordinarily high, amounting on a large number of articles to eighty per cent *ad valorem*. In the state of São Paulo the necessity of drawing the needed supplies of the means of life from abroad has been considerably reduced: yet the rapid industrialization of the country has led to such an increase in the population that the rents on dwellings and business sites have been known to rise seventy per cent in a few months. As a result, domestic production was in a position to take full advantage of the duty and freight protection. The most important articles of consumption reached exorbitant prices.[1] Wages also are correspondingly high. Agricultural labourers receive on the average three milreis (four marks) per day, industrial labourers four to eight milreis (5.30 to 10.60 marks), mechanics ten, lithographers twelve, and stone-cutters fifteen milreis (twenty marks) per day.

In the previous inquiry only the formation of the domestic price and its relation to the world market price have been considered. But this world market price must be very different when determined by the interaction of markets affected by tariff protection from what it would be under entirely free competition of all producing regions. Particularly in the first moment of introduction or increase in protection the commodities destined for the world market experience a reaction which operates to depress the price; hence the assumption, hitherto frequently made, is fully justified, that while the duty produces a difference between the domestic · price and the world market price, it does, however, at the same time reduce the latter. But whether and to what extent this reduction will actually appear in a given case is another question, whose solution depends on how production adapts itself to the change. If much fixed capital is invested in the business, a diminution in the amount produced is difficult or impossible, and the result may even be

---

[1] *Berichte der k. u. k. österr.-ung. Konsulatämter*, Jahrgang 1912. Handelsbericht des k. u. k. Konsulates in São Paolo, p. 3.

a very disastrous crisis. Thus the crisis in wine culture in southern France was mainly due to the fact that the European market districts had rapidly extended their agrarian protection to viticulture. In the field of industrial production at least a gradual diminution of output will occasionally be possible. It may happen, too, that by an enormous concentration of enterprises production costs may be so reduced that an extension in consumption in the markets remaining open may replace those lost.

The Effect of Protective Duties on Production Costs. But unless the investigation of the effects of tariff protection is to be very incomplete, it must not be limited to the effect on prices. The decisive factor for productive enterprise is not the price of the commodity, but the profit, which depends on the difference between the price of the goods and the cost of production. If an import duty, while in fact raising the price, at the same time increased production costs in the same or higher degree, the branch of production affected could derive no advantage from it. It is therefore necessary to determine the influence of protective duties on productive costs also. Two issues are here involved: (1) the relation between domestic and foreign production costs, and (2) the relation between domestic production and domestic needs. These two relations, again, must be regarded not merely in a static sense, according to their condition at any moment of time, but also dynamically, in their developmental tendencies.

The costs of production vary from one plant to another in the same country, but free competition will tend to concentrate productive capacity in the plants with the lowest costs. Hence it will be more accurate to speak of a standard than of an average cost of production in a country. Its relation to production costs in other countries is subject to constant variations. Thus in the case of agricultural products every harvest brings a shift, since with an equal total outlay for seed, labour, use of tools and machinery, &c., the yield of every year is different, and the share in the cost to be imputed to each unit of the product must vary accordingly. Passing variations will not, however, change the productive relations, as the adherents of the classical school assume. When the standard production cost in America rises above that in Italy, there will follow no increase in grain culture in Italy, which would have to disappear when the production costs in America settled back.[1] Capital and labour will turn exclusively to those branches of production which offer permanent possibilities of employment. Such possibilities are afforded by commodity protection, as the domestic market is thereby secured to home production against foreign competition. The question now arises as to how production costs will be affected when this security is afforded.

The answer to the question depends on the situation of domestic production with regard to supplying the home demand. If it is inadequate to this purpose, attraction will be exerted on capital and labour to enter the protected branch of production, though this can of course take place only on condition that the country controls sufficient capital and labour, whether by actual possession or through its ability to secure them abroad. Again, only movable capital can be obtained from abroad, and not the immovable capital of land. Hence, when a branch of production requires much land, and new virgin soil is not to be had in a country, protection cannot result in an increase in the land capital, but only in a more intensive utilization of that already at hand. As a result, it has been observed in Europe that duties on grain have not increased the profits of agriculture; they have indeed raised the prices obtained for grain, but they have increased production costs to an equal or greater extent through the resulting rise in value of land. The higher prices of grain have been simply capitalized into higher land values.[2]

---

[1] Luigi Fontana-Russo, *Grundzüge der Handelspolitik* (German translation, Leipsic, 1911), p. 155.

[2] Bruno Heinrich Roncador, *Wesen und Wirkung der Agrarzölle* (Jena, 1911), pp. 62 ff.

If movable capital is in question, as in the case of manufactures, protection will bring about an increase in capital, an intensification of competition within the country, and hence a decrease in production costs. This downward tendency cannot be prevented except by deficiency in the capital and labour called forth. The duty therefore furnishes only one of the conditions for the development of an industry, namely, the assurance of a definite market, but never the industry itself, as many south European countries have had to learn from indiscriminate increases in their duty rates. A lower duty on iron manufactures has been more effective in Germany and the United States than has a higher one in Spain and Russia.

If the domestic production is sufficient for the needs of the country, the competition between establishments will operate in the direction of gradually excluding the smaller plants working under higher production costs. With an increase in the size of an enterprise the production costs decrease, but the risk increases; an ever-increasing proportion of the entrepreneur's capital must be converted into investment capital, which in the case of suspension of operations must be almost entirely lost. A factory is suitable for but one use. The building may, in the unusual case in which it is located in a city, be adapted to some other kind of manufacturing or for utilization for dwelling purposes, while the machinery used has in general only the value of junk. The risk may be lessened by various forms of concentration—fusion, combination, community of interest, trade agreement (Kartell) or trust—in connexion, frequently, with a manipulation of foreign markets. The main interest centres in stability, i. e. in securing regular employment of the plant, as any reduction, even, means that machines must lie idle with labour losses, &c., and so raises production costs. But the domestic demand, again, is far from being a constant quantity; it changes with the purchasing power of the population and with the degree of activity in elaborating industries producing articles for export. If a sharp decrease in demand takes place, foreign markets must be sought, so that for many branches of production, as, for example, for the whole mining industry, exportation forms a sort of safety-valve.

The case in which an industry produces a surplus beyond domestic requirements may not, however, merely accidentally supervene, but may also be brought about deliberately and systematically. This is especially true of those smaller special articles, of which almost every country produces certain varieties for the world market, such as toys in Germany, fezes in Austria, watches and clocks in Switzerland, laces in Belgium, &c. Such specifically exporting industries will not merely not desire protection, but will even repudiate it, in order not to offer foreign countries an incentive to imitation. On the other hand, there are export industries which rest primarily on the home market, and hence will require protection, but which will yet struggle for foreign markets, because by an increase in the size of establishments and a specialization of their products, production costs may be further reduced, and in this way consumption stimulated even in the home country. Exportation itself is a means of promoting domestic consumption, a principle of which the beet-sugar industry affords a conspicuous example. Without increasing its export capacity, this industry would not have found it possible, in the short period since it was established, to reduce production costs, and with them prices (exclusive of consumption taxes) to about one-fifth the original figures. Agriculture now buys its implements and machinery cheaper by half than it did thirty or forty years ago, because the market has been extended. Tariff protection and commercial treaties are therefore not contradictory policies ; both aim to secure a market, protective duties an internal and commercial treaties an external one.

The Effect of Export Duties. The fiscal object of export duties, which aim at the shifting of the tax to the foreign buyer, will be attained only in case the country has an absolute or at least a relative monopoly in the goods in question. The monopoly may consist in a special quality of product, or of a favourable commercial location, which gives the country a dominant position in the particular markets. But the export duty will promote at the same time all efforts of such markets to free themselves from the monopoly, and the latter must become less and less secure in view of the active spirit of invention and of enterprise characteristic of the present time.

The commercial policy effect of the duty is still more difficult of achievement; the aim here is to secure advantage to domestic industries in providing themselves with raw materials. We have isolated examples in the case of timber and mineral ores. Even when the supply is rendered less easy to obtain by the competing foreign manufactures—which is possible only in the case of monopoly—the advantage achieved is often too small to remove other obstacles in the way of the development of the domestic industry. In Spain export duties on iron ore failed to accelerate the development of the iron industry, for the reason that coal and also the general conditions necessary for modern large-scale manufacturing are wanting in the country. The export duty on wood in the Canadian provinces of Quebec and Ontario has, on the other hand, led to a rapid growth in the domestic manufacture of wood-pulp, the American paper mills being forced by the difficulty in procuring raw wood to purchase their half-manufactures. Of the Canadian output, of which four-fifths consist of planing mill products and one-fifth of cellulose (chiefly sulphite cellulose), about seventy per cent is exported. In the year 1911, 847,939 cords of unmanufactured wood were exported, as opposed to 672,288 cords in an improved condition sent out by the fifty-four factories of the country (twenty-eight in Quebec and fourteen in Ontario). Three-fourths of the exports are taken by the United States, where, moreover, Germany and Sweden also compete to an increasing extent. It will be seen that the economic protective policy can employ export duties only in rather special cases.

The Effect of Freight-rate Protection. Discriminating rates for imports on the railways to the disadvantage of foreign goods operate in the same way as import duties to the amount of the difference between the transportation charges on the foreign commodity from the frontier to the consumption point, and the charge on the domestic product from the place where it is produced to the consumption point. The effect will diminish with the rise in the value of the goods, as the basis for computation for import duties and for railway freights is essentially different. Duties, to be sure, are to-day usually levied according to the quantity of the goods imported, principally according to their weight, but this only on grounds of technical administration, the amount of the duty fixed in the customs tariff being really based on the value of the goods. The relation between the value of the goods and the duty is translated into a relation between quantity and duty merely for purposes of collection. The basis of present-day railway rates is, on the other hand, a car-space system depending on bulk and weight. It looks to the highest utilization of the means of transportation, and hence the charge is fixed according to the amount of car capacity taken up. A ton of iron is treated in general in the same way as a ton of needles. Alongside this system, indeed, particularly in the case of special and exceptional rates, remnants still subsist of the older system of classification by value, adjusting the transportation charge according to the worth of the goods. This adjustment, however, is made in a very rude fashion, as goods economically more or less similar are grouped into a few classes which have rates applied to them whose graduation is far behind the complicated classification of the customs tariff. The unit rates on freight shipments in Austria vary between 0.16 and 1.22 heller per 100 kilograms per kilometre, while the duty rates in the Austro-Hungarian tariff on cotton goods alone—all treated alike in the railway schedule—are graduated from 65 to 800 kronen per 100 kilograms. As a result, freight-rate protection is chiefly applied to bulky commodities of small value and handled in large quantities, such as grain, timber, coal, and the like, and for the same reason it has been manipulated in a one-sided way in the interest of agrarian protection.

The Effect of Administrative Protection and of Protection by Concerted Popular Action. The indirect protective measures connected with the political administration, such as the manipulation of veterinary and food products regulations, exclusion of foreign countries from public contracts, &c., as well as the protective instrument afforded by concerted private action, the boycott, and national propagandas, have shown themselves efficient but very imperfect weapons. They afford no gradation of protection such as is demanded by modern economic life, but work prohibitively, and so grant to domestic producers a dangerous monopolistic position. Further- more, they usually represent hostile acts directed against a specific foreign state, which they consequently incite to retaliation. For these reasons their application is usually restricted to cases in which the regular protective instrument of customs duties fails through peculiarities of the political constitution forbidding the erection of a customs line, or through theoretical prejudices against the use of tariff pro- tection or the like.

2. Effects of the Positive Measures

The Effect of Export Bounties. The immediate effect of bounties on exports is a differentiation of the domestic and foreign prices of the commodity affected. The domestic price will be higher than that on the world market by about the amount of the export bounty, though allowance must be made for transportation costs. The producer will sell his goods abroad so long as the domestic consumer does not bear the whole burden of the bounty, as by this means he secures the bounty in addition to the foreign price. Transportation costs are, to be sure, deducted, and in the case of goods of great weight in proportion to their value, such as grain and iron, it may happen that the freight to the frontier may offset the effect of the export bounty either entirely or for certain parts of the country. An indispensable accompaniment of the bounty is of course an import duty on the commodity affected at least equal to the amount of the bounty, since the latter tends to raise the selling price of the domestic goods only and not of the foreign product. Under complete free trade goods exported under a bounty would immediately return into the country in order to profit by the higher prices. Thus the branches of production which have been provided with export bounties have also been protected with prohibitive import duties, and this in spite of an efficiency which would otherwise have made tariff protection seem quite superfluous to them. An example is afforded by the sugar industry. Governmental export bounties have, however, the further effect that in spite of the persistent difference between domestic price and foreign price, they none the less bring about a price reduction at home. That is, they reduce the amount of production cost imputed to each unit of the commodity, and intensify competition on the world market by favouring selectively the most effective establishments, and by making possible greater specialization through the extension of the market. The domestic price naturally falls along with that obtaining on the world market, as only the difference between the two is constant. The sugar industry again affords an example; in spite of the bounty, the domestic price is finally lower than it was before the bounty was introduced. But the consequence, ultimately unavoidable, is that in the world market a contest between the nations ensues, not merely for low production costs, but also for high export bounties, as no country will consent to be left behind in the governmental encouragement of its industries.

In regard to the effect of export bounties, a lively discussion was carried on even in the classic literature of political economy. Adam Smith maintained that an export bounty on grain must result in a sharp increase in price, since it would stimulate exportation, while an increase in the production of grain in the country he regarded as impossible. Yet the farmer would derive no advantage from this increase in the price, for wages would rise accordingly. The worth of a given quantity of wheat Smith regarded as equal to the quantity of labour which it would support in the person of the labourer. The prices of grain had, in fact, been very low in England for a long time, in spite of the bounty; but this he attributed to the increase in the value of silver. In manufactures, on the other hand, an extension of production is easily possible, and hence a rise in price would not be the necessary consequence of a bounty; yet the bounty would be injurious in this case also, as such exportation would be carried on only at a loss, and besides, capital would be artificially diverted from its most advantageous employment. Ricardo disputed the assertion with regard to grain bounties. He viewed an extension of grain production as possible through the cultivation of new land and improved cultivation of the old; hence the influence of the bounty on prices would not be permanent. Moreover, grain forms only a part of the means of subsistence of the labourer, and therefore the farmer might also profit in part by the bounty. In fact, grain production is neither inextensible nor extensible at will. In countries with tariff protection, however, the price-moderating effect will be restricted to the world market price, while within the customs domain, as already explained, the price must be higher than that on the world market by the amount of the duty.

A great difficulty lies in the indeterminate fiscal effects of the governmental export bounty. Alleviation has repeatedly been sought, especially in the field of the sugar and shipping bounties, through arbitrary limitation on the sum to be paid out during a year. The result of adopting this policy must be that claims to bounties cannot be decided until after the expiration of the year, when, in case the determined sum has been exceeded, a reduction in the rate must be made. But to exert a real stimulating effect the bounty must not be uncertain, but must be susceptible to accurate computation in connexion with each business transaction. It may even exert a contrary effect in a case where favourable conditions would justify an extension of the industry, but where producers may be led to divert investments to other fields in order not to exceed the allotted sum for the year in question.

In the case of governmental export bounties, as in that of production bounties, the recipient is not always the only person favoured. It is possible to speak of a shifting of bounties after the analogy of the shifting of taxes. This shifting arises from the fact that the state grants favourable conditions to other domestic interest-groups, as, for example, when it prescribes the purchase of raw materials within a country, the payment of higher wages, granting of shorter hours of work, or the like. With each such increase in costs a portion of the bounty is passed on to other hands. Illuminating examples of this character might be drawn from the field of the shipping bounties. The fundamental idea was to encourage the shipyards by building-bounties, based on the tonnage capacity of the ships constructed, and the navigation company by service bounties based on the commercial performance in the course of a year. But when now the bounty to the shipping companies comes to be granted only on ships purchased within the country, the shipyards receive a second bounty, namely, that part of the service bounty represented by the difference in price between vessels purchased at home and abroad. If the ship operators also receive the service bounty wholly or in part on foreign-built ships, no shifting of the bounty in favour of the foreign shipyards takes place, as the latter are not in a position to utilize any artificial condition brought about by the law, and

hence cannot change their prices. A protective effect may
follow from this shifting, even in the case of production
bounties. The French law of April 2, 1898, renewed the
production bounty on silk-spinning mills which had been
introduced in the law of January 13, 1892, but provided
different rates according to whether domestic or foreign
cocoons were used, the rates being respectively 400 francs
and 340 francs per basin.[1] By such a differentiation, the
demand for the domestic product is increased, and its price
raised so that only the bounty of 340 francs is retained by
the spinnery, the difference of sixty francs going to the
domestic silk-grower, upon whom it acts as a protection
against foreign competition.

The effects on the various interest-groups at home and
abroad are most clearly seen in the case of private export
bounties, which at the present time have achieved a greater
significance than state bounties. The interest-groups to be
considered are the producers and their organizations, the
elaborating industries, the working-men, and the organs of
public economic policy.

The producers aim at continuous employment without over-
loading the domestic market. Export bounties are a means
adapted to this end, since they distribute among all producers,
and so lighten, the loss arising from the difference in price
at home and abroad. The combine will take care that the
possibility of exportation shall not lead to any expansion in
production at home, exportation being regarded in such cases
strictly as an emergency expedient for co-ordinating domestic
production and domestic demand. Only governmental export
bounties which aim at exportation itself will lead to such an
expansion.

Quite different is the situation of the elaborating industries.
If the export bounties are paid inside the combine alone, then
the foreign competitors in these industries receive their raw
materials or part manufactures cheaper than do the home

---

[1] A. de Lavison, *La Protection par les primes*, Paris, 1900, p. 117.

producers. Thus the German shipbuilding industry entered complaint in the year 1902 because of the favouring of Dutch competition by the German *Kartelle*; as a result of this favouritism, the shipbuilders had found it cheaper to purchase their raw materials in the markets of Holland rather than directly in Germany. The Remscheider steel toolmakers pointed to the same disadvantage which they were under in comparison with competition from Sheffield. English competitors obtained German spirits delivered cheaper than German firms. The state sugar bounties had a similar effect, and manufactures using sugar, such as the production of cakes, marmalades, candies, and chocolate, developed much more rapidly in England than on the Continent. In the German trust investigation (*Kartellenquete*), it was even asserted that manufacturing industries had been compelled to build establishments in foreign countries in order to take advantage of the marketing of raw materials abroad at low prices by the German producers' organizations. In view of the variable character of direct export bounties, however, such an effect is to be observed on a considerable scale only in the case of cut-price exportations supported by high duties.

If export bounties are paid to the elaborating industries, that is, to the domestic customers of the product controlled by the combine, discrimination against them in comparison with foreign competition will be avoided, but other evils will arise from such a course. In the first place, the export bounty never amounts to the difference between domestic price and foreign price. For example, in November 1900 the wire-rod association sold wire-rod in Germany at 185 marks per ton and abroad at 115 marks. It granted an export bounty of fifteen marks to domestic buyers who used the material in manufacturing for exportation, thus making the price 170 instead of 185 marks, but the foreign manufacturer still received the commodity fifty-five marks cheaper. Furthermore, there is a dangerous relation of dependence among the various branches of production; this is shown by the fact that the combine grants the export bounty as a favour and not as a right, and hence often in connexion with burdensome conditions. Discriminations with no justification in fact between individual establishments are frequently met with. The plants are commonly compelled to procure their entire supply from the combine, and even to order it directly, a condition which is especially oppressive when the combine itself delivers only fixed minimum quantities, as in the case of the Rhenish-Westphalian Coal Syndicate, which does not fill orders for less than a minimum supply of 5,000 tons per year. Further pressure is often brought to bear to compel the organization of the purchasing industries, though this is more difficult to accomplish, in proportion as the product is advanced on the road from raw material to finished article. The right of examining accounts reserved by the Düsseldorf clearing house seems to have been only a moral safeguard, as no use has in fact been made of it.

The effect on the national economy in general, as also and more particularly that on the working-class, is a much disputed point. On the one hand, the cheap sales abroad are looked upon as a squandering of the national wealth. This conclusion follows directly from the classical theory of international trade, and has been drawn in particular by Brentano.[1]

The foreign country where importation takes place under the stimulus of export bounties and reduced freight charges or exports in other countries, receives more in foreign goods, labour products and capital utilization than it gives in return ; conversely, the country from which the exportation takes place gives up more value than it receives from abroad. Export bounties therefore involve a reduction in the yield of the national productive forces, of the compensation of the nation's labour and of the profits of its capital, together with a lessened increase in the national wealth. They represent a systematic squandering of the national labour and of the national capital. They signify a loss for the national economy, increasing the wealth of a few at the expense of the welfare of a vastly greater number.

[1] L. Brentano, ' Über Ausfuhrprämien,' *Patria, Jahrbuch der Hilfe* (1904), p. 86.

This view stands or falls with the assumption that the value of a commodity is a summation of production costs. On the other hand, if the value is regarded not as inherent in the commodity but as something added to it from without, derived from the demand and supply relations of the market, the question will be raised as to how these value relations are in fact affected by the payment of bounties. It has already been pointed out that only the existing difference between domestic price and foreign price is overcome by such payments. The domestic value will be higher than if the goods exported had been sold inland. A depression of consumption can take place, however, only when a protective import duty makes possible an unjustified rise in the price. The injury is then to be attributed to the duty and not to the export bounty. The foreign value will fall as a result of the influence of the export bounty, and with it the domestic value also gradually declines, as it is of course compounded of the foreign value and the export bounty. The supporters of the export policy of the combines emphasize the fact that as a result of cut-price sales abroad the total labour force remains employed and is fully paid ; hence such foreign sales unfavourably affect the entrepreneur's profit alone, and not the income of the working people or employees. This contention holds good only with respect to the branch of production which follows the exporting policy. For other branches of production a stabilization of conditions of employment achieved by export bounties is in itself no disadvantage, as such continuity represents the general interest of the national economy, and an injurious effect does not become possible unless the domestic price is artificially raised above the necessary level, which again can only be the result of a protective duty.

On the world market, competition will be considerably intensified by the export bounties, and this again will furnish a strong incentive toward technical improvement on the part of the industries of all countries. But export bounties incite not merely to imitation but also to defensive action. They are always regarded as an interference by a foreign state in the economic development of a country, and lead to retaliatory measures until finally, as has been seen in the case of the sugar bounties, no possible course is left but their general abolition by mutual agreement.

The Effect of Measures for the Encouragement of Shipping. It is still more difficult to pass judgement on ship subsidies and shipping bounties, as in this case considerations affecting the means of transportation themselves are added to the numerous complications of the international commodity market. As the measures of encouragement must be undertaken in the way of legislation, and so be fixed for a period of years, their provisions cannot remain permanently in harmony with the advancing economic and technical situation, and hence may lead to restriction instead of stimulating expansion. When, for example, the sum appropriated for a particular year is exhausted, the shipping enterprises will endeavour to postpone new investments to another year, and in this way may leave a momentary favourable conjuncture entirely or in part unutilized. In any case, such bounties represent an interference in business development which is very likely to be taken advantage of in the service of individual interests. It has not infrequently happened on the passage of bounty laws that the first few years witnessed a greatly increased activity by which ship-builders and operators sought to exploit the advantages offered, followed in later years by an all the more critical period of stagnation. The phenomenon of bounty shifting between ship-builders and operators has been discussed in connexion with export bounties.

In the distribution of subsidies and bounties, legislative and administrative organs have really fallen into a dangerous dilemma in an age like the present, saturated with social and political strivings. If they support the large enterprises, they lay themselves open to the reproach of wishing to accentuate the already existing overdominance of the economically strong. As a result, they have usually fallen into the error of discriminating in favour of antiquated types, such as ships of small tonnage capacity, and especially sailing-vessels. The operation of sailing-vessels enjoys the reputation of being ' the best school for the seamen ', but from an economic point of view they must be regarded as having outlived their usefulness for ocean service. The fact is readily overlooked that the protection of the weak is justified only on the grounds of maintaining human lives, and not when the question relates to the support of competitively inefficient business enterprises. The development of French bounty legislation in particular offers aggravated instances of this procedure. Italy also, in spite of great expenditures, has not been particularly successful in this field. In the decade from 1900 to 1909 the share of Italian shipping in the water traffic of the country increased from 4,100,000 tons to 5,000,000 tons, or by twenty-four per cent, while the portion under foreign flags increased from 7,800,000 to 14,400,000 tons, or eighty-six per cent.

A further disadvantage is that under the influence of international competition the expenditures of the different countries on their merchant marines mount higher and higher, while at the same time they become of less and less effect as the measures counterbalance each other. In the case of bounties the money sums necessary cannot be accurately estimated in advance, so that difficulties arise in the framing of budgets. For this reason the principle of limiting the amounts has been introduced into the Italian, French, and Austrian legislation. But in this way the end is in part defeated, as the enterprises must reckon with the possibility that the amount granted may be exceeded and the bounties correspondingly reduced. Finally, there is an unmistakable tendency on the part of shipping bounties to become transformed into export bounties on commodities, as the emphasis is constantly shifted from the transportation medium to the goods exported. In the bonus on freights (*Frachtzuschuss*) contemplated in the case of certain goods in a recent Italian bill, and in the Austrian subsidy agreement with the Austro-Americana, only a poor disguise remained of the original character of the payments. This policy, however, must afford opportunity to the country to which the subsidized exportation takes place to throw difficulties in the form of customs regulations in the way of the policies.

On account of these grave disadvantages, statesmen have frequently turned their backs on the whole policy of shipping bounties, and declared that a real encouragement of the merchant marine is possible only by an indirect procedure, that is by means of manipulation of regulations in the field of commercial policy and domestic trade policy. Ships are in any case transportation media, and must profit by every change which stimulates the commerce on which they live. The building of good roads leading to port towns, the establishment of combined railway and ship transportation tariffs, the seeking out of new market regions, and in general every measure promoting exportation, as well as the encouragement of indirect commerce by the provision of free zones in port towns—such measures must necessarily bring prosperity to the national shipping. Ship-building may be aided by exemption from duty on all materials used, by making as light as possible the precautionary conditions of such exemption, by assistance in securing orders, and by the best possible distribution of orders over moderately long periods of time. Still, the reciprocal reactions between commerce and means of transportation must not be overlooked. If men had always waited to provide new transportation media until the growing traffic had placed beyond any doubt the question of their proving profitable, we should to-day possess but a fraction of our present world-commerce. For it must not be forgotten that here, as in the case of production, a better-developed foreign competition is constantly on the alert, if granted freedom of access, to nip in the bud any manifestation of activity, however well justified, on the part of the national spirit of enterprise. Hence, it will not in the near future be possible to dispense with subsidies and bounties, as after all they make possible and stimulate the creation of new transportation media, which in turn are an important instrument of national economic policy.

II

THE EFFECTS OF CAPITAL PROTECTION

1. Effects of the Negative Measures

The Effect of Discouraging the Importation of Capital.
Means of combating foreign capital are applied only in case
it is used to establish the influence of the foreign enterpriser
and owner of capital. But the countries economically un-
developed, and politically only partially independent, will be
forced to take their choice between admitting foreign influence
along with foreign capital and dispensing with foreign capital
altogether. In the latter case, however, the country would
be deprived of that productive factor which in the course
of modern development has become most important. If the
country increases in strength to the point where'it possesses
the necessary technical and mercantile power to carry on its
own affairs, attention must first be given to freeing from
foreign influence the enterprises most intimately connected
with the public economic interest. In this connexion the
governmental initiative will be useful and necessary, provided
that foreign capital is not frightened away, or that it can be
replaced by domestic. That foresight is in order in such
a situation has been abundantly shown by the experience
of China, where, after the vehement nationalization movement, the Government was forced to adopt the expedient
of mixed enterprises conducted by foreigners and Chinese
together. The purely private economic enterprises will
succumb of themselves to the nationalization process when
the time comes. No encouragement in this direction
through economic protective measures has proved itself
desirable.

The Effect of the Discouragement of Capital Exportation.
The means of combating the exportation of capital have
proved of but little value. Capital does not possess the
substantial character of the other factor of production, labour
power, and moreover is transferred·in the form of commodities whose exportation appears desirable, and hence flows
irresistibly to the place where it yields the highest return.
But the yield will be higher the farther the region where the
capital is used is below the cultural level of the place where
it is produced. The force of public opinion can operate only
on the agencies for transmitting the capital, that is to say,
the banks, whose business operations are subject to public
control, and very little on the real owners of the capital, who
ultimately control it but whose relations of ownership are not
generally known. In any case the political motive will never
be so powerful that it will not be outweighed in the mind
of the capitalist by the material advantages of a loan. As to
influencing the technical institutions for capital transmission,
this becomes less and less possible as time goes on, for the
reason that the institutions under the control of the State
steadily lose their dominant position in relation to the capital
market. The bank of issue possesses a monopoly solely in
the issuance of notes, while in the discounting of exchange
and making of loans it must compete with private banks.
The stock exchange is indeed indispensable for speculation,
but it has long since ceased to be so for the marketing of
new securities among the people. Issuance without recourse
to the exchange, by public advertising or even by means of
private circulars to bank customers, has taken on its present
large proportions chiefly for the very reason that exchange
trading has been so hedged about with restrictions. The
number of securities not quoted on the exchange—the
' exotic ' paper—constantly increases. Moreover, domestic
capitalists may share in foreign issues and leave the securities
purchased in a foreign place of deposit, and then any possibility of political influence is excluded.

2. Effects of the Positive Measures

The Effect of the Encouragement of Capital Importation.
Special devices for enticing the inflow of foreign capital must fail, as they will be without effect if the economic and political conditions of the country do not promise a higher yield on capital, and will be superfluous if such a yield is to be counted upon. That, nevertheless, they are met with is explained by the fact that particular points or regions of the country seek to direct the flow of capital in a specific direction. One city offers attractions to those foreigners who as bondholders intend to live on the interest of their capital, and another offers advantages for the location of new factories. These local extensions of inducements may, however, not be limited in their effects to the distribution of a capital immigration independently taking place from foreign countries, but may also, especially in the case of the attraction of bondholders, actually bring about such an immigration of capital. The colonizing of persons living on an income is, however, unfavourable to the development of large-scale industry, and will be free from danger to the national economy only on condition that the development of other parts of the country into out-and-out industrial districts is not interfered with.

The Effect of the Encouragement of Capital Exportation.
The exportation of capital needs to be encouraged only in those cases in which other and greater advantages are to be achieved by it, especially when by the strengthening of political influence in a foreign country a road may be opened to an increased exportation of commodities through the participation in public contracts and the like. The indispensable pre-supposition in this case is, however, that sufficient and cheaper capital is at the disposal of the home national economy, so that the question shall ultimately relate solely to an influencing of the direction taken by a capital outflow and not to the artificial production of such a movement. The consideration just named places narrow limits on this field of economic policy.

III

THE EFFECTS OF LABOUR PROTECTION

1. Effects of the Negative Measures

The Effect of the Restriction of Emigration. In modern civilized countries emigration cannot be effectively prevented; aside from the question of safeguarding personal liberty, the density of modern traffic renders impossible the maintenance of any strict control. Such a control would be most likely to succeed in a country occupying an insular position, as water transportation, in view of its sharp concentration in individual vehicles and in commercial centres, is more easily supervised than railway traffic. If with a view to higher interests—especially the obligation to military service—the State is forced to forbid emigration in certain cases, its prohibition will be much more effectively enforced by means of penalties which it can threaten in the case of return, for nearly every emigrant cherishes a secret hope of sometime seeing his home again.

The Effect of the Restriction of Immigration. In the first place, it must be settled that the interest of the national economy in need of protection is a purely economic one. Ethical grounds of restriction, arising from the different characteristics of races and nations, we may pass over, as they usually serve merely as disguises. The physical and moral dangers depicted with much satisfaction have not in themselves been strong enough to have led nations to oppose foreign immigration. But for the ruinous competition arising in the labour market, even the hated Chinese would be patiently endured, as has been shown in the American States of Oregon and Washington, as well as in the Hawaiian Islands, where, by the influx of the yellow race, the whites have been elevated to a sort of labour aristocracy. The interest requiring protection is exclusively that of maintaining the existing equilibrium between wages and the cost of living for the working-class. When, as has been repeatedly proved by statistics, the Chinese in California is content, on account of his restricted needs, with half or a third of the wages which the native labourer receives, the national economy is threatened with the danger of retrogression. The private enterpriser will find it immediately profitable to substitute cheap labour power for dear, but from the national economic standpoint it is not desirable to have a relation once established between the two productive factors, labour and capital, so distorted that machine power is displaced by human power instead of the reverse. Moreover, the factor which is decisive of the extent of the domestic market open to production is neither land area nor density of population but domestic consumption, and this must undoubtedly be diminished when foreigners with a low standard of life displace the home labour force, and even with the reduced wages accumulate savings which they send out of the country.

When an interest requiring protection is not present, the restriction of immigration must be injurious, as the soil and all other capital in a country can only be made fruitful by human labour. An economic domain which lacks the labour force necessary to develop its resources will be forced to look about for immigrants, except in so far as the state of technical knowledge permits a substitution of machinery for human labour. Conditions in many States will not be uniform, and conflicts of interest will result such as are seen in the contemporary protective policy. For example, immigration restriction in the United States encounters the determined opposition of the tobacco- and cotton-growing Southern States. Moreover, the exclusion policy itself cannot be uniform and permanent, but must be directed according to the need against specific classes of immigrants, and laid aside when the economic grounds no longer require its enforcement. Australia restricts by drastic measures the influx of population at a lower cultural level than its own, but shows a strong increase of immigration from England. It has also taken other measures against the Chinese, and against the Polynesians or Kanakas. Finally, we can observe in the legislation of different countries a distinct periodic rise and fall in the stringency of the protective provisions.

The effect of all protective measures is further prejudiced by the fact that evasion can never be entirely prevented. Even in the case of immigration restriction, smuggling flourishes. Thus, it is known that on the Mexican border whole towns live by smuggling yellow labour into the neighbouring States of the Union, that Canada is the headquarters for a smuggling trade into the United States, not of goods alone but of immigrants as well, &c. But the difficulty of enforcement is no argument against a regulation otherwise justifiable. Economic policy can never compute its effects with mathematical accuracy, and so, as in this case, must be guided by the results of experience.

The adherents of the free-trade theory reject labour protection as well as protective duties. Every artificial obstacle which adds to the inevitable enormous natural barriers to the transfer of human labour force, forms in their eyes a manifest injury to the world economy, and especially to the working-classes.[1] It merely contributes to divert labour from its natural directions of application, and to cause it to be used in countries where it is less productive. But in fact there are no such natural directions; wage-levels, which exert the attractive force on the immigrant, are in no case a gift of nature, but a hard-won boon of the nation's civilization. The individual State must not inquire what is good for the world, but exclusively what is good for itself. It may be objected that the working-class cannot permanently main-

[1] Giuseppe Prato, *Il protezionismo operaio*; *L'esclusione del lavoro straniero* (Turin, 1910), pp. 187 ff.

tain a wage standard notably higher than that of surrounding countries, for if it did capital would emigrate, and the opportunities of labour be reduced. A tendency to such an equalization undoubtedly exists, but the process works itself out only in slow and gradual changes. Chinese labour is cheap, yet all new cotton-spinneries are not on that account built in China, for in that country, as a result of defective political institutions, many other conditions indispensable for industrial growth are wanting. The accession of cheap labour power leads to the further result that the lower and less productive occupations are turned over to the new-comers, and the native working force can turn to the higher and more remunerative callings. The latter may find their cost of living actually reduced, since many articles, such as clothing, can be manufactured more cheaply than before. The possibility of such a differentiation of labour will, however, serve as a check upon protective measures for discouraging immigration, or will permit of so limited an advantage being gained through the policy by the national economy that the disadvantages will predominate.

As protective measures are not directed against foreign immigration in general, but only against certain of its effects, such measures may be rendered superfluous by international treaties preventing these effects. Just as protective duties may become unnecessary in case the industrial organizations of competing countries reach an understanding as to their respective market territory, so also opposition to immigration may cease if by mutual agreement the immigrants are directed to points where they do not disadvantageously affect the domestic labour market. In 1909, the President of the American Federation of Labour, Samuel Gompers, proposed to the Italian labour organizations that each Italian immigrant should be enrolled in the American Federation, which would then undertake the direction of the immigrant stream. Italian economists were opposed to the plan on the ground that the American organization would merely seek to protect its own interests. It goes without saying that this would have been the case, but it is this interest which now gets safeguarded, the only difference being that it is done by one-sided protective measures instead of by mutual agreement.

International agreements between governments, interested organizations, and transportation enterprises afford the sole possibility of taking from protective measures their odious character and avoiding reprisals on the part of affected foreign countries. The anti-Chinese legislation of the United States of America led in the year 1905 to the boycotting of American goods in China, but when a conflict of the same character arose with Japan in 1907 a *modus vivendi* was reached. Japan itself prohibited the shipping companies from transporting immigrants, and stopped the issuance of passports to labourers.

2. EFFECTS OF THE POSITIVE MEASURES

The Effect of the Encouragement of Emigration. The encouragement of emigration, whether on political, religious, or economic grounds, always involves an economic loss, as was copiously demonstrated even in the Middle Ages by the expulsion of the Jews from Spain, and by the struggles between Protestants and Catholics. It is usually the efficient and enterprising elements which are driven out, involving a double loss to the country, which misses both their valuable production ability and the incentive of their example to the rest of the population. Pressure on the domestic labour market cannot be artificially relieved in this way unless at the same time measures for excluding immigration are carried through. In any case, the process is dangerous, as labour power is a productive factor, and by unduly enhancing its price production itself may be handicapped. The repatriation of undesirable immigrants is to be judged by the same standards as the restriction of immigration.

The Effect of Encouraging Immigration. The encouragement of immigration has taken its place alongside of protective duties as the most important measure of economic protective policy for the development of humanity. In this way America, Australia, and Africa have been settled, and opened up to economic activity; thus were overcome the natural barriers which separated two important elements in production, natural resources and labour power. The material sacrifices made by the oversea countries to this end have been insignificant in comparison with the results achieved. In the execution, it is true, the self-interest of administrative organs has reduced the efficiency of many measures of encouragement, and even transformed them at times into their opposites, but such technical shortcomings do not affect the principle itself.

Unpleasant results follow in the emigrant lands, especially in cases where private enterprises overrun the country with an army of agents for soliciting the people. The productivity of the country may be seriously set back while still higher interests are affected, if the immigrants are solicited for regions where fever and other diseases claim many victims before the land can be made productive.

THE EFFECTS OF ECONOMIC PROTECTIONISM IN GENERAL

Increase in the Productive Power of the National Economy.
The protective policy is a means of consolidating and unifying a country in an economic sense, and enabling it to ward off dangers from without, and to develop in accordance with its own laws. If the classical free-trade ideal of the development of the international division of labour on the basis of varied natural productive conditions were correct, the protective policy would necessarily represent an obstacle to the growth of world-trade. If, on the contrary, as we have attempted to show, the natural conditions of production are at the present time progressively less and less important, and artificial conditions more and more decisive; if cotton is not manufactured in the place where it grows, or iron ore in the place where it is mined, but rather in the place where the market for the products in question exists, then the economic protective policy, as belonging to these artificial conditions of production, must be regarded as a means of developing the productive power of a country. If the natural conditions of production were decisive, Italy would be forced to restrict itself to the cultivation of wine, tropical fruits, and the like, while, as a matter of fact, it has manifested a notable growth in prosperity only since the time when by the aid of foreign coal, cotton, wool, &c., it secured for itself large-scale manufacturing industries.

The relation of exchange between agricultural and industrial countries which was so attractive to the classical theory, is, we mean to say, no permanent condition given by nature, but merely a stage in the general process of industrialization.

in which materials derived from nature undergo the application of an ever-increasing quantity of labour and capital
before they are finally used in the satisfaction of human
wants.　Manufactured goods displace raw material, and
manufactures of higher value those of lower.　Even in technical consumption, that is, in the use of goods for the purposes
of further elaboration, the place of natural substances is
constantly taken by artificial.　Examples are—coal-tar dyes,
artificial indigo, synthetic camphor, cryolite, Norwegian saltpetre, celluloid, galalite, artificial silk, &c.　By this change
the supply is rendered independent of the frequently scanty
deposits of the natural materials ; the quantity which can
be produced is unlimited, and so can be adjusted to any
demand ; the quality is pure and uniform, while in nature
numerous foreign substances cause difficulty, and finally
a considerable cheapening of the raw material supply is
usually possible.　The process of industrialization is affecting
agriculture also.　In the industrial region of Western Europe
a transition is taking place from grain culture to truck
farming ; there is a steady improvement in the breeds of
live-stock, and a remarkable development of dairying,
poultry-raising, and the like.[1]　The causes are to be found
in the increasing scarcity of land and of labour, which has
raised rents and wages to such an extent that the sole condition of profitable culture is the employment of larger and
larger amounts of capital.　But the investment of capital
can be advantageous only on condition that production can
be specialized, and the possibility of specialization again
depends on the extent of the market.　The problem to be
solved in each individual case is accordingly that of realizing
the maximum marketable product from a minimum of land
area and with a minimum expenditure of human labour.
Industrialization makes possible an improvement in the scale
of living, as capital can be multiplied more rapidly than

[1] For a fuller discussion see Josef Grunzel, *Sieg des Industrialismus*,
Leipsic, 1911.

population, and can be made productive in a much higher degree than the natural soil and human labour force. It also assures a greater stability of economic conditions, as it renders production less dependent upon natural vicissitudes such as changes of weather, elemental catastrophes, &c. Finally, its use promotes culture in the highest degree, substituting as it does for coarse physical labour the lighter but more effective mental effort and providing leisure for physical and mental recreation.

Protective duties and their substitutes are a means of industrialization, as they assure and stabilize the domestic market in the interest of industries actual or potential, and so provide the necessary conditions for their development. It is only when they are held to be always and everywhere necessary that the value of protective duties is overestimated. They can only secure the market, not create it; and, in addition, they cannot conjure forth the two productive factors, labour and capital. They can, moreover, after having done good service in one period, become positively injurious in case at a later time the home market becomes too narrow for the industry in question.

Growth of World-Economy. Judgements passed on economic protectionism have usually suffered from the erroneous conception that the policy is equivalent to exclusion from the world-economic sphere. In reality, it leads to a greater multiplication of world-economic relations, inasmuch as it enables and compels the individual economic domain to participate more energetically in such activity. Industrialization necessarily outgrows the domestic market, as a point will be reached beyond which the specialization of production and concentration of establishments cannot be carried further without extending the market to foreign fields. Besides, even under limitation of the domestic market, exportation will become indispensable when large productive establishments require to be continuously occupied and the risk of a decrease in consumption at home is to be avoided. In addition, an increase in the demand more rapid than the growth of population can be achieved by no other means than by refining the demand, which again strengthens the endeavour toward specialization. In the place of the international division of labour between agriculture and manufactures, assumed by classical economics, a division of labour within the sphere of manufacturing appears. If now the development of the productive capacity of a country leads to industrialization, and if industrialization increases the participation of the country in world-economic dealings, it follows that the protective policy, as an important aid to industrialization, must under proper manipulation lead to an extension of world-economic relations.

The foreign-trade statistics of the most important nations pursuing a protective policy show that when first introduced it may indeed reduce importation momentarily, but that an increase all the more rapid subsequently results if other influences do not intervene to produce a disturbing effect. If we compute the imports in billions of marks by annual averages for five-year periods for the time since 1850, which includes approximately thirty years of free trade (1850–80) and thirty years of protection (1880–1910), the changes may be represented by the curves below :—

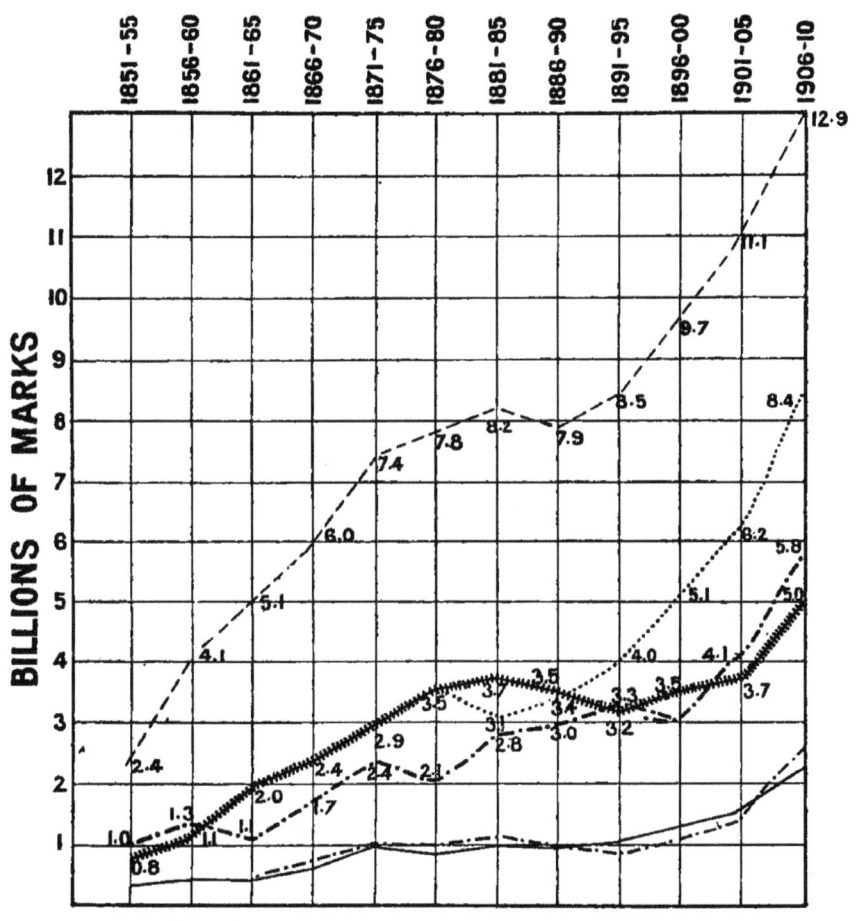

IMPORTS OF LEADING COUNTRIES

Great Britain ------------
Germany   ....
France   ++++++++++++++++++++++++++
The United States .-..-..-..-
Italy   -..-..-..-..-
Austria - Hungary_____

Increase and Equalization of the Mutual Dependence of Nations. The growth of world-economic relations means an increase in the dependence of each country on those foreign nations which purchase from or furnish to it commodities, capital, or labour power. This dependence, however, is in itself no economic disadvantage, as is demonstrated each day of our lives. Very few civilized persons would to-day be in a position to provide for their own needs if thrown upon their individual resources. Even the different social strata of the population cannot to-day be so sharply opposed to each other as was the case in the Middle Ages. The only question is whether the dependence resulting from economic relations grows more undesirable in character; the answer depends not merely on how much is obtained from foreign nations or how much must be marketed abroad, but also on the number of countries among which this dependence for supplies or for markets is divided.

In the first place, world-commerce shows a tendency, in the multiplication of trade connexions, to mitigate any relation of too close dependence of one country upon another. Great Britain has the closest commercial relations with the United States of America; but the share of the latter in the total trade of England, imports and exports, has sunk from 20·8 per cent in the year 1880, to which figure it had risen under the influence of the sudden increase of grain importation, to 15 per cent in the year 1910. The most important source of imports for Belgium was formerly Holland, which in the year 1860 still furnished more than 20 per cent of the imports; in the year 1910, however, its share was less than 9 per cent, and was surpassed by the shares of several other countries. In the exports of Belgium, France formerly stood at the head with 38 4 per cent in 1861; at present the shares of France, Germany, England, and Holland are not far from equal. France also had at one time the largest share of the foreign trade of Spain, amounting to more than 40 per cent; but now its part is surpassed by that of Great Britain, and even the latter country has not more than 20 per cent. Another familiar example is the progressive emancipation of the Balkan countries from Austria-Hungary. While in the decade of the 'seventies fully half the foreign trade of Roumania was carried on with the Dual Monarchy, its share at present is hardly a fourth. In Servia, for the period of 1884–92, imports from Austria-Hungary averaged 86·8 per cent, and exports to the same country 66·3 per cent of the total for the kingdom ; in the year 1909 the proportions had sunk to 24·4 per cent and 31·4 per cent respectively. A tabulation of the more important commercial nations of the world with the figures for the largest shares of individual foreign nations in their imports and exports will further show that these national quotas are smaller the more advanced is the country in its economic development. Such a tabulation is given below for the year 1910 (in some cases 1909).

DISTRIBUTION OF IMPORTS AND EXPORTS OF LEADING NATIONS

Country.	Most important Import Countries and their Shares (%) in Country's Total.		Most important Export Countries and their Shares (%) in Country's Total.	
		Per Cent.		Per Cent.
Great Britain .	United States of America .	. 17·7	United States of America .	. 11·6
	France .	. 7·6	Germany .	. 10·3
	Russia .	. 6·4	British India .	8·8
	British India .	6·3	France .	. 6·3
	Germany .	. 6·1		
Germany .	Russia .	. 14·8	Great Britain .	13·4
	United States of America .	. 13·3	Austria-Hungary .	11·0
	Great Britain .	8·6	United States of America .	. 8·4
	Austria-Hungary .	8·1	France .	. 7·3
	France .	. 5·7	Russia .	. 7·2
France . .	Great Britain .	13·0	Great Britain .	20·4
	Germany .	. 12·0	Belgium .	. 16·1
	United States of America .	. 8·5	Germany .	. 12·9
	Belgium .	. 6·5	United States of America .	. . 7·3

Country.	Most important Import Countries and their Shares (%) in Country's Total.		Most important Export Countries and their Shares (%) in Country's Total.	
		Per Cent.		Per Cent.
Belgium . .	France . .	15·2	Germany . .	26·1
	Germany . .	13·4	France . .	18·3
	Great Britain .	12·4	Great Britain .	13·4
Russia . .	Germany . .	46·3	Germany . .	28·4
	Great Britain .	16·1	Great Britain .	22·9
Roumania .	Germany . .	33 8	Belgium . .	26·1
	Austria-Hungary	23·3	Austria-Hungary .	24·7
	Great Britain .	15·7	Netherlands .	10·7
Bulgaria . .	Austria-Hungary	29·6	Turkey . .	30·0
	Germany . .	16·0	Belgium . .	19·6
	Turkey . .	14·8	Germany . .	10·4
Servia . .	Germany . .	41·0	Germany . .	18·8
	Austria-Hungary	19·1	Austria-Hungary .	15·2
	Great Britain .	13·5	Belgium . .	13·8
Greece . .	Great Britain .	22·9	Great Britain .	25·1
	Russia . .	19·6	Austria-Hungary .	10·1
	Austria-Hungary	12·6	Germany . .	10·0
United States of America .	Great Britain .	17·4	Great Britain .	29·6
	Germany . .	10·7	Germany . .	14·0
	France . .	7·8	France . .	6·2
Japan . .	British India .	22·4	China . . .	19·7
	Great Britain .	20·4	Germany . .	9·8
	China . .	14·8	Great Britain .	5·6
	Germany . .	9·4		
Switzerland .	Germany . .	33·4	Germany . .	23·2
	France . .	19·1	Great Britain .	16·6
	Italy . . .	11·5	France . .	11·0
Italy . .	Germany . .	15·5	Germany . .	14·1
	Great Britain .	15·1	United States of America . .	12·7
	France . .	10·1	France . .	10·5
	Austria-Hungary	9·5	Switzerland .	10·4
			Great Britain .	10·1
Austria-Hungary	Germany . .	39·0	Germany . .	43·2
	United States of America . .	8·4	Great Britain .	10·2
	Great Britain .	7·9	Italy . . .	9·6
Spain . .	Great Britain .	20·5	Great Britain .	27·5
	France . .	18 8	France . .	27·1
	Germany . .	11 6		
	United States of America . .	11·1		

Country.	Most important Import Countries and their Shares (%) in Country's Total.		Most important Export Countries and their Shares (%) in Country's Total.	
		Per Cent		Per Cent.
Portugal . .	Great Britain .	26·9	Great Britain .	23·5
	Germany . .	15 3	Spain . . .	17·9
	United States of America . .	10·6	Brazil . . .	16·6
Sweden . .	Germany . .	34·4	Great Britain ,	32·2
	Great Britain .	24·5	Germany .	21·0
Norway . .	Germany . .	30·9	Great Britain .	26·2
	Great Britain .	23·9	Germany .	25·7
	Sweden . .	12·1	Sweden .	10·1
Denmark . .	Germany . .	41·9	Great Britain .	67·2
	Great Britain .	20·3	Germany .	22·4
Argentina . .	Great Britain .	31·1	Great Britain .	21·7
	Germany . .	17·4	Germany .	12·1
	United States of America . .	13 8	France . .	10·1
			Belgium . .	9·8
Brazil . .	Great Britain .	26 9	United States of America .	40·2
	Germany . .	15 6	Great Britain .	16·2
	United States of America . .	12·4	Germany . .	15·6
	France . .	10 4		

In a similar way it can be shown with reference to the articles which enter into the world-trade that their production becomes distributed over more and more regions, or else that, in case the monopolistic position of a single country cannot be broken, substitution products or artificial substances are brought into use. The form of production most universally carried on is that of breadstuffs and meat, the most important articles for human nourishment. In the coal and iron industries, the dominant position of England, far surpassing all other countries down to the middle of the nineteenth century, has been seriously undermined. In the most important textile material, cotton, a certain oppressive dependence upon the United States of America still subsists, but in Russian Asia and in the African colonies experiments full of promise in the direction of emancipation have been undertaken. In the next most important raw material, wool, a sharp competition has arisen between non-European countries, greatly reducing prices on European markets in the second half of the last century. In rubber, we have seen in recent years an extension into Eastern Asia of the production which had formerly been concentrated in Brazil. Similar examples might be multiplied at length.

Intensification of Conflicts of Interest. Economic protectionism, in promoting the interests of one country, may readily come into conflict with the efforts of another country directed toward a different goal. The immediate consequence is that the threatened country adopts reprisal tactics, and to this end similarly draws its weapons from the arsenal of the protective policy. Duties placed too high by foreign countries will be answered with increases in duties at home, and eventually even with special retaliatory duties; high freight rates for imports on the railways of a foreign country will be rendered ineffective by low rates on exports in the homeland, and occasionally hostile measures may be taken in quite other fields for forcing the opponent into submission. Under some circumstances the opposition may grow into a struggle in economic policy, and finally into a purely political conflict. The closer are the world-economic connexions, and the more complicated the protective measures become, the better is the opportunity for such an issue.

Most conflicts have arisen from the protection of commodities. Thus the protective tariff programme sketched in a communication of December 15, 1878, from the German Imperial Chancellor to the Bundesrat, added to the repeated failure of treaty negotiations, considerably cooled the relations between Germany and Austria. But the necessity of political harmony between the two States led Bismarck to propose the famous reciprocal arrangements, in order that political friendship should not have to keep company with economic hostility.

Heated political controversies have, however, arisen on

economic grounds between Austria-Hungary and the Balkan States, because the former maintained stringent veterinary police exclusions while the latter countries were struggling energetically to promote industrialization.   The ill-feeling engendered by the tariff war with Roumania of 1886–90 was removed by the movement of Roumania toward the Triple Alliance.   But with Servia, after the breaking off of treaty negotiations in the year 1906, relations took so disastrous a turn that every new political event, as the annexation of Bosnia in 1908 and the Balkan War of 1912–13, threatened to cause the outbreak of war between the two countries.

On the other hand, political occurrences have frequently led to an intensification of tariff protection.   The inauguration of the tariff war between Italy and France was due in large part to the resentment aroused by the entrance of Italy into the Triple Alliance.   Similarly, the co-operation of the Triple-Alliance powers in the conclusion of the December Treaties of 1891 was designed to afford for the political alliance a strong basis of co-operation in the field of commercial policy.

With regard to the protection of capital, there have thus far been misunderstandings but no open conflicts.   Evidence of such conflicts was afforded, however, by the hostile attitude of Germany to Russian loans, and of France to loans of the Triple Alliance countries.

On the other hand, protection against immigration has led to friction between the United States of America and Japan, and has embittered relations between America and China.   Even the measures taken against seasonal migration in Germany, France, and Switzerland have not been without political reactions on the countries affected, Austria and Italy.

Strengthening of International Community of Interest.   While it is no doubt true that in the future development of the world-economy conflicts of interest will never be wanting, and that as they are frequently reconciled they will invariably re-appear, yet there is no mistaking the fact that at the same time the complex of communities of interest in the world-economic sphere must grow at a still more rapid rate. The latter will probably never develop so far as to eliminate all conflicts of interest, but time must bring a constant increase in the responsibility of every country, and arouse it to the danger of destroying an existing community of interest. Ever more frequently will the way of compromise be sought and found.

This course of development is clearly foreshadowed in the rapidly growing number of international agreements in the field of economic policy. With regard to commodity protection in particular, the numerous commercial treaties have aimed at a compromise between the clashing interests. Many countries, it is true, such as the United States of America, Russia, and the countries of the Iberian and Balkan peninsulas, have frequently set up as their ideal a completely autonomous commercial policy, but they have always been forced to fall back on the treaty policy. The international agreements affecting means of communication, the mails, telegraph service, railways, and navigation, immediately serve only the technical ends of trade, and hence do not as yet take into account such protective measures as special freight rates and ship subsidies. The same applies to international treaties for the protection of industrial property and those relating to weights and measures, &c. On the other hand, the international corporation agreements extend into the field of protective policy as they are able to replace protective duties levied by the State.

The protection of capital has not yet been brought under international control, but the necessity of protective measures relating to migratory movements of population is becoming more and more manifest. Moreover, as already mentioned, the immigration laws of the United States of America and of the Australian Federation have opened the way to such action.

Conclusion. The protective policy promotes the economic development of a country as it makes possible an industrialization which is not the result of natural conditions but of the productive energy of its civilization.   It increases the activity of a country in world-trade for the reason that an industrialized nation cannot rest content with domestic markets, but requires exportation in order to secure that minimizing of risk which is so valuable in every field of modern economic life.   The more active participation in world-economic relations increases indeed the dependency of each country upon its neighbours, but at the same time it lessens the danger of this dependency by distributing both purchases and sales among many economic domains.   It is true that conflicts of interest arise from the clashing of the protective policy measures of different countries, but in view of a steadily growing community of interest, these show themselves on the road to settlement by international agreement.

The protective policy embodies a permanent principle which varies only in its application, and one which in general must be so manipulated that national-economy and world-economy development must be brought into the closest harmony.   National-economy and world-economy do not stand in a relation of hostile opposition, but rather condition each other.   In an economic sense also the truth holds good that he most benefits the world who best serves his own people.

INDEX

GENERAL APPENDIX

PUBLICATIONS OF THE DIVISION OF ECONOMICS AND HISTORY

THE Conference which met at Berne in 1911, under the auspices of the Division of Economics and History of the Carnegie Endowment for International Peace, appointed three Commissions to draft the questions and problems to be dealt with by competent authorities in all countries. The first Commission was entrusted with *The Economic and Historical Causes and Effects of War*; the second with *Armaments in Time of Peace*; the third with *The Unifying Influences in International Life*. Subsequently the suggestions of the three Commissions were considered and approved by the entire Conference.

The questions are to be discussed scientifically, and as far as possible without prejudice either for or against war; and their discussion may have such important consequences that the questions are presented below *in extenso*.

Report of the First Commission

THE ECONOMIC AND HISTORICAL CAUSES AND EFFECTS OF WAR

The Conference recommends the following researches :

1. Historical presentation of the causes of war in modern times, tracing especially the influence exercised by the striving for greater political power, by the growth of the national idea, by the political aspirations of races and by economic interests.

2. Conflicts of economic interests in the present age :

(*a*) The influence of the growth of population and of the industrial development upon the expansion of States.

(*b*) The protectionist policy ; its origin and basis ; its method of application and its influence upon the relations between countries ; bounties (open and disguised, public and private); most-favoured-nation treatment ; the attitude towards foreign goods and foreign capital ; the boycott ; discouragement of foreign immigration.

(c) International loans ; the policy of guarantees ; the relations of the creditor to the debtor States ; the use of loans for gaining influence over other States.

(d) Rivalry among States with respect to capitalist investments in foreign countries :

1. The endeavour to obtain a privileged position in banking enterprises, in the opening and development of mines, in the letting of public contracts, in the execution of public works, in the building of railways (Siberian, Manchurian, Persian Bagdad Railway, Adriatic Railway, &c.) ; in short, the organization of larger capitalistic enterprises in foreign countries.

2. The hindering of foreign countries by convention from executing productive enterprises on their own soil, e. g. from building railways in their own countries.

3. The anti-militarist movement, considered in its religious and political manifestations. (Only opposition to all military organization is here to be considered.)

4. The position of organized labour and the socialists in the various States on the questions of war and armaments.

5. Is it possible to determine a special interest of individual classes making for or against war, for or against standing armies ?

6. The influence of women and woman suffrage upon war and armaments.

7. The extension of obligatory military service in the different States, in times both of war and of peace.

(a) The conditions of military service ; the system of enlistment and of general obligatory service, the actual position of aliens.

(b) The ratio of the persons obliged to render military service to the entire population.

(c) The influence of the present system of military obligation and the organization of armies upon warfare and upon its duration.

8. The economic effects of the right of capture and its influence upon the development of navies.

9. War loans provided by neutral countries ; their extent and influence on recent warfare.

10. The effects of war :

(a) Financial cost of war. The methods of meeting it : Taxation ; International Loans ; External Loans.

(b) Losses and gains from the point of view of public and private economic interests ; checks to production and the destruction of productive forces ; reduction of opportunities for business enterprises ; interruption of foreign trade and of the imports of food ; the destruction of property ; shrinkage of values of property, including securities ; financial burden caused by new taxes, debts, and war indemnities ; effects upon private credit and upon savings banks ; advantages to those industries which furnish military materials ; advantages and disadvantages to neutral countries.

(c) The effects of war upon the supply of the world with food and raw materials, with special reference to those States which are in large degree dependent upon other countries for such supplies, e.g. Great Britain and Germany ; by diversion of capital from those countries which produce food and raw materials (especially the stoppage of railway building and of new investments in agriculture and other industries).

(d) The condition of the victorious State : manner of levy and use of contributions and war indemnities ; influence upon industry and social life.

(e) The manner in which the energy of nations is stimulated or depressed by war.

11. Loss of human life in war and as a result of war : influence upon population (birth-rate, relation between the sexes, ratio of the various ages, sanitary conditions).

12. The influence of war and of the possibility of war upon the protective policy, upon banking conditions (especially upon banks of issue), and upon monetary systems.

13. The influence of annexation upon the economic life of the annexing States, and upon the State whose territory has been annexed.

14. The annexation of half-civilized or uncivilized peoples, considered especially from the point of view of the economic interests, which act as motive powers ; the methods through which private enterprises take root in such regions and through which they bring influence to bear upon their own governments ; the effects of such annexations upon the development of trade with the annexing State and with other countries, as well as upon the economic and social life of the natives.

15. The progressive exemption of commercial and industrial activities from losses and interferences through war.

16. Influence of the open-door policy upon war and peace.

GENERAL APPENDIX

Report of the Second Commission

ARMAMENTS IN TIME OF PEACE. MILITARY AND NAVAL ESTABLISH-
MENTS. THE THEORY, PRACTICE, AND HISTORY OF MODERN
ARMAMENTS.

1. **Definition.** Armaments might be described as ' the preparations made by a State either for defence or for attack '. These would include the provision of food, financial preparations, and also semi-military railways, canals, docks, &c.

2. **Causes of armaments.** Motives for increasing or commencing them, distinguishing the great from the small powers.

3. **Rivalry and competition in armaments.** Motives and consequences of rivalry, with the possibilities of limitation.

4. **Modern history of armaments, with special fullness from 1872.** To be noted as important landmarks :

(a) The introduction of conscription into Germany, France, Austria, Italy, Japan, &c.

(b) Modern inventions affecting war.

(c) The question of privateering and private property at sea.

(d) Duration of military service.

(e) The traffic in arms.

5. **Military budgets from 1872** (distinguishing ordinary from extra-ordinary expenditures).

6. **The burden of armaments in recent times.**

(a) The proportion of military to civil expenditure.

(b) Military expenditure per capita.

(c) Military expenditure from loans in time of peace, i. e. a comparison of expenditure from taxes with expenditure from borrowed money.

(d) Comparative burdens of individual taxpayers in different countries and the extent to which the differences are due to armaments.

(e) Military pensions.

(f) It is desirable to ascertain where possible the ratio between the total income of each nation and the total expenditure on armament at various times.

7. **The effects of war preparations upon the economic and social life of a nation :**

(a) On the sustenance of the entire population of a country at war.

(*b*) On railway policy.

(*c*) On public administration and on social legislation.

8. The economic effects of withdrawing young men from industrial pursuits, into the army and navy :

(*a*) Compulsory.

(*b*) Of non-compulsory service (specially in the case of mercenary troops).

(Allowance being made for the industrial value of military education and training.)

9. The influence of changes in the occupations of a people upon the composition and efficiency of armies, and the influence of the changes in the composition of armies on the economic life.

10. Loans for armaments (participation of domestic and foreign capital).

11 The industries of war, i. e. the various manufactures and other industries which are promoted and encouraged by military and naval establishments, distinguishing between :

(*a*) Government undertakings (arsenals, dockyards, &c.).

(*b*) Private undertakings, including the history and working of the great armament firms, which sell to foreign customers as well as to their own governments.

12. War materials (munitions of war). Their recent development and their cost. This includes arms, ammunition, armour-plate, warships, guns of all kinds, military airships, &c. So far as possible the effect of recent inventions upon offensive and defensive war should be indicated.

Report of the Third Commission

THE UNIFYING INFLUENCES IN INTERNATIONAL LIFE

1. The Conference is of the opinion that the economic life of individual countries has definitely ceased to be self-contained ; and that, notwithstanding the barriers raised by fiscal duties, it is becoming in ever-increasing measure a part of an economic life in which the whole world participates.

2. It desires that this change be studied with the object of ascertaining to what extent the economic life of individual nations has ceased to be self-contained, and the causes which are bringing about the greater interdependence of nations.

3. Special attention should be paid to the following factors :

(*a*) How far the growth of population is responsible for the changes that have occurred and are in progress.

(*b*) The extent to which the insufficiency of the natural resources of individual countries for their own requirements has contributed to it.

(*c*) Whether the increasing economic unity of the world is the cause or the result of the rising in the standard of living, and how far the increasing welfare of nations has been caused by the growing unity.

(*d*) In what measure the need of individual countries to obtain materials of production from other lands and to find new markets for their own products is responsible for the growth of international dependence.

4. The Conference desires that investigations be made into :

(*a*) The volume of the world's production of all the many articles of food, of the various raw materials, and of the principal manufactures.

(*b*) The productions of individual countries, and the extent to which they are retained for home consumption or are exported.

(*c*) The consumption of individual countries, and the extent to which the various articles are supplied from home productions or are imported.

5. The Conference wishes to ascertain to what extent the economy of production by large units, instead of by small units, has contributed to the international dependence of nations.

6. The development of this world-embracing economy has taken place in great measure in consequence of the investment of capital by rich countries in less developed lands. Through this there have arisen close relations and a great increase of wealth, not only for the lending and the borrowing countries, but for all nations. The Conference is of the opinion that researches should be made into the extent of the interdependence of the nations in the matter of capital.

7. The Conference desires to institute inquiries into the interdependence of the financial centres of the world.

8. The Conference desires to make the unifying effects of international trade, the building of railways, the progress of shipping, the improvement and extension of all means of communication and the progress of inventions, the subjects of careful investigation.

9. The Conference is in favour of making a comprehensive study of the various international unions and associations, in which the social and economic interests of all classes of society are now either organized or in process of organization, through official or private action.